AutoCAD®: The Drawing Tool

AutoCAD®

THE DRAWING TOOL

Charles F. Rubenstein, P.E.
Assistant Professor EE7
Cuyahoga Community College
Cleveland, Ohio

 Delmar Publishers Inc.

NOTICE TO THE READER

Publisher does not warrant or guarantee any of the products described herein or perform any independent analysis in connection with any of the product information contained herein. Publisher does not assume, and expressly disclaims, any obligation to obtain and include information other than that provided to it by the manufacturer.

The reader is expressly warned to consider and adopt all safety precautions that might be indicated by the activities described herein and to avoid all potential hazards. By following the instructions contained herein, the reader willingly assumes all risks in connection with such instructions.

The publisher makes no representations or warranties of any kind, including but not limited to, the warranties of fitness for particular purpose or merchantability, nor are any such representations implied with respect to the material set forth herein, and the publisher takes no responsibility with respect to such material. The publisher shall not be liable for any special, consequential or exemplary damages resulting, in whole or in part, from the readers' use of, or reliance upon, this material.

ACAD, AutoCAD, and DXF are the trademarks of AutoDesk, Inc.
IBM is the trademark of the International Business Machine Corporation.
MS DOS is the trademark of Microsoft Corporation.
DMP61 is the trademark of Houston Instruments.
KX-P1124 is the trademark of Panasonic Industrial Company, Computer Products Division.

Cover design by Nancy Gworek.

Delmar Staff
Associate Editor: Kevin Johnson
Editing Supervisor: Marlene McHugh Pratt
Project Editor: Ward David Dales
Production Supervisor: Wendy A. Troeger

For information, address
Delmar Publishers Inc.
2 Computer Drive West, Box 15-015
Albany, New York 12212

Printed in the United States of America
Published simultaneously in Canada
by Nelson Canada,
a division of The Thomson Corporation

10 9 8 7 6 5 4 3 2 1

Libraary of Congress Cataloging-in-Publication Data
Rubenstein, Charles F.
    AutoCAD, the drawing tool/Charles F. Rubenstein
        p. cm.
    Includes index.
    ISBN 0-8273-4885-1
    1. Computer graphics. 2. AutoCAD (Computer program) I. Title
    II. Title: AutoCAD.
T385.R843 1992
620'.0042'02855369—dc20   91-46224
                                                              CIP

Table of Contents

Preface

This book was written to answer the needs of the student about to enter into the area of computers and the application of the AutoCAD program. The majority of the manuals dealing with AutoCAD assumes that the individual, sitting down at the workstation, has some knowledge of DOS and AutoCAD. For the majority of students this is not the case.

This text assumes that the student has not been exposed to a computer. Therefore, an overview of the computer workstation, the Disk Operating System (DOS), and how to bring the AutoCAD Main Menu to the screen must be discussed prior to any of AutoCAD's commands. These topics are detailed in Chapters 1 and 2. How to use AutoCAD's command structure and procedures are discussed in Chapters 3 to 21.

When AutoCAD's Main Menu appears on the screen (refer to Chapter 2) the instructor and the textbook must be able to provide answers to the three challenges the student will face:

1. What command do I use?
2. Where is the command located?
3. How do I implement the command?

The command application is detailed starting in Chapter 3 for Line, Arc, Circle, Erase, and Save to Dimensioning, Attributes, Hatching and the use of the Template (Chapter 21). The Instructional Objectives (listed at the start of each chapter) provide a listing of the commands discussed in that chapter. Although the text has been designed to start with the basic commands and then the more difficult commands, the instructor has the option to select the sequence of commands best suited for a given curriculum.

Prehaps the most difficult task that the student must learn is the location of each command. The Root Screen Menu (the menu shown on the screen after a drawing has been named) has 19 listings, and within these listings there are 8 to 35 separate commands. The Menu Map technique is used to show the student the location of each command. Each command location is illustrated starting from the Root Screen Menu (the first menu item after the stars [****] is BLOCKS), through the various submenus, to the specified command. In some cases, the command will have one or more options. These options are also illustrated. The Menu Map starts with the Root Screen Menu and illustrates, with the use of arrows, how to find the command. Using this technique, the student's learning period is significantly reduced.

The third challenge (How to implement the command?) is answered by listing a typical Command Sequence for a given command. Where applicable, one or more examples are used to show the student how to apply the command. If there are several options in the implementation of the command, the long way is first described and then the short cuts, if available, are described, along with any restriction that may apply.

In some institutions, the curriculum calls for the use of a special Template (designed by Autodesk) to be used with the Tablet and Tablet Command. (Refer to Chapter 21.) The Template is an overlay, displaying the majority of AutoCAD's commands. The Tablet (sometimes called a Digitizer) is implemented by using the Tablet command. The locations of the Template commands are crosshatched and appear at the end of each chapter. The use of the Template and the location of each command is unique to this text. In addition to the Template, this text illustrates the chapter commands that are listed in the Pull Down Menus. The commands are highlighted by an arrow.

Where possible, one or more examples are used to illustrate a specific command. These examples use prior commands as well as the current commands, thereby enhancing the educational process. The sequence of commands are based on the successful course given at Cuyahoga Community College, Cleveland, Ohio, called Introduction to CAD (ENGR 130A). At the time of this writing, approximately 1100 students have successfully completed this course. *AutoCAD: the Drawing Tool, Command EXERCISE Workbook* was developed to provide additional problems to futher enhance the book examples and problems at the end of each chapter. This workbook may be purchased from Delmar Publishers Inc., Albany, N.Y.

I would like to express my appreciation to Dr. Curtis Gooden, Dean of Instruction at Cuyahoga Community College, who offered me the opportunity to develop this and other advanced courses using AutoCAD. I would like to thank the students of my 1987 winter class who used and critiqued this text.

The illustrations (approximately 400) were plotted using the Houston Instruments Plotter DMP61. To the individuals at Houston Instruments, Ms. Lynn M. Johnson and Mr. K. Pflaum, you are absolutely correct, the Plotter performance meets and beats the specifications. A salute to the staff at Autodesk, and to Patricia Peper, Arul Arangan, and Gloria A. Bastidas for their help and assistance in the writing of this text.

To those listed below, my heartfelt thank you for your diligent work in the review of this text.

Brent J. Sorensen
Metropolitan Community College
Omaha, Nebraska

David H. Brown
Biglerville High School
Biglerville, Pennsylvania

Thomas J. Whistler
Saint Mary College
Leavenworth, Kansas

Lawrence Krauter
Clover Park Voc. Tech. Inst.
Tacoma, Washington

Robert H. Walder
Clark State Community College
Springfield, Ohio

Dr. Ralph Dirksen
Western Illinois University
Macomb, Illinois

Without the help and guidance of the staff at Delmar Publishers Inc., and in particular to Mike McDermott, Kevin Johnson, and Mary Beth Ray, this book would not have seen the light of day.

This book is dedicated to my grandchildren:
Brian Gary, Alan David, and Rebecca Leigh Rubenstein

1 Workstation of the Future

1.1 Introduction

The drafting workstation of the 1980s consisted of a large drafting table, movable parallel rule, reference table, chair, pencils, pencil sharpener, and the electric eraser machine. The drafting workstation of the future will be completely different. (In fact, the drafting workstation of the future is in use today.) The computer is the key element of the Computer Aided Design and Drafting (CADD) workstation. The drafting workstation (called workstation) will consist of a Control Processor Unit (CPU), one or more input devices, special software designed for drafting application, one or more output devices, and an individual who is skilled in applying the fundamentals of drafting combined with the ability to use one or more drafting software packages.

At a minimum, the new workstation will include a CPU with special features (enhanced graphics capability and math co-processor) and associated peripherals. Peripherals are those devices that will provide either input data or output data to/from the computer and are compatible with the software package used for the drafting applications. The Mouse, Pointer, and/or Digitizer are considered input peripherals. The keyboard, which is part of the CPU, also provides input data. The output peripherals will provide either a visual picture on a video Monitor or a print copy (sometimes called a hard copy) from either a Plotter or dot matrix Printer.

The computer requires at least two software packages. One of these packages programs the computer and provides some of the operational functions (eg, turning on or booting up the computer, making copies of the files, renaming files, deleting files, etc). This operational program is called the Disk Operating System (DOS).

The second software package is AutoCAD. The AutoCAD software program is a unique drafting system designed by AutoDesk to assist the individual in his or her design or drafting activities. In a sense, the drafting pencil has been replaced by the computer workstation.

1.2 Peripheral Equipment

Input devices may include one or more of the following items:

Alpha-Numeric keyboard

Stylus

Mouse

1

Menu Tablet

Digitizer

The output devices may include one or more of the following items:

Video Monitor

Dot Matrix Printer

Single or multi-pen Plotter

A typical flow diagram of the proposed workstation is shown in Figure 1–1.

AutoCAD software is designed to work with a large number of peripherals. The specific make and model numbers of the individual devices are listed in the AutoCAD supplementary manual entitled *Installation and Performance Guide for the AutoCAD Drafting Package.* Typical input devices are:

CALcomp Series 2500 and 9100 series

Hitachi HICOMSCAN HDG series

IBM PS/2 Mouse

Summagraphics SummaSketch MM series tablet

Typical output devices that will produce hard copy are:

Plotters	*Printers*
Houston Instruments	Panasonic
Hewlett Packard	Epson
IBM	Okidata

The video Monitors provide a visual presentation. Many companies make

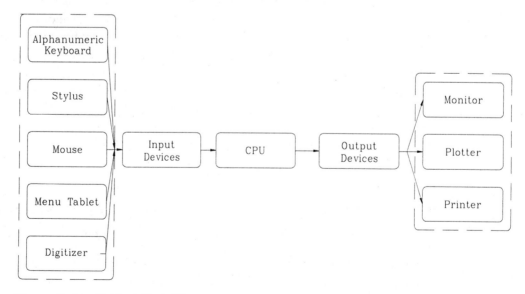

Figure 1–1   Typical Flow Diagram

these units. A sample list taken from the AutoCAD manual is shown below:

MONITORS

IBM	WYSE
HP	HITACHI
SIGMA DESIGN	SONY
VERTICOM	

A number of Plotters, Printers and Monitors are available. The prime Printer's considerations are (1) the size of the hard copy (usually limited to 8.5" × 11") and (2) the number of dots per inch (dpi). For the Plotters, in addition to the size of the hard copy (from A size, 8.5" × 11" to D size, 24" × 36") the need for a multi-pen and/or color capability will depend upon the individual's requirements. The Monitor specification will call out the display size, video card adapter, color, and resolution. Listings of the specific Monitor, Printer or Plotter are growing daily. The equipment manufacturer will provide sufficient data to make its equipment work with the AutoCAD drafting package.

1.3 Computer Interface

It is imperative that the CAD operator have some working knowledge of the Computer ON/OFF switches, drives, and cable locations. For those who will be using the computer for the first time, a few definitions are in order:

Standard Floppy Disk is a magnetic film disk housed in a nonmagnetic cover and used to store computer information. The disk (sometimes called a "floppy") must be formatted to accept information from the computer. Currently the floppy disks come in two sizes: 5 ¼" and the 3 ½". AutoCAD's Release 11 is available in either size. These floppies come in two options and are shown in Table 1-1.

Table 1-1

Disk Size	5 ¼"	3 ½"
Low Density	360 kB	720 kB
High Density	1.20MB	1.44 MB

NOTE: k represents 1000, B represents Bytes or a unit of magnetic disk storage, and M represents 1,000,000.

Care must be taken to choose the correct floppy for your CPU. The 286 and 386 computers will usually work with either floppy size or density. The older XT computers, unless modified, were designed to use the low density 5 ¼" floppy. The setting of the magnetic disk structure or formatting of the disk is based on the DOS software and is discussed in Chapter 2. It is possible to have two floppy disk drives installed in the same computer. The top drive is usually designated as drive A and the lower drive is called drive B.

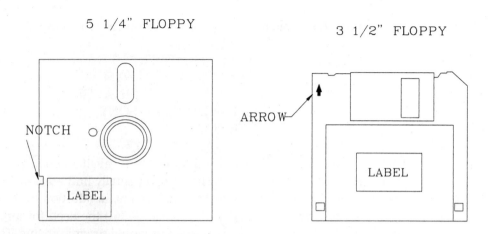

Figure 1–2   Typical Floppy Disks

The computer operator must be careful when the disk is placed in the drive. Always place the 5 ¼″ disk with the label side up and the notch on the operator's left side. The 3 ½″ disk is placed label up and arrow on the left side. Then lower the handle or bar. Figure 1–2 shows both floppy disks.

Hi-Density Floppy Disk is a disk generally used in the 286 or 386 computers. It has the storage capability of 1.2 MegaBytes (1.2 MB).

Disk Drives The disk drives are used to rotate the disks and to input and recall computer data.

Hard Disk Drive is a drive similar to the floppy disk drive except for its storage space. Typical storage space will range from 30 MB to 150 MB or greater. The hard disk is usually called drive C, D, or E. The hard disk and its disk drive are housed inside the computer and cannot be removed except for repair and maintenance.

Disk Operating System (DOS) is software designed to operate the computer. The DOS system is discussed in Chapter 2.

1.3.1 Workstation

The computer as shown in Figure 1–3 is one of the key elements of any workstation. In turn, the computer is divided into two specific items: The CPU, or main chassis, and the keyboard. The keyboard is not considered a peripheral device but rather an integral part of the computer. Figure 1–3 shows an IBM PS/2 Computer.

The computer shown in Figure 1–3 has 2 disk drives. The top disk drive is called drive A. The bottom drive is labeled drive B. Notice that the keyboard is connected to the computer and is considered part of the computer.

Figure 1–4 shows a typical video Monitor. This Monitor is similar to your TV receiver and is used to display text and/or graphics in either black and white or color.

Most video Monitors have two cables connected to the back of the Monitor.

Figure 1–3 IBM Personal Computer PS/2

Cable 1 is the power cable and may be plugged into a convenient power source. The second cable must be connected to the CPU in the area shown in Figure 1–9.

The Plotter will also provide an output similar to that of the Video Monitor. However, the Plotter will provide a copy of a drawing displayed on the screen to a specified scale. Figure 1–5 shows a high resolution Plotter, Houston Instruments Model DMP 61. This Plotter may be equipped with an eight-pen holder and plot drawings (A size to D size). The output of the Plotter is sometimes referred to as "hard copy."

All illustrations for this text were plotted using the Houston Instruments DMP 61 Plotter.

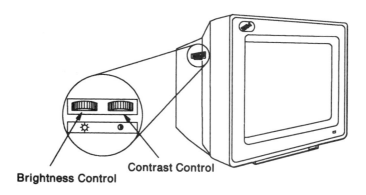

Brightness Control   Contrast Control

Figure 1–4 IBM Model 8514 Monitor

Figure 1–5   Houston Instruments DMP 61 Series Plotter

Another type of hard copy is obtained through the use of a dot matrix Printer as shown in Figure 1–6. This Printer is a Panasonic KX-P1124. Usually, a check print (made by the dot matrix Printer) is used to determine if the drawing is correct before plotting.

The computer accepts input data from either the keyboard, a Mouse, or a tablet/Digitizer as shown in Figure 1–7. The tablet comes in a number of different sizes.

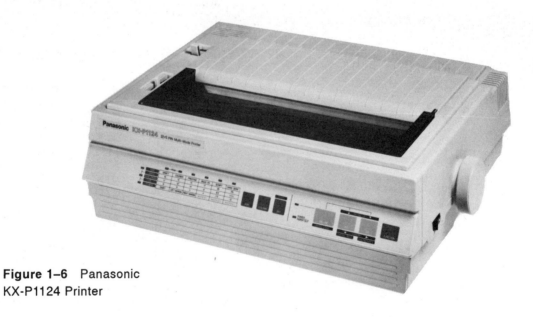

Figure 1–6   Panasonic
KX-P1124 Printer

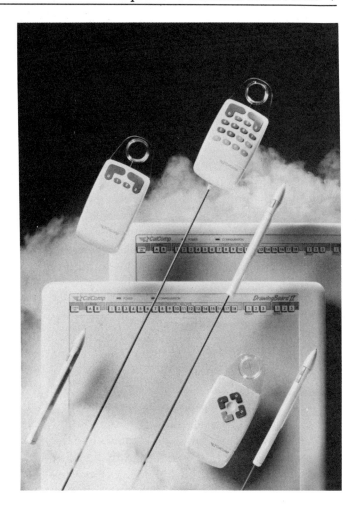

Figure 1–7 A family of
CalComp Tablet/Digitizers

1.4 Minimum Computer Specifications

The selected computer capability used to operate as a CADD workstation will be a compromise between the latest state of the art devices and the overall cost of the workstation. The computer should have the following minimum characteristics:

    40 MB hard drive
    Math co-processor
    16 MegaHz clock
    Special graphics adapter keyed to the Monitor specifications
    1 floppy disk drive
    2 parallel and 2 serial ports

1.5 Typical Workstation

The typical workstation consists of a computer (Figure 1–3), Monitor (Figure 1–4), and a tablet (Figure 1–7). The selection of the Plotter and/or the Printer will depend on company requirements. The exact configuration, including the furniture to house the equipment, will depend upon the available business, cash flow, and other business-related requirements.

1.6 Location of Switches, Cables, Etc.

When the installation of the workstation has been completed, the first-time user will look around and say "How do I turn this system on?" Questions such as "Where is the Power ON/OFF switch? How do I load a floppy disk?" or "Where do these cables go?" might pose a problem.

Figure 1–8 shows the location of the Power ON/OFF switch with reference to the right front corner of the computer. The switch is labeled in accordance with the international convention where 1 indicates the ON position and 0 indicates the OFF position.

In most applications, all cables are connected to the back of the computer as shown in Figure 1–9. Although the keyboard may be used for data input, it is considered part of the computer and not a peripheral device. Depending upon the configuration, one or more cable terminals may not be connected. For peace of mind, it is a good practice to make a sketch of the back of the computer and indicate which type of cable is connected to which terminal.

The proper insertion of the floppy disk will make the operator's life easier. Figure 1–10 is a front view of the computer showing the disk drives. Hold the 5 ¼" disk with the label up and the notch to the left side of the operator. If a 3 ½" disk is being used, hold the disk with the label up and the arrow on the operator's left. Gently insert the disk into its respective drive. After the disk is in the drive, move either the handle or bar to lock the disk in place.

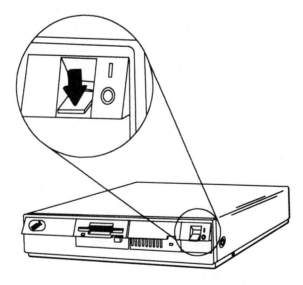

Figure 1–8 Location of the Power ON/OFF Switch

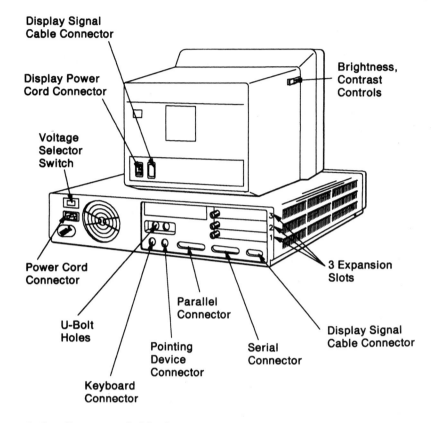

Figure 1-9 Computer Cable Connectors

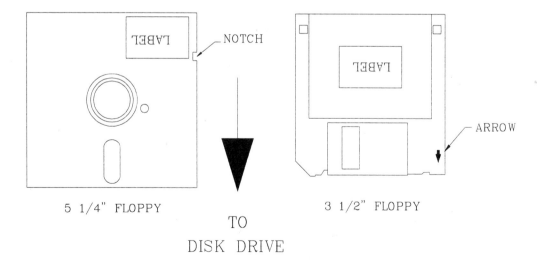

Figure 1-10 Floppy Disk Insertion

GLOSSARY

DOS: Disk Operating System

Floppy disk: A disk containing a magnetic film within a nonmagnetic case. Disks are used to store information. There are two disk sizes (3 ½" and 5 ¼"). Storage capability is from 360 kB to 1.44 MB.

Floppy disk drive: The disk drive is used to house the floppy disks.

Format: The magnetic structure required for storage of information in either a floppy or hard disk.

Hard disk: The hard disk is similar to the floppy disk with two differences: Greater storage capability (20 MB to 100 MB).

Mouse: An input device, shown on the screen as cross hairs or as an arrow.

Peripherals: Major components of a workstation (eg, Printer, Plotter, Mouse, etc.).

2 Computer Fundamentals

Instructional Objectives

1. To understand that DOS is a software program that enables the computer to communicate with the peripherals to perform a given operation or program
2. To become familiar with the prime DOS commands
3. To be aware of the potential danger in the use of the FORMAT and/or DELETE DOS commands
4. To become familiar with the procedures necessary to log on to the computer and bring up the AutoCAD program
5. To become familiar with the use and handling of the floppy disk

2.1 Introduction

The DOS software provides for the communication link between the computer (CPU), the peripheral equipment, and the operator. If the DOS program is not present, then the computer is not functional. In the industrial environment, the CAD workstation uses a hard disk drive and the DOS program is resident on the hard drive. In the dual floppy configuration, the DOS program is resident on a disk in drive A. Although there are many DOS commands, the CADD operator should be knowledgeable of at least six basic commands.

Format

Change in drive

Listing of files within a directory

Copy a file from one drive to another drive

Delete a file

Rename a file

Before going into these commands, let us spend a few moments discussing the term *file*. A file consists of a completed operation either in word processing (such as a letter) or a completed program (such as a Basic program for a mathematical problem) or a completed drawing as found in AutoCAD.

The computer operator must assign a name to each file. The DOS software restricts the filename to a maximum of eight characters (any combination of letters, numbers, $, -, or _). The name may be extended (depending upon circumstances) by adding a period and three more characters after the eight character filename. The three additional letters or numbers are called the extension. An example of a filename would be 1234ABCD.123.

CAUTION: (1) Do not place a space, comma or period between the letters or numbers of the filename and (2) Certain extension names are not acceptable since they are used in the software (either in the DOS program or AutoCAD program). A sample list of the restricted names include

BAK, DWG, OVL, EXE, BAS, SHP, COM

2.2 Disk Drive Change Command

At a minimum, the average workstation designed for CADD has a floppy disk drive called drive A and a hard disk called drive C. During the normal operation of the computer, the operator may be required to change from drive A to drive C or drive C to drive A. The command to change from drive A to drive C is

A:\>C: (R)

NOTE: (R) = depress ENTER key (sometimes labeled RETURN)

The disk drive that is in current use is the first letter to be typed. Then the colon is typed. If drive A is now showing and we want to change to drive C, type A:. Next type the prompt symbol (\>). The combination of A:\> is the statement that drive A is active. (The light on drive A will be lit.) The next two characters (C:) to be typed indicate the new drive name. In this example, we want drive C to become active. The colon (:) is an essential part of the command structure. In normal CADD work, the operator uses drive C except when a copy of the drawing is required for safe-keeping. The command structure for copying files is discussed in subparagraph 2.5 of the text.

2.3 FORMAT Command

When the FORMAT command is used, the CPU will: (1) erase all the files on the disk, (2) inspect the disk for defects, and then (3) initialize the magnetic film enabling it to accept information from the computer.

CAUTION: When a disk is formatted, all information on the disk has been erased.

NOTE: The command structure assumes that the DOS software is loaded into the computer and that the drive that contains the DOS program is active. The drive that is active is usually shown with a drive letter (A, B, or C) followed by the prompt sign (:\>). If the DOS is loaded onto the hard disk, the command structure for formatting the disk in drive A (without a label) is

C:\DOS>format A: (R)

REMEMBER: (R) = Press the ENTER key

The computer interprets the command as follows: the DOS formatting program is in a directory called DOS located on the hard disk (drive C). If the operator wants to format the disk that is in drive A (a label or name may be placed on the disk in drive A) the command structure is

C:\DOS>format A:/V (R)

At the end of the format cycle, the computer will prompt you (place a message on the screen), asking, " FORMAT ANOTHER (Y/N)?". Press N for NO or Y for YES. Then the prompt will change to "PLACE LABEL (Y/N)?" Answer Y. Type a disk name with a maximum of 11 characters or less and then (R).

2.4 Directory Listing

The term *directory* has two applications. The first application is to designate a section in the disk called a directory. The term directory is also used to request a listing of all filenames within a specified section of the disk.

The individual who installs the workstation will program the hard disk. In most cases, there is a *root directory* that will serve as the focal point for all directories. The root directory is designated as CD\.

The computer will store information (text and/or graphics) within a specific area of the hard disk or floppy disk. A filename is the only means of identifying files. The floppy disk usually has one directory but a hard disk is divided into a number of segments called *directories*. These directories contain the files that represent the end product of the computer system (ie, word processing, Basic programming, AutoCAD drawings).

The Command Sequence to change directories requires two commands. The first command is used to leave the current directory and go to the root directory. The second command will be used to go from the root directory to the desired directory. Assume that we are in the BUG directory (C:\BUG>) and want to go to the BIRD directory (C:\BIRD>). The root directory is designated as C:\>. To go from the BUG directory to the root directory, type either CD.. or CD\. The letters CD stand for "change directory." The first command would either be C:\BUG>CD.. or C:\BUG>CD\. The second command (to go from the root directory to the BIRD directory) would look like this: C:\>CD BIRD (R). There is a space between CD and BIRD. This will activate the required directory and the prompt sign will read C:\BIRD>.

To obtain the listing for any directory, the operator must be able to select a directory where the files are located.

The operator must (1) activate the drive that contains the required directory and (2) select the correct directory. Once the drive and directory have been activated, the command structure to bring up the directory listing (the second use of the word directory) is

C:\BIRD>DIR (R)

If there are more than 25 files, the listing will scroll up the screen. There are several ways to stop the scrolling:

1. To view the directory on a page-by-page sequence, add /P to the above command (the resulting listing will be limited to a page length):

    C:\BIRD>DIR/P (R)

    The information that is presented on the Monitor is the filename, number of bytes used, and the date and time of the last effort.

2. For a number of applications, only the filenames are important, therefore replace the /P with /W:

    C:\BIRD>DIR/W (R)

The video presentation will be a horizontal listing, with only the filename showing. If the number of files exceeds 100, then the screen will scroll again.

3. To prevent scrolling use /W/P:

    C:\BIRD>DIR /W/P (R)

2.5 Copy Command

Whenever a file or files are to be copied (either from the hard disk to the floppy or vice versa), the operator must first activate the drive and directory where the file is listed. Then the operator will call for the Copy command. The command structure is

C:\BIRD>copy filename A: (R)

The command reads this as follows: There is a file by the name of (filename) on drive C (directory whose name is BIRD) that is to be copied onto the floppy disk in drive A with the same filename. If a new filename is required, then place the new filename after A:.

NOTE: There is a space between copy and filename and another space between filename and A.

This command structure is used to copy one file at a time. It is possible to program the computer to copy more than one file, from the *same* directory, using a similiar command. The multiple copy command structure will make use of:

WILD CARD (?)

or

PATTERN MATCHING (*)

The wild card will replace one character within the filename. For example, we want to copy nine files with the filenames: Project1, Project2, Project3, Project4 . . . Project9. (The DOS software is not sensitive to the presence of a capital letter or lowercase letter.) Note that the only thing different in the filenames is the number. Therefore, the command structure is

C:\BIRD>Copy project? A: (R)

where the ? replaces the number.

The pattern matching (*) operates in the same way with one exception. The * could represent one or more characters. Using the same filenames as in the above example, the command would be

C:\BIRD>copy Proj* A: (R)

The wild card and pattern matching is usable with another command such as the DELETE command.

CAUTION: When using the *, it is possible to copy more files than required. For instance, if using the above example, the command had been

C:\BIRD>copy P* A:(R)

then all files beginning with P would be copied.

NOTE: It is not possible to copy a file in the same directory where it is originally listed. To copy a file from one directory on the hard disk to another directory on the hard disk use

C:\DIRECTORY NAME>copy filename C:\directory name (R)

2.6 DELETE Command

The DELETE command is the second most deadly command in the DOS program. The FORMAT command is the deadliest command where it is possible to erase a 40 MB hard disk in less than .5 seconds. The DELETE command removes the filename from the directory but is restricted to one filename. First, establish that the file in question is available (the drive and directory have been activated). The command to delete this file is

C:\BIRD>del filename (R)

The use of the wild card and pattern matching technique is applicable to the DELETE command.

2.7 RENAME Command

The RENAME command is used whenever the filename has to be changed. It is repetitious, but the file to be renamed must be located in the active drive and directory. The command structure is

A:\>REN filename1 filename2 (R)

The CADD operator has to change filename1 (cadd12, for example) to filename2 (dacc21). Note the space between REN and filename1 and the space between filename1 and filename2. Rewriting the command, we have:

A:\>Ren cadd12 dacc21 (R)

2.8 Log In Procedure

The Command Sequence required to boot up (apply power to the computer) and activate the AutoCAD program may be different depending upon the person who installed the equipment and the initial programming. In general, once the power is applied, the computer performs a self-test and upon successful completion of the self-test, displays a message on the Monitor showing the C:\> symbol. This means that the hard drive (C) has been activated and it is now up to the CAD operator to bring up the AutoCAD program. As indicated previously, all programs have their own directory. Therefore, what is now required is to instruct the computer to change directory (CD) from the current directory (assumed to be the root directory) to the AutoCAD directory. The Command Sequence is

C:\>CD ACAD (R)

The computer will select the AutoCAD directory and place a C:\ACAD> response on the screen. The operator responds with ACAD (R).

C:\ACAD>ACAD (R)

The computer then takes this information and brings up the AutoCAD program in two steps. The first step is a brief message and the second display is AutoCAD's Main Menu which is shown in Figure 2–1.

NOTE: AutoCAD Release 11 requires a special log in procedure. This procedure utilizes a code (eg., the name of the owner of the software, etc.). However, once the procedure has been performed and saved as a default, the Main Menu appears automatically. The details of the Main Menu are explained in Chapter 3.

```
Main  Menu
    0   Exit AutoCAD
    1   Begin a NEW drawing
    2   Edit an EXISTING drawing
    3   Plot a drawing
    4   Printer Plot a drawing
    5   Configure AutoCAD
    6   File Utilities
    7   Compile shape/font description file
    8   Convert old drawing file
    9   Recover damaged drawing


    Enter selection:
```

Figure 2–1 AutoCAD's MAIN MENU

2.9 Care and Treatment of the Floppy Disk

The floppy disk is a means of storing information from the computer for either short or long term. In the normal course of work, the floppy disk must be handled very carefully. If the disks are mishandled, then the stored information will either be modified or lost. For trouble-free operation, five rules should be followed:

1. Keep the disk in its envelope when not in use.
2. Do not place the disk in direct sunlight or near a magnetic field.
3. Do not touch the exposed magnetic film.
4. Do not bend, fold, or crease the disk.
5. When inserting a 5 ¼" floppy, make sure that the drive handle or drive door is in the UP position. Insert the floppy disk with the notch on the left side and the label showing. (Refer to Figure 2–2.) Gently push the disk to engage the back of the drive. Rotate the drive handle or lower the drive door to complete the loading procedure. If a 3 ½" floppy is used, place the floppy into the drive with the label up and the arrow to the operator's left. (Refer to Figure 2–2.) Push the disk into the drive until it falls into place. There are no handles or doors to be concerned about.

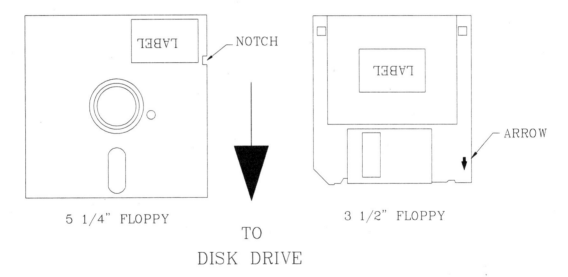

Figure 2–2 Floppy Disk

COMMAND SUMMARY

DOS Commands

DRIVE	COPY	DELETE	DIR	CD
FORMAT	RENAME	*	?	

GLOSSARY

Copy: To copy or reproduce a file or files in another directory.

Delete: To erase all data stored for a specified filename.

Directory: A listing of filenames or a section in the Hard Drive.

Drive: The housing for either a floppy drive (A or B) or the hard disk drive (C or D).

Format: To arrange the magnetic structure of the disk, in order to store information.

Rename: To change the name of a file.

PROBLEMS

1. List the procedure necessary to format a floppy disk in Drive B if the DOS commands are located in the hard drive (Drive C).
2. Are there any limitations or restrictions in establishing either a filename or directory name?
3. List the required procedures to copy a file (named school.dwg) from the AutoCAD directory in drive C to a floppy disk in drive A.
4. You want to copy four files from directory A on drive C to a floppy disk in drive A. The filenames are CNTL1, CRTL2, CATL3, and CCTL4. List the procedure and commands used to copy the four files using one command.
5. True or false. It is possible to copy a file onto the same directory that the file is listed.
6. The file named proto1 has to be renamed MANUF1. The file is located in directory 3 of the hard drive. List the procedure and commands necessary to accomplish the name change.
7. List the five rules for the use of the floppy disk.

3 Introduction to AutoCAD

Instructional Objectives

1. To understand AutoCAD's Main Menu options.
2. To be able to start a new drawing
3. To be able to edit an existing drawing
4. To be able to exit the AutoCAD program
5. To be able to use the File Utility Menu in lieu of DOS Commands
6. To be able to use the Monitor's video screen
7. To understand and be able to use AutoCAD's Units and Limits commands
8. To understand the difference between the SAVE and END commands
9. To understand the purpose of the QUIT command
10. To be able to find additional information of a command through the HELP commands

Starting with this chapter, a copy of the AutoCAD template is shown at the end of each chapter. The location of the commands listed in the chapter are highlighted by crosshatching. This illustration will assist those operators who will use the template instead of the screen menu to select applicable commands.

3.1 Introduction

The CAD operator must specify the correct directory before starting a work effort within the AutoCAD's program.

First, the current directory should be changed to the AutoCAD's directory. To accomplish this change answer the current prompt C:\> with CD ACAD (R). Complete the directory change by answering the second prompt with ACAD (R).

All information is typed, and a space between CD and ACAD must be used. The result of this log in procedure is the display of the Main Menu as shown in Figure 3–1 or a message from AutoCAD. If the message appears, press ENTER, or (R), to obtain the Main Menu.

The Main Menu lists 10 categories, tasks, or operational modes. These tasks are divided into 6 areas:

Tasks 0, 1, and 2 are considered drafting modes.

Tasks 3 and 4 provide the capability to obtain a hard copy of the drawing.

```
Main Menu
    0    Exit AutoCAD
    1    Begin a NEW drawing
    2    Edit an EXISTING drawing
    3    Plot a drawing
    4    Printer Plot a drawing
    5    Configure AutoCAD
    6    File Utilities
    7    Compile shape/font description file
    8    Convert old drawing file
    9    Recover damaged drawing


    Enter selection:
```

Figure 3–1   Main Menu

Task 5 is used for system configuration.

Task 6, File Utilities, provides for special DOS Commands (COPY, DELETE, RE-NAME, and DIRECTORY) to be accomplished without leaving the AutoCAD program.

Tasks 7 and 8 are reserved for special programs.

Task 9 recovers damaged input files.

NOTE: The extension .DWG is automatically inserted by the AutoCAD program. The AutoCAD program is "User friendly" and will tell you if a mistake has been made. Find the mistake and try the Command Sequence again.

Tasks 0, 1, and 2 are operational tasks and are discussed below. Tasks 3 and 4 are detailed in Chapter 7. Task 5, system configuration, is discussed in Appendix B. Tasks 7 and 8 are outlined in the system reference manual and not covered in this text. Task 9 is used when a drawing file has been damaged and is not acceptable to the AutoCAD software. Select Task 9 and input the filename of the damaged file. The AutoCAD software program will attempt to repair the damaged file. A screen message will indicate whether or not the file has been repaired and is usable.

3.2   Operational or Drafting Tasks

There are three operational tasks:

Start a NEW drawing

Edit an EXISTING drawing

Exit AutoCAD

3.2.1 Begin a NEW Drawing

The Operator must keep in mind that AutoCAD keeps track of the files by their filenames. The filename may consist of a maximum of eight characters [either letters (A to Z), numbers (0 to 9) or special characters, such as hyphens(-), dollar signs($), or underscoring(_)].

The AutoCAD program **automatically** adds the three character extension (.DWG) to all filenames.

Remember, that both DOS and AutoCAD treat uppercase and lowercase letters in the same way.

To start a new drawing, the operator inputs number 1 (Task 1) as shown in Figure 3–2. The system then asks for the file or drawing name. The operator types in the filename and depresses the ENTER button.

If the filename is already on file, the following message will be displayed.

**Warning! A drawing with this name already exists.

Do you want to replace it with the new drawing? <N>

The operator has a choice of either to replace the existing file or change the filename.

3.2.2 Edit an EXISTING Drawing

If the operator wants to recall an existing drawing, then number 2 is used to signify an existing drawing is required. Again, the prompt will ask for the filename. If the filename is not in the directory, then the following message will appear:

**Drawing (name) is not on file.

Press return to continue.

```
Main Menu
    0   Exit AutoCAD
    1   Begin a NEW drawing
    2   Edit an EXISTING drawing
    3   Plot a drawing
    4   Printer Plot a drawing
    5   Configure AutoCAD
    6   File Utilities
    7   Compile shape/font description file
    8   Convert old drawing file
    9   Recover damaged drawing


Enter selection:   1

Enter Name of drawing <default>: filename
```

Figure 3–2 Initiating a New Drawing

If this message appears, the operator has either made a mistake in the filename or the drawing may exist in another directory. If the drawing is located on a floppy disk, the operator must insert the floppy disk containing the drawing in drive A, input the number 2 (to instruct the program that the drawing is an existing file), then type A:filename(R). The A: instructs the program to look at the floppy disk in drive A for the file.

3.2.3 Exit AutoCAD

When the operator has completed the assigned work effort and wants to exit the AutoCAD program, the existing work effort must be Ended or Quit (refer to paragraph 3.8 of this chapter). Upon ending or quitting the drawing, the Main Menu reappears. The operator has to type ZERO (0) to exit the program. This results in a C:\> prompt.

3.3 File Utility Menu

Chapter 2 describes a number of DOS commands; however, AutoCAD has been designed to provide similar DOS functions without leaving the AutoCAD program. These commands are listed in Figure 3–3.

The selection of any of the File Utilities options is straightforward. Input the option number and follow the prompts on the screen.

CAUTION: When asked for the drawing name, remember that the name of the drawing has a maximum of eight characters plus the .DWG extension.

To obtain a listing or directory of .DWG, select 1 and (R). This input will provide a listing of all .DWG files in the existing directory. To obtain a listing for files on a floppy in drive A, select 1, then type A: and (R). File Utility 2 will list those filenames that do not have a .DWG extension. File numbers 3, 4, 5 (Delete, Rename, and Copy files) perform the same functions as the Dos Commands discussed in Chapter 2. Cat-

```
File Utility Menu
    0.  Exit File Utility Menu
    1.  List Drawing files
    2.  List user specified files
    3.  Delete files
    4.  Rename files
    5.  Copy files
    6.  Unlock files

Enter selection (0 to 6) <0>:
```

Figure 3–3 File Utilities Menu

egory 6 (Unlock Files) is used when the AutoCAD program is used in the Network mode. When a file is locked up (used by another operator), select this option and input the filename. Usually, the locked filename is the same as that shown on the screen with the exception of the extension. The last character of the extension is changed to k.

3.4   Operational Video Screen

You have now selected Option 1 of the Main Menu and have input the proper filename. After a short pause, the Monitor will display the operational video screen as shown in Figure 3–4.

The video screen is divided into four operational areas:

1. Status Line/Pull Down Menus
2. Root Screen Menu
3. Command Line
4. Drawing Area

The Status Line, located at the top of the screen, lists the Layer that is set, whether the SNAP and/or ORTHO options are active and the Coordinates of the cursor have been activated. If the Coordinates do not change when the Pointer is moved, press F6.

The Root Screen Menu is located on the right side of the screen and is one of several methods used to input a command to the AutoCAD's program. The Root Screen Menu consists of a number of alphabetized Menu Names and drafting commands. Those functions that have a colon (:) after the Menu Name (eg., LAYER:), are designated as a program command. The remaining Menu Names are titles of a submenu. There are approximately 25 submenus.

The Command Line, located on the bottom of the screen, is the area where an

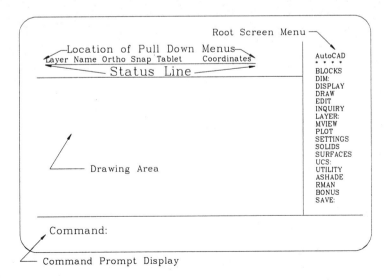

Figure 3–4   Operational Video Screen

interchange of information occurs. The operator inputs data to the CPU and the AutoCAD program, or answers the program prompts.

The Drawing Area takes up the majority of screen space. The space appears to be small, but you will be able to set the limits (either in inches or metric units) for an object as small as a pin head or as large as a skyscraper.

There is a Pull Down Menu located in the same area as the Status Line. This menu is activated (when in Task 1 or 2) by moving the Pointer or cursor (the crosshairs on the screen) to the top of the screen. This menu contains Menu Names that are the same as those shown in the Root Screen Menu. The selection of the command is accomplished by placing the arrow on the Menu Name and then on the command name.

3.5   The Pointer

AutoCAD is called a "Menu-driven program and user friendly." All the commands are listed on successive Screen Menus. The Root Screen Menu, shown in Figure 3–5, is used to select any program function that resides in the AutoCAD program.

The menus are organized as follows. All the Menu Names are alphabetized for easy selection. Use of a colon (:) after the name defines a drafting function. The remaining names are Menu Names and are used to select a submenu command list.

REMEMBER: The program will usually accept input commands from either the keyboard, the Screen Menu, or a Template. The term *Pointer* is a generic term used to describe a Mouse, Puck, Digitizer, or Stylus. The Pointer is used to select a command name or Menu Name from the Screen Menu or Template.

NOTE: Pointers have a minimum of one button (called a *Stylus* or *Pen*) to a maximum of 16 buttons or functions. The buttons are usually labeled

Figure 3–5   Root Screen Menu

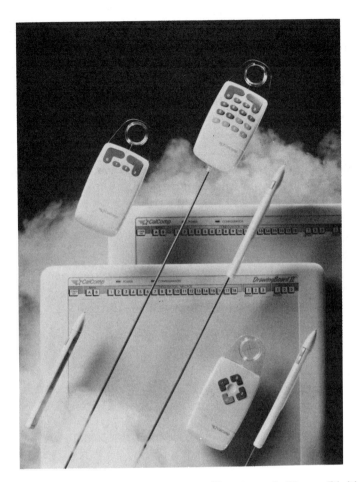

Figure 3–6   Available Pointers from CalComp (Courtesy CalComp Digitizer Products Group)

with a number or letter. Each button is programmed for a specific function. The Pick button, usually labeled zero (0), will pick a command from the Screen Menu or Template Menu. This selection is the same as typing the command. If the Pointer has more than one button, then the button labeled one (1) serves the same function as pressing the ENTER key (for most commands). If there are three buttons, then the third button labeled two (2) is usually reserved for the OSNAP command. The fourth button labeled three (3) functions to cancel the current command (called ^C). These button assignments are listed below:

Button 0: Selects the command.

Button 1: Acts the same way as the ENTER key.

Button 2: Brings up the OSNAP commands.

The remaining button functions are listed in the operations manual of the Pointer. Figure 3–6 shows a number of different Pointers.

When the Pointer is used to select a command from the Screen Menu area, the Menu Names are highlighted. After the command is highlighted, press the ENTER key. Another way to input a command is to use the Template. The Template has to be configured. (Refer to Chapter 20.) Use of the Template is reserved for experienced operators and is discussed later on in this text. An alternate method to pick a Screen command is to use the keyboard and the INS button and UP/DOWN arrows. When the proper command is highlighted, press the ENTER key (R).

There are approximately 25 submenus in the AutoCAD program. You should become familiar with the heading as shown in the Root Screen Menu. (Refer to Figure 3–5.) As you continue in this program, the menu selection will become easier. If the submenu's listings exceed the 20 command listings, the last listing will have the term *next*. Use the Pointer to pick "next." This will continue the submenu listing. Likewise, the term *previous* is used to return to the beginning of the submenu listing.

3.6   Establishing AutoCAD's System of Units

The operator should first establish the units (inches, feet, or feet/inches) for the drawing. The UNITS command is not listed on the Root Screen Menu (Figure 3–5). The UNITS command is located in the Settings Submenu. The SETTINGS Submenu (shown in Figure 3–7) has two pages.

The initial listing starts with DDEMODES to LIMITS and "next".

The term "next" means that the submenu is continued on the next or second page. When you highlight "next" with the Pointer, the second part of the SETTINGS Menu is displayed (starting with LTSCALE and ending with VPORTS). Highlight the command name (in this case, UNITS) and the Command Prompt Line becomes part of the Text Screen as shown in Figure 3–8.

The Text Screen is considered as the back of or the flipside of the Graphics or Drawing Screen. The Text Screen contains information in a text form, whereas the

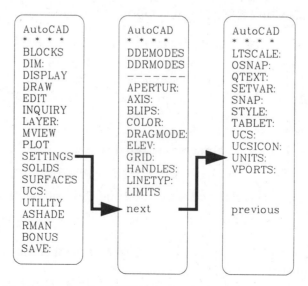

Figure 3–7 Menu Map for the UNITS Command

```
Command: units
System of units:            (Examples)

      1.  Scientific         1.55E+01
      2.  Decimal            15.50
      3.  Engineering        1'-3.50"
      4.  Architectural      1'-3 1/2"
      5.  Fractional         15 1/2

Enter choice, 1 to 5 <2>:
Number of digits to right of decimal point (0 to 8) <4>:
```

Figure 3–8   AutoCAD's System of Units

graphics Screen may contain graphical and text data. F1 (located on the keyboard) acts as a switch (to/from the Text Screen or to/from Graphics Screen).

The term *unit* is very difficult to define. In some AutoCAD applications unit represents a pure number. For engineering and architecture applications, the term unit may represent inches, feet, or feet and inches.

After the UNITS command has been selected, the resulting Text Screen automatically flips ON. The Text Screen is shown in Figure 3–8.

This figure lists five categories of units. The first deals with scientific notation and the second with a decimal notation. Because Scientific and Decimal systems do not have a defined unit of measurement, both are considered pure numeric systems. However, the next two unit categories deal with inches and/or feet. The Engineering units are expressed in decimal form. The fourth category, Architectural, is similar to the Engineering Units with the exception that the distance is expressed in feet, inches, and fractional inches. The majority of architectural drawings use fractions rather than decimals. The last category, Fractional, deals only in fractions.

Usually, the units are set for a given industry and not changed. The command shown in Figure 3–8 also requires the operator to establish the accuracy of the drawing by specifying the number of digits required to the right of the decimal point. You may select from 0 to 8 digits. The actual decimal point selection must be based on the type of drawing and the decimal point readout for that type of drawing effort. When the units are expressed in feet and inches, do not leave a space between feet and inches (ie., four feet six inches is expressed as 4'-6", 4'6" or 4'6; eight feet seven and one-half inches is expressed as 8'7.5" or 8'7.5).

NOTE: If the Metric System is to be used, select decimal from the Units Menu and upon print out (either plot or Printer plot) you may then specify Metric measurement.

The feet and inches displayed on the screen will show either a space or a dash between feet and inches. The space or dash is used for clarity only and is not to be used by the operator.

The command used to establish the type of units is also used to establish the system of Angle Measurements as shown in Figure 3–9.

```
Systems of angle measure:           (Examples)

     1.  Decimal degrees            45.0000
     2.  Degrees/minutes/seconds    45d0'0"
     3.  Grads                      50.0000g
     4.  Radians                    0.7854r
     5.  Surveyor's units           N 45d0'0" E

Enter choice, 1 to 5 <1>:
Number of fractional places for display of angles (0 to 8) <0>:
```

Figure 3–9   AutCAD's System of Angle Measurements

If you are doing work for an Engineering firm then selection 1, 2, 3, or 4 can be used. However, if you are working with land surveys then selection 5 is used. In addition to Angle measurement, a tolerance or number of digits to the right of the decimal point or the lowest fraction must be selected. All rotational drawings produced by AutoCAD are in a counterclockwise direction. (Refer to Figure 3–10.) Answering the next command message "Do you want angles measured Clockwise?" with a Y (for yes) changes most rotational drawings' rotation to clockwise. AutoDESK has established the drawing rotation as counterclockwise (CCW). My suggestion is to answer this question with its default <N>.

3.7   Establishing the Limits of a Drawing

CAUTION: If the limits are expressed in feet and/or inches, select the UNITS command first.

The operator may either type in the command from the keyboard or select the command LIMITS from the Settings Submenu as shown in Figure 3–11.

The lower left corner of the screen is specified as the origin where X = 0 and Y = 0. In AutoCAD, this is expressed as 0,0 (the X value is specified first then the Y

```
Direction for angle 0:
     East    3 o'clock  =   0
     North  12 o'clock  =   90
     West    9 o'clock  =   180
     South   6 o'clock  =   270

Enter direction for angle 0 <0>:
     Do you want angles measured clockwise? <n>
```

Figure 3–10   AutoCAD's System of Compass Direction

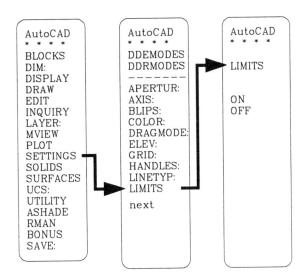

Figure 3–11 Menu Map for the LIMITS Command

value). These values *must* be separated by a comma (,). It is standard practice to specify the lower left corner of a drawing as 0,0. The actual command line message is shown in Figure 3–12.

The next command line (Figure 3–12) will ask for the upper right corner value. The default value is 12,9, [the drawing is 12 units wide (X direction) and 9 units high (Y direction)]. The ratio between X and Y (12:9 or 4:3) should be maintained. Whenever the limits are changed, this ratio must be maintained to provide a consistent drawing area. Whether the default value shown in < > is used or a different set of values are input, you must confirm the values by depressing the ENTER key or pushing button 1 on the Pointer.

If the default value that appears between < > is *not* used, then another value is substituted. Upon completion of the LIMITS' data, the ZOOM command must be used to adjust the screen display for the new limits. For the present either: type in ZOOM and depress the ENTER key and type A and (R), or answer the command line message with ALL and depress the ENTER key. If you are using a Pointer, then select DISPLAY from the Root Screen Menu (Figure 3–13), then ZOOM command from the Display Menu. (Pick ALL from the ZOOM Menu.)

```
Command:   LIMITS

ON/OFF/<Lower left corner><0.0000,0.0000>:

Upper right corner <12.0000,9.000>:
```

Figure 3–12 Command Sequence for the LIMITS Command

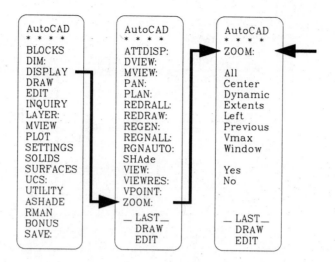

Figure 3–13 Menu Map for the ZOOM (ALL) Command

After this command has been completed, move the cursor to the upper right corner to check the upper limits. Make sure that the Coordinate Display (located in the Status Line) is activated. Use function key F6 to turn ON the Coordinate Display.

When used correctly, the LIMITS ON/OFF command will tell the CAD operator when a drawing function is not within the limits of the drawing. This command puts an electronic fence around the limits of the drawing. If ON is selected, then any drawing command that is drawn outside the limits or originates outside the limits of the drawing will not be drawn on the screen and the operator will see this message in the command prompt line:

**Outside Limits

3.8 Saving the Drawing

The CAD Operator must make sure that the information placed on the screen is not lost due to neglect, accident, or loss of electrical power. The following are two commands designed to minimize these problems:

1. SAVE command: This is an in-process save that permits the operator to continue the work effort.
2. END command: This command tells the program that the drawing has been completed. The drawing is placed into memory (on either the floppy or hard disk) and then the program is returned to the Main Menu.

3.8.1 SAVE Command

The SAVE command appears on the Root Screen Menu and is shown in Figure 3–14. The Command Sequence is shown in Figure 3–15.

Figure 3–15 displays a Dialogue Box. There are a number of these boxes used

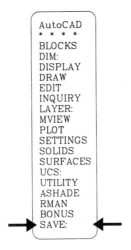

Figure 3–14 Menu Map for the SAVE Command

in this program. This box was developed by AutoDESK to minimize the number of key strokes the operator uses to activate a command. The four boxes on the right side act as Pointer buttons. Using the arrow on the screen, select the box to activate the command. However, when the "type it" box is activated, type in the drive and filename of the drawing to be saved.

It takes approximately 45 seconds to complete the SAVE sequence. This is an ideal way to invest your time in saving drawing information that has taken you 15 minutes to develop. The general rule for saving a drawing is to do so once every 15 minutes. There are a number of ways a drawing may be lost. Leading the list is power outages.

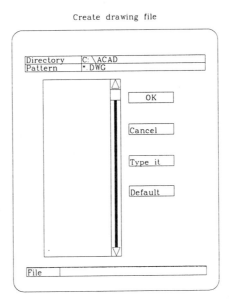

Figure 3–15 Dialogue Box for the SAVE Command

```
Command: Save (R)
File name <abcdef>: (R)
```

Figure 3–16 Command Sequence for the SAVE Command

The SAVE command is also used to make a copy of a drawing for updating without changing the original or reference drawing. Refer to the Command Sequence for the SAVE command in Figure 3–16. The second line lists the current drawing as a default. A copy of the reference drawing may be made by inputting the name of the new drawing and pressing (R). When the command line returns, input the command QUIT and answer the next line with Y. (Refer to Figure 3–17 for the Command Sequence for the QUIT command.) The CPU then returns the AutoCAD program to the Main Menu. Select option 2 (Edit an EXISTING drawing) and use the new drawing name.

3.8.2 QUIT command

The QUIT command may be used to leave the drawing without saving the drawing. The QUIT command is used when a drawing is reviewed but no changes are made or the drawing effort has so many errors that it pays to start over again. The QUIT command is found in the Utility Submenu as shown in Figure 3–18.

CAUTION: Make sure that you want to discard the drawing. AutoCAD gives you a second chance when the command prompt states "Really want to discard all changes to the drawing?" If the answer is yes, input Y. All information during this drawing effort will be erased. If you have second thoughts about discarding the drawing data, reply with N for NO and the drawing remains.

3.8.3 END Command

The END command is found in the Utilities Submenu and is illustrated in Figure 3–19 (Menu Map for the END Command).

```
Command: QUIT (R)
 Really want to discard all changes to Drawing? Yes (R)
```

Figure 3–17 Command Sequence for the QUIT Command

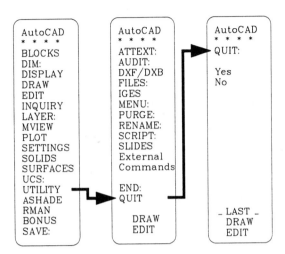

Figure 3–18   Menu Map for the QUIT Command

This command is used when the drawing effort has been completed and the operator wants to go on to another work effort. The Command Sequence (shown in Figure 3–20) is simple.

When the END command is picked or typed, the screen goes blank and returns with the Main Menu (Figure 3–1).

If the current drawing is new, the program takes all the data and places it in the hard disk under the drawing name. If this drawing is an update or revision of an existing drawing, then a different process is initiated. The initial or original drawing that was placed on the screen will be saved under the same drawing name but with a new extension: .BAK (back up). The drawing that was ended would have the same drawing name and the .DWG extension. In this way, there will be a backup

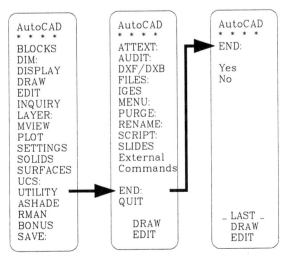

Figure 3–19   Menu Map for the END Command

Command: END

Figure 3–20 Command Sequence for the END Command

drawing. If the backup drawing has to be used, then the extension name must be changed to .DWG. Chapter 2 and the File Utilities (subparagraph 3.2) provides for the change in extension name (RENAME command).

3.9 HELP Command

The AutoCAD software is user friendly. The operator has the capability of obtaining command information by the use of the HELP command. The Command Sequence for the HELP command is shown in Figure 3–21.

Make sure that the Command prompt will accept a new command. The HELP command is located in the Inquiry Submenu and shown in Figure 3–22. The Command Sequence is illustrated in Figure 3–21. The important rule to remember is to first input a request for HELP, then input the Command name. If the operator is uncertain of the command spelling, place a ? for the second input.

Command: HELP
Command name (RETURN for list):

Figure 3–21 Command Sequence for the HELP Command

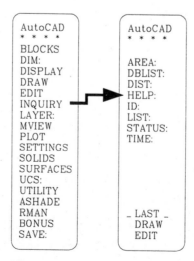

Figure 3–22 Menu Map for the HELP Command

3.10 Template Reference—Chapter 3

Figure 3-23 is the Template Reference for Chapter 3.

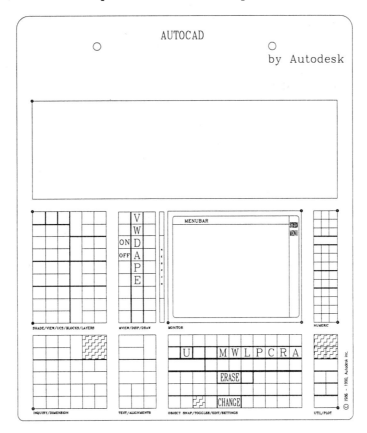

Figure 3–23 Template Reference for Chapter 3

COMMAND SUMMARY

The commands described in this chapter are as follows

UNITS	LIMITS
SAVE	END
QUIT	HELP

GLOSSARY

Command Line: Located at the bottom of the Monitor Screen. Used to input and receive messages from the program.

Limits: Defines the size of the drawing. Provides for the setting of the lower left corner (origin) of the drawing as well as the upper right corner.

Mouse: A peripheral device used to input data to the program.

Pick: To highlight and select a command or menu name from the Screen Menu.

Pointer: Generic name for an input device, such as the Mouse.

Puck: A device similar to a Mouse or Pointer.

Units: Units of a drawing when using the Scientific or Decimal option.

PROBLEMS

1. There are six categories listed in the File Utilities Menu. Name three categories and explain their functions.
2. List the peripherals that go into a CAD workstation.
3. Define the terms SAVE, END, and QUIT.
4. Describe the procedure necessary to use the HELP command.
5. The Main Menu contains nine listings. Name four listings and explain their functions.

4 The Basics of Computer Drafting

Instructional Objectives

1. To be able to use AutoCAD's drafting aids effectively
2. To be able to designate and locate a point on the screen
3. To be able to draw a line, circle, or arc to a given set of specifications
4. To be able to letter or place text information on the screen
5. To be able to erase a portion or all of a drawing
6. To be able to use the Function keys and Control keys effectively
7. To be able to use the Pull Down Menus effectively

4.1 Introduction

AutoCAD has been designed to assist the CAD operator in the drawing effort by providing the electronic equivalent of a pencil, ruler, and quad ruled pad. This assistance comes in the form of four Commands: GRID, SNAP, AXIS, and SPECIAL COMMANDS. The SNAP command controls the placement of the cursor. Usually the GRID spacing is a multiple of the SNAP spacing.

The GRID command displays a series of dots on the Video Monitor, similar to the boxes used in the quad rule pads. The operator can make the dots visible or invisible, or change the spacing between dots (whether the dots are visible or not). The GRID options are discussed in paragraph 4.2. Occasionally the GRID and SNAP spacing are the same, depending upon the drawing requirements. The GRID and SNAP commands are described in paragraphs 4.2 and 4.3, respectively.

4.2 GRID Command

The GRID command places a grid of dots (these dots will not be seen on the printout) spaced at specified intervals. The spacing may be equal to, less than, or greater than the SNAP setting. The GRID command is located in the Settings Submenu and a menu map for the GRID command is shown in Figure 4–1.

The Command Sequence lists four selections or choices that are available to the operator. (See Figure 4–2.)

The GRID spacing may either be in numerical units, decimal inches, or fractional inches. (Again, the GRID units will be the same as those established for the drawing.) However, by using the X response, it is possible to make the GRID spacing

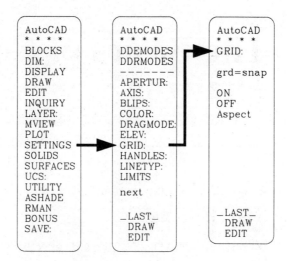

Figure 4–1   Menu Map for the GRID Command

```
Command: GRID
    Grid spacing(X) or ON/OFF/Snap/Aspect <0.0000>:
```

Figure 4–2   Command Sequence for the GRID Command

a multiple of the SNAP setting. For example, an input of 0.1X would provide a grid whose spacing would be 0.1 of the SNAP setting. A return of zero (0), automatically sets the GRID spacing equal to the SNAP spacing.

The GRID may be turned ON or OFF by the proper response to the command prompt. However, there are two other means to activate this command from the keyboard: F7 or ^G act as a toggle switch for the ON or OFF action.

When the operator replies to the Command Sequence with S, the GRID setting is automatically equal to the SNAP setting. The input of S has the same effect as inputting a 0 for GRID spacing. This feature (GRID spacing = SNAP spacing) becomes a time-saving feature when working with a large drawing.

The Aspect option provides a grid whose horizontal value (X) is not equal to the vertical value (Y). A is the answer to the command prompt. The prompt then requests a horizontal value and then a vertical value. The results of these values will be seen on the screen, if the grid is visible. The appearance of the grid depends not only on the command activated but also the size or limits of the drawing. If the drawing represents a 12 × 9 area, then a 0.25 grid is visible, but if the limits are 24 × 18 the grid appears to be too dense and the program will (1) not display the grid and (2) place the following message on the command line:

Grid too dense to display

4.3 SNAP Command

Although the grid might be visible or invisible, the effect of the SNAP command can be seen as the cursor is moved across the screen. The cursor will appear to hesitate and move from one GRID point to another (in SNAP increments as set by the operator). The SNAP command is located in the SETTING Submenu as shown in Figure 4–3. Figure 4–4 illustrates the Command Sequence that is used by AutoCAD.

Referring to Figure 4–4, the operator will select one of several modes:

1. Snap spacing
2. Turn ON/OFF the Snap command.
3. Change the Aspect ratio.
4. Rotate the Snap axis.
5. Set Snap style.

Mode 1 sets the spacing for the SNAP Command. This spacing will use the same UNITS specification (refer to Chapter 3) as input at the start of the drawing. Mode 2: The SNAP function may be turned ON or OFF by (A) using the SNAP command, (B) pressing the F9 function key or (C) pressing Ctrl and B keys (together) on the keyboard. The symbol for Ctrl is ^ (shifted 6). From this point in the text, the word Ctrl is replaced with ^ (eg., Ctrl C is written as ^C).

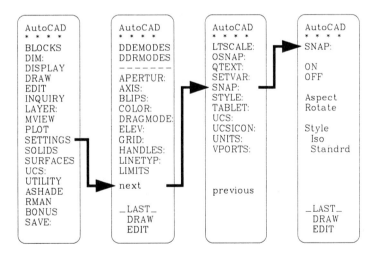

Figure 4–3 Menu Map for the SNAP Command

```
Command: SNAP
Snap spacing or ON/OFF/Snap/Aspect/Rotate/Style <0.0000>:
```

Figure 4–4 Command Sequence for the SNAP Command

```
Command: SNAP

 Snap spacing or ON/OFF/Aspect/Rotate/Style<0.0000>:  ASPECT
 Horizontal spacing <0.0000>:  1
 Vertical spacing(X) <0.0000>:  2
```

Figure 4–5 Command Sequence for the SNAP Command, Aspect Option

CAUTION: When the SNAP mode is turned ON, the Cursor (when moved) appears to jump from point to point and may be difficult to place the cursor at a position that is not a SNAP intersection. If this occurs, turn OFF the SNAP function (use either F9 or ^B).

Mode 3: The term Aspect (ratio) takes into account the relative SNAP distance established for the X-axis and the Y-axis. Usually, the ratio is 1 (X=Y). For those applications where the value of X SNAP is different from the Y SNAP, the operator responds to the command prompt with A. The command prompt will then ask for the horizontal (X) distance, then the vertical distance (Y) as shown in Figure 4–5.

The fourth selection, or Mode 4, provides the operator with the ability to rotate the SNAP axis. The rotation of the SNAP axis is similar to rotating the graph paper by a specific angle.

The last selection, Mode 5, depends upon whether the drawing is to be isometric or standard. If the operator is drawing on an isometric plane, then the reply is S for Style, then I for Isometric or S for Standard. Once the SNAP command is set, the customary command is either ON or OFF.

4.4 AXIS Command

When activated, the AXIS command simulates a ruler line across the bottom and on the right side of the screen as shown in Figure 4–6.

The command is found in the Settings Submenu. Figure 4–7 presents the Menu Map for the AXIS command.

The Command Sequence is listed in Figure 4–8.

The Command Sequence for the AXIS, GRID and SNAP commands are similar. The AXIS settings can be locked to the SNAP settings by answering the command prompt with zero (0) or the letter S. Usually the value of the AXIS setting is some multiple of the SNAP setting. In most cases the multiple is 10.The answer to the command prompt would be 10X.

The AXIS presentation may be turned ON or OFF by typing the command AXIS from the keyboard.

NOTE: Where the drawing limits are large as compared to the GRID or AXIS spacing, the program will not process the AXIS or GRID commands but will return a prompt message that reads "The GRID or AXIS is too

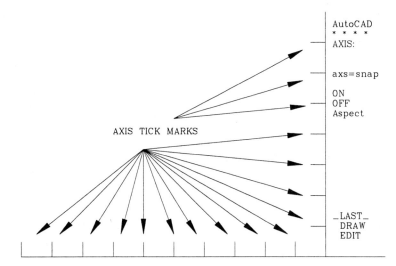

Figure 4–6   AXIS Line Display

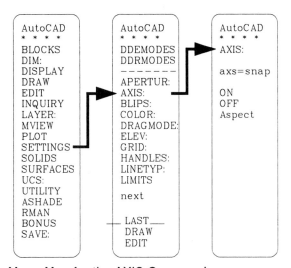

Figure 4–7   Menu Map for the AXIS Command

Command: AXIS
Tick spacing (X) or ON/OFF/Snap/Aspect <0.1000>:

Figure 4–8   Command Sequence for the AXIS Command

dense to display". The operator may either turn off the GRID or AXIS commands or change the individual settings.

4.5 SPECIAL Commands

In the event that the operator wants to interrupt a Command Sequence, do *not* shut off the power to the computer. For most applications, the use of ^C or the corresponding button on the pointing device will stop the command and return the command line for the next command.

If the program has stalled and the cursor cannot be moved and ^C has no effect, the next step is to depress the Ctrl Alt and Del keys at the same time. The first letter of each key (CAD) calls out the word CAD but does not have anything to do with the CAD program. The CAD keys will function for any program. When these keys are depressed, the computer will warm reboot and go back to the initial display (blank screen with the C prompt).

NOTE: When the Ctrl, Alt, and Del keys are used, the drawing on the screen will be lost. Therefore, this procedure should be used for Emergency *only*.

The other special command keys were discussed in the preceeding sections and are listed below for reference.

	ON/OFF FUNCTION	
Command	F key	^key
Snap	F9	^B
Grid	F7	^G
Flip Screen	F1	
Ortho	F8	^O
Coordinates	F6	^D
Cancel		^C
Delete		^X
Template	F10	^T

The ORTHO command restricts the movement of the line to either the X- or Y-axis, F8 or ^O turns this command ON or OFF. If the SNAP is rotated, then the ORTHO will be rotated accordingly.

4.6 Basic Drafting Commands

The basic drafting commands that are used most frequently are: place a point, make a line, develop a circle, and draw an arc.

4.6.1 POINT Command

The POINT command enables the operator to place a dot at a given location on the screen display. The location of this point is specified by a value for X (called X1) and for Y (called Y1). In the language of AutoCAD, the X value is given first followed by a comma and then the Y value. If the comma is omitted or a period is used, the command prompt will ask for the information again with the message "Invalid point." The location of the point is specified as a distance from the origin. AutoCAD assumes that the origin (0,0 where X = 0 and Y = 0) is located at the lower left corner of the drawing. The origin may be changed to another value and implemented when setting the Limits of the drawing. Figure 4–9 illustrates the point location of 4,2 as well as the location and value of the origin. These points are called Absolute or Cartesian Coordinates.

Notice that the units for this example are numeric. The X value of the point is 4 units to the right of the origin. (A negative sign in front of the 4 would mean that the point is 4 units to the left of the origin.) The Y value of the point is 2 units above the origin. (A negative sign in front of the 2 would mean that the point is below the origin.)

The POINT command is located in the Draw Menu and the Menu Map for the POINT command is shown in Figure 4–10. The Command Sequence for this command is given in Figure 4–11.

The location of the point may either be input from the keyboard in the form X,Y or placed on the screen by using the Pointer. When the Pointer's pick button (usually number 0) is depressed, a value of X and Y is determined by the program. The size of the point, when plotted will be the size of the pen tip. In the case of a Printer plot, the size will be one dot of the dot matrix. It should be noted that the symbol for a POINT is usually a small dot. However, AutoCAD has developed 15 additional symbols that are used to designate a POINT. These symbols are discussed in Chapter 12 (SETVAR Commands).

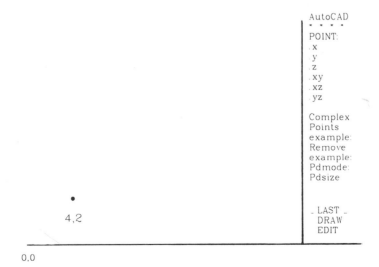

Figure 4–9 Point Location

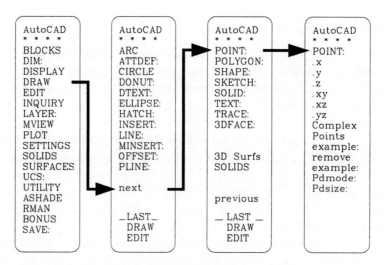

Figure 4–10 Menu Map for the POINT Command

Command: POINT Point: 4,2 (R)

Figure 4–11 Command Sequence for the POINT Command

4.6.2 LINE Command

The LINE command enables the operator to draw a line between two specific points. The LINE command is located in the Draw Submenu. The Menu Map for the LINE command is given in Figure 4–12.

The LINE command is one of several repetitive commands that prompt or ask the operator for the next "To point". When the LINE command is used (see Figure 4–13) the first statement in the Command line requests "From point". The answer must always be in Cartesian or Absolute Coordinates (X1,Y1) or the operator may place a point on the screen using the Pointer. After the first point or From point is specified, the answer to the To point may take one of four answers:

1. Cartesian Coordinates (X,Y)
2. Relative Coordinates specified as @X,Y
3. Polar notation specified as @M<angle
4. Pointer

The LINE command From point is specified in the same way that the point was described in paragraph 4.6.1. The values of X and Y are called the Cartesian or Absolute Coordinates.

The second method of specifying a point is called Relative Coordinates. These Coordinates specify the new To point with reference to the previous From point. The new point will be a certain distance in the horizontal direction (delta X) and a certain

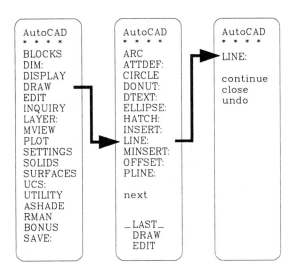

Figure 4–12   Menu Map for the LINE Command

distance in the vertical direction (delta Y). If a negative sign is placed before the value, such as -5,-3, then the delta X point will move to the left and the delta Y point will move down. Figure 4–14 illustrates the From point (3,1) and the relative value of X = 5 and Y = 2. The symbol @ (shifted 2), placed at the start of the inputted value, notifies the program that the next "To" location will use the Relative system. The information that is input will be in the form @5,2. No spaces are used between the @, X value, comma, or Y value. The location of the new point will be the addition of the values of X (3 + 5) or 8 and the addition of the Y values (1 + 2) or 3. The Cartesian or Absolute Coordinates for the second point are 8,3.

Example 4–1:   From point: = 2,3; To point: #1 = @4,5; To point: #2 = @-2,-3. Figure 4–15 shows the placement of these points. The last To point of the line is located at 4,5.

Polar notation (the second relative method) provides for the distance (magnitude) from the initial From point to the new To point and the relative angle. The typed data has the form @M<angle. If the distance to the next point is @4<45, the program will interpret this information as taking a line whose length is 4 units and an angle of 45° from the reference point.

REMEMBER: East direction is zero degrees (0°).

Figure 4–16 illustrates the From point of 3,3. The location of the To point (end of the line @4<45) is 5.284,5.284.

```
Command: Line  From  point:  X,Y
To  point:  X1,Y1
```

Figure 4–13   Command Sequence for the LINE Command

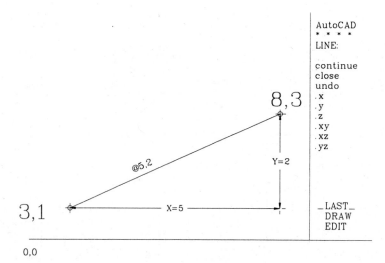

Figure 4–14 Relative Coordinate (@X,Y) System

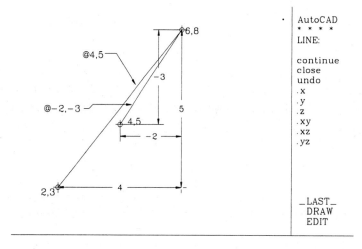

Figure 4–15 Solution to Example 4–1

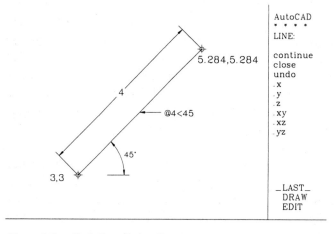

Figure 4–16 Use of the Relative Polar System

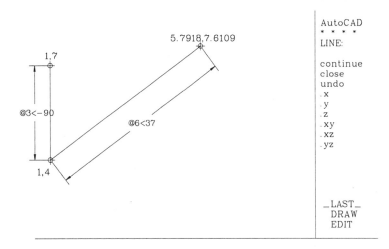

Figure 4-17 Solution to Example 4-2

REMEMBER: The input data should *not* have any spaces between @, <, and 45.

Example 4-2: From point = 0,7; distance to first To point = @3<-90; distance to the next To point = @6<37. The negative sign before the angle value means that the rotation will be clockwise. [Normal rotation for AutoCAD is counterclockwise (CCW). Figure 4-17 shows the solution. (The location of the last To point @6<37 is 5.7918,7.6109.

CAUTION: The LINE command requires either a new value of X,Y or a null value. If a null value is used (depress the ENTER key or space bar), the program will interpret this input as the end of the LINE command.

The ability of the program to remember and retain the location of every point used in the drawing provides the operator with a unique capability called Continue option. The Continue option is listed in the LINE Submenu as shown in Figure 4-18.

The Continue option places the cursor at the end of the last line providing that the LINE Command Sequence was not broken. If the operator wants to continue a line, the LINE command is activated as in the normal operation but the location of the From point is null (depress the space bar or the ENTER key). The alternative method is to pick the Continue option from the Screen Menu. Another use of the Continue option is to go from LINE command to an ARC command.

Since the computer remembers the location of every point that has been specified, AutoCAD provides for a special feature called Close option. For example: Draw a box of 4 sides. After the third side is drawn, you may either draw the last line or use the Close option by selecting C from the keyboard or Close from the Screen Menu. The program remembers the location of the start point and all other points. The AutoCAD program will draw a line from the last To point to the first From point. The selection of the Close option may also be picked from the LINE Submenu.

```
AutoCAD
* * * *
LINE:

continue
close
undo
. x
. y
. z
. xy
. xz
. yz



_LAST_
DRAW
EDIT
```

Figure 4–18 Line Command Submenu

CAUTION: AutoCAD assumes that the line commands have not been broken. If the LINE Command Sequence was terminated, the closing Line from the last point will go to the first point of the new sequence.

Try this example: LINE command; From point = 2,5; To point = 4,6; To point = @-2,0. Close the drawing using the Close option.

4.6.3 CIRCLE Commands

AutoCAD has 5 different methods for drawing a circle:

1. Given Center and Radius

2. Given Center and Diameter

3. Given 3 points

4. Given 2 points

5. Tangent, Tangent and Radius (TTR)

Each method has its own Menu Map and Command Sequence. The operator should select the correct method based on available data.

4.6.3.1 *Center and Radius (Method 1)*

If the Center point and Radius are given, use the Menu Map for the Circle as shown in Figure 4–19 and the Command Sequence as shown in Figure 4–20.

The Center of the circle is given in Cartesian (Absolute) Coordinates or by the use of the Pointer for a screen pick. The Radius is input either through the keyboard or by pointing.

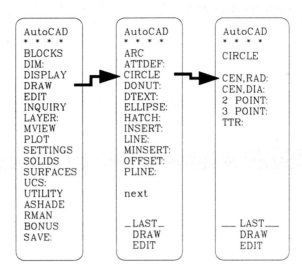

Figure 4–19   Menu Map for a Circle (Method 1)

```
Command:  CIRCLE 3P/2P/TTR/<Center point>:
     Diameter/<Radius>:
```

Figure 4–20   Command Sequence for a Circle (Method 1)

Example 4–3: Draw a Circle whose Center is located at 5.5,5.5 with a Radius of 4. The solution is shown in Figure 4–21.

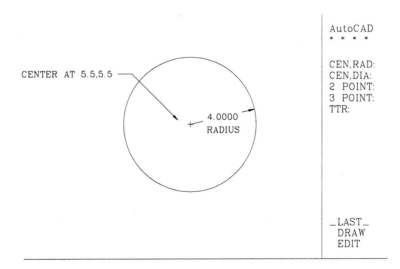

Figure 4–21   Solution to Example 4–3

4.6.3.2   Center and DIAMETER (Method 2)

The Menu Map and the Command Sequence for the Method 2 Circle is the same as Method 1 with the one exception. The Diameter of the circle is used instead of the Radius. Figure 4–22 is the Menu Map for the Circle drawn using Method 2 and Figure 4–23 is the Command Sequence for this method.

Repeat Example 4–3, but change the Radius of 4 to a diameter of 8. The two circles will appear as one line.

4.6.3.3   THREE POINT CIRCLE (Method 3)

The AutoCAD program makes an assumption that the 3 points are located on the circumference of the circle. The Menu Map for the 3 Point Circle is shown in Figure 4–24, while Figure 4–25 describes the Command Sequence.

The location of the first point may either be in Cartesian Coordinates or designated by using the Pointer (to place that point on the screen). The two remaining points may be specified by using Cartesian Coordinates, relative delta, relative polar, or pointing.

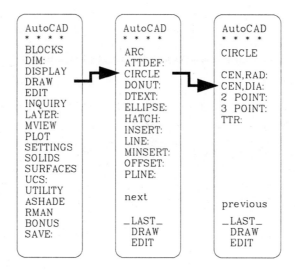

Figure 4–22   Menu Map for the Circle Command (Method 2)

```
Command: CIRCLE 3P/2P/TTR/<Center point>:
   Diameter/<Radius>: D Diameter:
```

Figure 4–23   Command Sequence for the Circle Menu (Method 2)

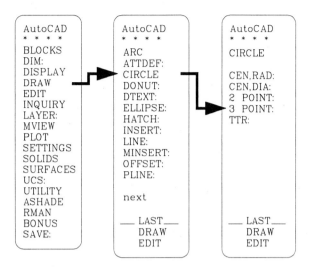

Figure 4–24 Menu Map for the 3 Point Circle (Method 3)

```
Command: CIRCLE 3P/2P/TTR/<Center point>: 3P First point: 4,2
Second point: @3<90
Third point: @3,-3
```

Figure 4–25 Command Sequence for the 3 Point Circle (Method 3)

Example 4–4: The following data are used to draw a 3P Circle: 3P First point = 4,2; Second point = @3<90 and Third point = @3,-3. Figure 4–26 shows the solution to this example.

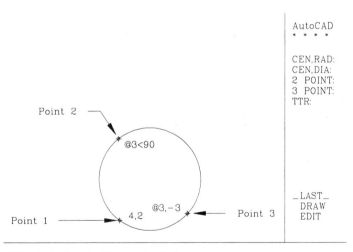

Figure 4–26 Solution to Example 4–4

4.6.3.4 TWO POINT CIRCLE (Method 4)

In order to construct a circle using two points, AutoCAD assumes that these points are on the diameter of the circle. Figure 4–27 is the Menu Map for the 2 Point Circle (Method 4).

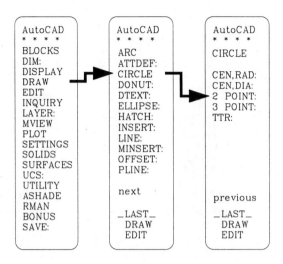

Figure 4–27   Menu Map for a 2 Point Circle (Method 4)

```
Command: CIRCLE 3P/2P/TTR/<Center point>: 2P First point on diameter: 1.5,4
Second point on diameter: 5,5
```

Figure 4–28   Command Sequence for the 2 Point Circle

The Command Sequence is similar to the three point method and is shown in Figure 4–28. The first point may either be the Absolute Coordinates or may be specified using the Pointer.

Example 4–5: 2P First point on diameter = 1.5,4 and Second point on diameter = 5,5. Figure 4–29 gives the solution.

NOTE: For the 3P and 2P Circles, we will use Point 1, Point 2, or Point 3 to specify the point location.

4.6.3.5 *TANGENT, TANGENT and Radius (TTR) (Method 5)*

The circle generated by this command will be based on the following: Drawing a line that is tangent to a point on a circle, drawing a circle that is tangent to two lines, or drawing a circle that is tangent to another circle and arc. In any of these cases, the Radius of the circle must be input by a numerical value or by use of the Pointing device. Figure 4–30 shows the Menu Map for the TTR Circle. Figure 4–31 reflects the Command Sequence for this command.

Example 4–6: Given a line (A) and a Circle (B), construct another circle tangent to the line and first circle with a Radius of 1. Line A: 3,2 to 5,3; Circle B is centered at

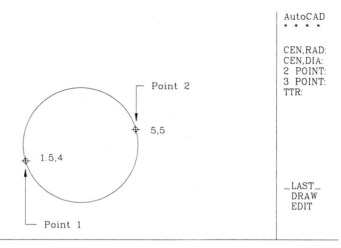

Figure 4–29 Solution to Example 4–5

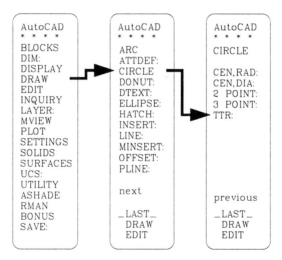

Figure 4–30 Menu Map for the TTR Circle (Method 5)

```
Command: CIRCLE 3P/2P/TTR<Center point>: TTR
Enter Tangent spec:
Enter Second Tangent spec:      Radius:
```

Figure 4–31 Command Sequence for the TTR Circle (Method 5)

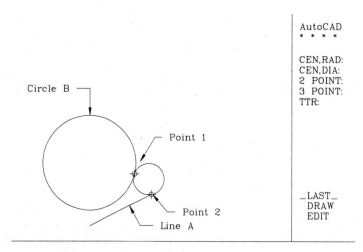

Figure 4–32   Solution to Example 4–6

3,4 with a Radius of 1.5. Construct Circle C tangent to Line A at Point 2 and tangent to Circle B at Point 1 with a Radius of 0.5. Figure 4–32 shows the solution.

The process above shows the basic sequence. There are other configurations of TTR circle construction but they require the use of another command (OSNAP). If the circle cannot be drawn, the operator will see the following message in the command line area: "Circle does not exist."

4.7 ARC Commands

The designers of the AutoCAD program were very careful in establishing many methods to construct an arc. Five methods are available for circle construction, but 11 methods are called out for the construction of an arc.

REMEMBER: The ARC is a segment of a circle.

The information to construct an arc is usually based on three data points and the methods listed below:

1. 3–Points
2. Start point, Center , endpoint
3. Start point, Center, Included angle
4. Start point, Center, Length of chord
5. Start point, endpoint, Radius
6. Start point, endpoint, Included angle
7. Start point, endpoint, Starting Direction
8. Center, Start point, endpoint
9. Center, Start point, Included angle
10. Center, Start point, Length of chord
11. Continuation of a Line and endpoint

The ARC commands are abbreviated in the ARC Submenu. The letters used in the abbreviations are listed below with their definitions:

A = Included angle
C = Center
D = Starting Direction
S = Start point

E = End point
L = Length of chord
R = Radius

The ARC Submenu is self-explanatory. Determine what information is available (A, E, S, R, etc.) and match the information on hand with one of the 11 methods listed above. Once the method is selected, answer the command prompts. Figure 4–33 is the Menu Map for the ARC command. The ARC command is found in the DRAW Submenu. Figures 4–34 to 4–41 are the Command Sequence for the 11 ARC commands.

Methods 8,9 and 10, follow a similar procedure to that listed above.

The terms *chord* and *direction* should be defined before the ARC commands are used. The chord is defined by the straight-line distance connecting the Arc's Starting point and endpoint. A positive sign prior to the chord length provides for the minor axis (less than 180°) drawn CCW. However, a negative value of the chord's length will draw the major axis of the arc CCW.

The direction of the arc is specified by an angle (90° means above the point) or the use of the Pointer.

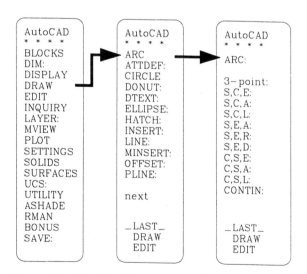

Figure 4–33 Menu Map for the ARC Commands

```
Command:   ARC Center/<Start point>:
Center/End/<Second point>:
End point:
```

Figure 4–34 Command Sequence for the 3-Point Arc

```
Command:   ARC Center/<Start point>:
Center/End/<Second point>: C Center:
Angle/Length of chord/<End point>:
```

Figure 4–35 Command Sequence for the SCE Arc

```
Command: ARC Center/<Start point>:
Center/End/<Second point>: C Center:
Angle/Length of chord/<End point>: A Included angle:
```

Figure 4–36 Command Sequence for the SCA Arc

```
Command: ARC  Center/<Start point>:
Center/End/<Second point>: C Center:
Angle/Length of chord/<End point>: L Length of chord:
```

Figure 4–37 Command Sequence for the SCL Arc

```
Command: ARC Center/<Start point>:
Center/End/<Second point>: E
End point:
Angle/Direction/Radius/<Center point>: R Radius:
```

Figure 4–38 Command Sequence for the SER Arc

```
Command:   ARC Center/<Start point>:
Center/End/<Second point>: End
End point:
Angle/Direction/Radius/<Center point>: A Included angle:
```

Figure 4–39 Command Sequence for the SEA Arc

```
Command:   ARC Center/<Start point>:
Center/End/<Second point>: E
End point:
Angle/Direction/Radius/<Center point>: D Direction from start point
```

Figure 4–40 Command Sequence for the SED Arc

```
Command: ARC Center/<Start point>:
End point:
 NOTE: START POINT = END OF LINE
```

Figure 4–41 Command Sequence for the Continue Line Arc

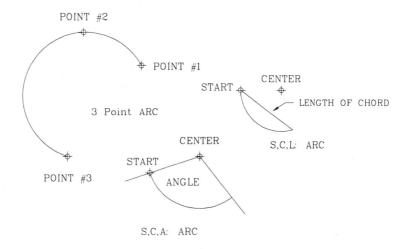

Figure 4–42   Solutions to Examples 4–7, 4–8, and 4–9

Method 11 (Continuation of line and endpoint) is a special case of SED (Start, End, Direction). When Method 11 is used, select the ARC Menu and CONTIN. This will automatically input the last point (from the LINE command) and direction of the arc. The command is completed by inputting the endpoint. This method is used to draw an Arc tangent to a Line.

Try these examples using the ARC commands:

Example 4–7:   Draw a 3–point Arc: Point 1 (start point) = 3.75,6.75; Point 2 (second point) = 2,7.75; Point 3 (end point) = 1.5,4.

Example 4–8:   Draw SCA Arc: Start point = 4,3.5; Center = 5.5,4: Angle = 105.

Example 4–9:   Draw SCL Arc: Start point = 6.75,6; Center = 8,6; length of chord = 1.

Example 4–10:   Draw an SER Arc: Start point = 2.25,6; endpoint = 3,4.25; Radius = 1.

Example 4–11:   Draw CSA Arc: Center = 4.5,4.5; Start point = 3,5.25; Angle = 270.

The solution to Examples 4–7 to 4–9 are shown in Figure 4–42.

4.8   TEXT Command

The placement of text material on a drawing requires two separate commands: STYLE and TEXT. The Style command is discussed in Chapter 7. The TEXT command gives the draftperson a new tool to reduce the most exacting drafting chore. The TEXT command is found on the flip or reverse side of the DRAW Submenu as shown in Figure 4–43.

AutoCAD gives the operator versatility in the placement of the text material. There are two methods used to place the textstring at a particular location. The first method called Option 1 provides for eight specific locations for the textstring placement. These locations are detailed below and are illustrated in Figure 4–44.

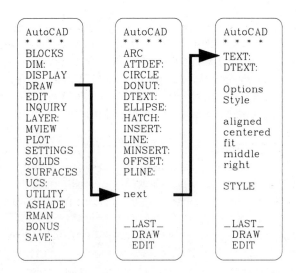

Figure 4–43 Menu Map for the TEXT Command

Start point or left justified

      Centered Text

   Middle Text Location

   Aligned Text

     Fit Text

       Right point or right justified

= Start, mid, centered, aligned, fit, or right end points

Figure 4–44 Method 1 Text Placement Options

1. Start point: This option places the start of the text material at a specified point (lower left corner of the text letter) for Left Justification. (All lines of text will start at the same point on a new line.)
2. Align (A): permits the operator to select the starting and ending point of the text. The program determines the height and width of the characters. The Align points must be specified for each line of text.
3. Center (C): permits the operator to Center the bottom of the text at a specified point.
4. Fit (F): The Fit option is similar to the Align option with the exception that the operator must specify the text height.
5. Middle (M): This option is similar to the Center option with the exception that the text is centered in the middle of the characters and not at the bottom of the characters.

6. Right (R): is similar to the Starting point option except the text is Right Justified. (The end of the sentence will be even on the right side.)
7. Style (s): This Style option is different from the STYLE command. This option shows the operator which STYLE command is current.
8. Double Null Reply (R): This option bypasses the Command Sequence and places the new text line beneath the preceeding line with the exception of the Align option.

Figure 4–44 provides a sample line of text for each option listed above.

When the Pull Down Menu is activated and the Options box is selected, the operator has the capability to select a number of modes including DTEXT Options. This selection provides a menu of four Text options (Font, Alignment, Height, and Rotation). Select the Text Alignment option to determine where the text location point will be if Method 2 Placement Options (Justify, or J) is used. Figure 4–45 shows the text placement points similar to that shown in the Text Placement Dialogue Box. The six Method 2 categories are listed in Table 4–1.

Table 4–1 Method 2 Text Location Statements

COLUMN 1	COLUMN 2
TOP (T)	LEFT (L)
MIDDLE (M)	CENTER (C)
BOTTOM (B)	RIGHT (R)

The text location is derived from the selection of one from each column. Therefore, if TLeft (TL) is selected, the Start point would be the top left corner of the textstring.

Example 4–12: The textstring ("AutoCAD is here to stay") is to be placed at 5,5 using the TCenter location. Select TEXT command, (refer to Figure 4–43) and select the Justify option. This selection results in another Command Sequence. (Refer to Figure 4–46 Command Sequence for Method 2 Text Placement Options.)

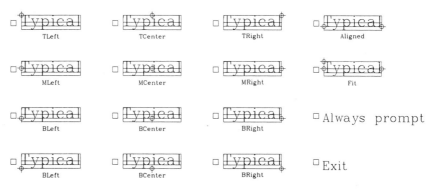

NOTE: Pick the Text Alignment by picking the small box

Figure 4–45 Dialogue Box for Text Alignment Selections

```
Command: TEXT Justify/Style/<start point>:  J
Align/Fit/Center/Middle/Right/TL/TC/TR/ML/MC/MR/BL/BC/BR:  TL
Top/left point: 5,5
Height <0.2000>:  0.2
Rotation angle <0>:  0
AutoCAD is here to stay
```

Figure 4-46   Command Sequence for Method 2 Text Location Option

Select Top and Center TC. Input 5,5 as the text location and 0.2 for the letter height. The textstring will be drawn so that the top Center of the textstring is located at 5,5. Figure 4-47 illustrates the solution to this example.

The Command Sequence for the TEXT command is listed in Figure 4-48. All TEXT options, with the exception of the Align and Fit modes will require height and the rotational angle for the characters. The Align option requires the Start point (point 1) and the endpoint (point 2) for each line of text. The program computes the height and width of each character and the rotational angle of the line is given by the location of points 1 and 2. The Align and Fit options are similar. When the Align option is used, the program computes both the height and width for each character. When the Fit option is used, however, the operator must specify the height and the program calculates the width of each character.

The Multi-Line Text option may be used by inputting a NULL (R) twice, after each line of text has been completed. As stated before, the automatic Multi-Line option is not available for the Align option.

4.9   EDIT Command Prompt Response

When using the EDIT commands, such as ERASE, COPY, FILLET, etc., you must first identify the object (one or more entities) that will be edited or changed and then confirm the selection by pressing (R). When the object is first identified, the screen presentation of the selected object becomes dotted in appearance. This is the same

```
AutoCAD is here to stay
```

Figure 4-47   Solution to Example 4-12

```
Command: Justify/Style/<Start point>:  Aligned
First line point: 2,2
Second line point: 2,4
Text: AutoCAD is here to stay
```

Figure 4-48   Command Sequence for the TEXT Command

as if the program is asking you if these items (shown in dotted form) are the items to be edited. If the answer is Yes, then reply with (R). If the answer is No, use ^C to cancel the command.

The operator has several ways to select the object(s) to be edited. The operator may either pick each object with the Pointer, or make a temporary box or window around the objects (by selecting Window then inputting the first corner point (Co-ordinates or Pointer) and then the other corner. Most EDIT Submenus have a minimum of the following four choices:

1. **Window:** A window is a box drawn around the entities (lines, circles, or arcs) to be edited. The Command Sequence, will call for the location of the first corner. This location may either be input by the Pointer or by use of Cartesian Coordinates. The second corner location is similar to the first corner. When the box or window has been drawn, the objects selected appear in dotted form. The command prompt will display, "Select Objects": Reply with (R).
2. **Last (L):** This term refers to the last entity drawn. If L is input then the object last drawn will be selected.
3. **Previous:** This statement refers to the most recent selection of entities.
4. **Crossing:** This command is similar to the Window command.

The Crossing option edits any entities inside the window and those that lie on the crossing window boundaries.

There are two remaining terms that are sometimes included in the EDIT Sub-menu: Remove and Add. The Remove option removes an entity from the selection. The Add option adds entities to the selection. The terms *Remove* and *Add* are discussed in detail in Chapter 9.

4.10 ERASE Command

The ERASE command is one of the most used commands in the EDIT Menu. It acts like an electronic eraser to remove unwanted drawing entities (including text material). This command is found in the EDIT Submenu and is shown in Figure 4–49.

As indicated in paragraph 4.9, the Command Sequence for Object Selection offers the operator a choice of five options. These options, shown in Figure 4–50, are:

1. Pick an object(s) using the Pointer. Some operators prefer to select the individual entities by pointing to them on the screen.
2. Use the Window option (W). Draw a window or a box that will capture or enclose the drawing entities by calling out the first corner location of the window and then the second corner location. The corner location may either be input through the keyboard or pointed to by the Pointer.
3. Use Last (L). If Last (L) is selected, then the last entity drawn on the screen will be erased.
4. Select the Crossing (C) option. This option erases whatever is inside the window, but also erases those lines that cross the window boundaries.
5. Erase the Previous selection of entities (P).

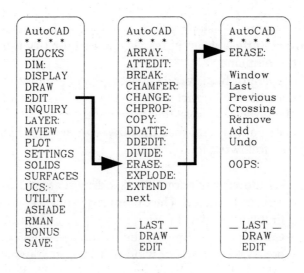

Figure 4–49   Menu Map for the ERASE Command

```
Command: ERASE
Select object: 1 selected, 1 found
Select object: (R)
```

Figure 4–50   Command Sequence for the ERASE Command

After the ERASE command has been completed, there will be a number of "blips" (dots on the screen). The REDRAW command, chosen from the Display Menu or typed in, cleans off the blips to give a clear screen.

4.11   Pull Down Menu Commands for Chapter 4

AutoDESK has developed a series of Pull Down Menus (special menus) that will either minimize the time to activate a Screen Menu listing or provide a Dialogue/Icon Box.

CAUTION: Not all the commands that are listed on the Screen Menus for a given submenu are listed on the Pull Down Menus. Figure 4–51 illustrates the initial Pull Down Menu headings.

Move the cursor (cross hairs) towards the Status Line area located at the top portion of the video screen. The cursor automatically changes to an arrow and another list of names appears in the Status Line area, starting with Assist and ending with Solids.

Assist	Draw	Modify	Display	Settings	Options	Utility	File	Solids

Figure 4–51 Initial Pull Down Menu Headings

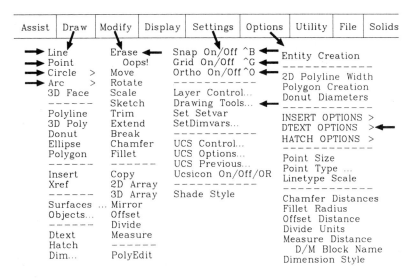

Figure 4–52 Pull Down Menus for Chapter 4

(Refer to Figure 4–51.) Place the arrow on the Menu Name and pick the word. The background color, as well as the letter color, will change. This color change informs the operator that the Menu Name has been selected. A list of available commands appears for that menu. Pick the command as you would if the command was listed on the Screen Menu.

At the end of each chapter, the Pull Down Menu commands are listed and highlighted by an arrow. If a Dialogue Box or Icon is keyed to the highlighted command, it will be listed and displayed. In Chapter 4, the DRAW and MODIFY Menus were discussed. The commands POINT, LINE, CIRCLE, ARC, and ERASE were discussed. Figure 4–52 shows the Pull Down Menus for this chapter.

NOTE: When certain commands (LINE, POINT, and ERASE) are picked, the Pull Down Menu disappears and the Screen Menu for the selected command appears. However, for the ARC and CIRCLE commands, the operator selects the command options directly from the Pull Down Menu. Figures 4–53 and 4–54 are additional Pull Down Menu selections.

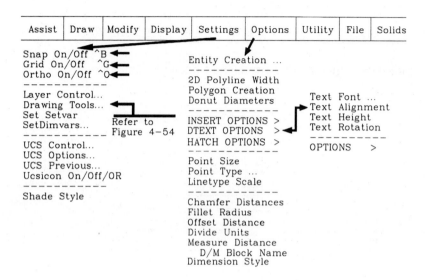

Figure 4–53   Pull Down Menus for Chapter 4 (Continued)

Snap			
X Spacing	0.1000	Snap	
Y Spacing	0.1000	Grid	
		Axis	
Snap Angle	0.0000	Ortho	
X Base	0.0000	Blips	
Y Base	0.0000		

Grid

| X Spacing | 0.2000 |
| Y Spacing | 0.2000 |

Axis

| X Spacing | 0.0000 |
| Y Spacing | 0.0000 |

Isoplane

Left
Top
Right

Isometric

OK   Cancel

Figure 4–54   Dialogue Box Called Drawing Tools

4.12   Template Reference—Chapter 4

Figure 4-55 is the Template Reference for Chapter 4.

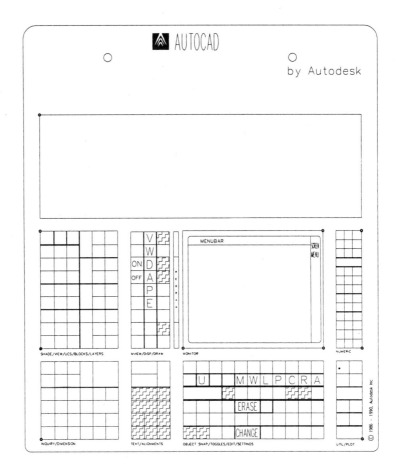

Figure 4–55   Template Reference—Chapter 4

COMMAND SUMMARY

The commands discussed in this chapter are as follows:

ARC	FUNCTION KEYS	POINT
AXIS	GRID	REDRAW
CIRCLE	TEXT	SNAP
CONTROL KEYS	LINE	ERASE
PULL DOWN MENUS	ORTHO	

GLOSSARY

BAK: This file is used as a backup to a current file.

Blip: The dots that remain on the screen after a line is erased.

Chord: The linear distance between the start and end of an arc.

Null: No input value. Accomplished by pressing the ENTER key or depressing the space bar.

Text: The command used to place alphanumeric characters on the screen.

PROBLEMS

1. Draw the following lines and add the textstring:
   2,2; @2.65<50; @2,0; @0,3; @-3,0; close
   Place the following textstring: "Problem 4–1".
   Use the TXT font; Align mode: point 1 = 3,5.5; point 2 = 5.5,5.5
2. Draw the following items and add the text data as listed:
   Circle 1: Center at 3,7; Radius (rad) = 1.25
   Circle 2: Center at 3,3.25; Diameter (dia) = 1.25
   Box: Lower left corner 6,6; upper right corner 8,8
   Circle 3: 2P method: Use the midpoint of the vertical lines of the box above. Draw a triangle: 6,3; 8,3; 7,4.5; close
   Circle 4: 3P method: Circumscribe the triangle using the intersection of each.
   Place the textstring: "Problem 4–2," Middle location at 5,5; height (hgt) = 0.2.
3. Draw the following arcs, lines and text:
   Arc 1: Using the 3P method, point 1 = 9,7.5; point 2 = 7.25,6.25; point 3 = 0,-3.
   Arc 2: Using the SCA: Start (S) point = 1.27,7.79; Center (C) = @2,-1; Angle (A) = 90.
   Arc 3: Using the SER: S = 2.63,6.52; End (E) = 4.5,8; Radius =1.5.
   Continue function: Line 1.48,2; 5.43,1.45; (R), then ARC Continue; endpoint = @3.06<87.5.
   Text: "Problem 4–3" :font = complex; Center option, at 3,6; hgt = .25 printer plot (PRPLOT): Using extents and half scale.

5 Advanced Drawing Commands

Instructional Objectives

1. To be able to use the three Polygon Command options
2. To be able to draw an Ellipse
3. To understand and use the OBJECT SNAP (OSNAP) commands
4. To properly use the UNDO commands (part A)
5. To understand the limitations and usage of the REDO command

5.1 POLYGON Command

The POLYGON command is listed under the DRAW Submenu and the Menu Map for this command is shown in Figure 5–1. The operator may use one of the three command options to draw a polygon. These options are:

1. Edge method
2. Inscribed method
3. Circumscribed method

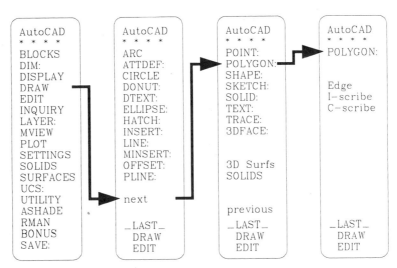

Figure 5–1 Menu Map for the POLYGON Command

```
Command: POLYGON Number of sides:  4

Edge/<Center of polygon>:  E or Edge
First endpoint of edge:  3,5
Second endpoint of edge:  @1<0
```

Figure 5–2   Command Sequence for the POLYGON Edge Option

```
Command: POLYGON Number of sides:  5

Edge/<Center of polygon>:  3,4
Inscribed in circle/Circumscribed about circle (I/C):  I
Radius of circle:  2
```

Figure 5–3   Command Sequence for the POLYGON Inscribed Option

```
Command: POLYGON Number of sides:  7

Edge/<Center of polygon>:  4,6
Inscribed in circle/Circumscribed about circle <I/C>:  C
Radius of circle:  .75
```

Figure 5–4   Command Sequence for the POLYGON Circumscribed Option

Each option has it's own Command Sequence. Figure 5–2 refers to the Command Sequence for the Edge option, Figure 5–3 illustrates the Inscribed option, and Figure 5–4 is the Command Sequence for the Circumscribed option.

NOTE: The initial prompt of all three options is the same, namely, "number of sides."

Any number of sides (3 to 1024) may be selected. After the number of edges (sides) has been selected, then choose the command option. If the Edge option is required, type E and then input the specified Coordinates of the Starting point of the edge. The Absolute Coordinates may be input from the keyboard or pointed to on the screen. The second point may be specified in one of four ways: Absolute Coordinates, Relative Delta X and Delta Y, Relative Polar, or by the use of the Pointing device. When both edge points are input, the POLYGON is drawn.

Example 5–1: The operator needs a seven-sided polygon where the Starting point of the edge is 2,5 and the second Endpoint is 3,5. This polygon is shown in Figure 5–5(a). If the Endpoints were specified as 3,5 for the first Endpoint and 2,5 for the second Endpoint, then the polygon would appear as a mirror image, as shown in Figure 5–5(b).

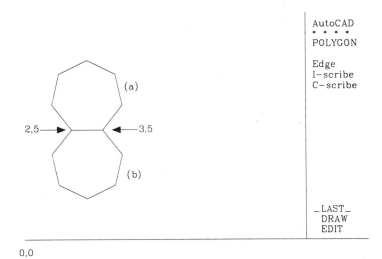

Figure 5–5 Solution to Example 5–1

The SCRIBED Methods [Inscribed (I) or Circumscribed (C)] are activated automatically when the operator responds with the Coordinates of the Center of the polygon instead of E for Edge. Once the Coordinates are specified, the operator selects either Inscribed (I) mode or Circumscribed (C) mode by typing I or C or selecting the commands from the Screen Menu. (Refer to Figure 5–1.) Figure 5–6(a) shows the I selection while Figure 5–6(b) is the resulting polygon from the C mode. Both polygons used the same Center point. The Inscribed option is defined when a polygon is drawn or inscribed inside the circle, while the Circumscribed option is defined when a polygon is drawn outside the circle. The second response to either the I or C option is the Radius of the circle.

Example 5–2: Draw a five-sided polygon using the I option, with Center of the circle at 5,4 and a Radius of 2 units. The resulting polygon will look like that in Figure

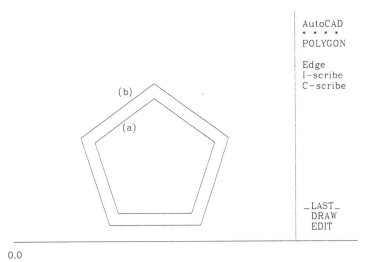

Figure 5–6 Solution to Example 5–2

5–6(a). Now draw the five-sided polygon using the C option, using the same Radius and Center. This polygon is shown in Figure 5–6(b).

5.2 ELLIPSE Command

The ELLIPSE command is listed under the DRAW Submenu as shown in Figure 5–7.

The operator should know the location of either the ellipse Center and two Endpoints (P1 and P2) or three Endpoints (P1, P2, and P3). The Command Sequence (Figures 5–8 and 5–11) are divided into three options. If the Center Coordinates are known, the operator responds to the first Command prompt ("Axis Endpoint 1>/Center:") with C for Center, then the Coordinates (either from the keyboard or from the pointing device) followed by the values of P1 and P2. An example of this option is shown in Figure 5–9. If three points are known, the response to the first prompt is the location of P1, followed by the Coordinates of P2 and P3.

Example 5–3: Draw an ellipse whose Center is at 4,5; P1 is located at 2,4 and P2 is located at 3,2. Figure 5–9 shows this example worked out.

Example 5–4: A second ellipse is specified using the three point method: P1 = 2,3; P2 = @4<60; and P3 = 4,5. This ellipse is shown in Figure 5–10.

The third ellipse option will require a rotation angle about the major axis. The Command Sequence is given in Figure 5–11. The Command Sequence requires the location of P1 and P2 but R replaces P3.

Example 5–5: Draw an ellipse where P1 = 2,5; P2 = 7,3; and R. R = 15 (degrees). Figure 5–12a illustrates this ellipse. However if R = 45°, the ellipse will look like Figure 5–12b. If R is increased to 75°, the ellipse appears as shown in Figure 5–12c.

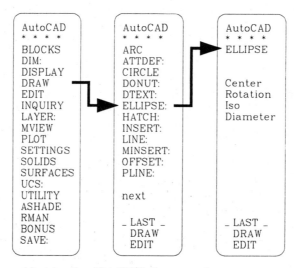

Figure 5–7 Menu Map for the ELLIPSE Command

```
Command: ELLIPSE
<Axis endpoint 1>/Center:    C
Center of ellipse: 3,5
Axis endpoint: 2,3
<Other axis distance>/Rotation:  4,2

                        (a)



Command: ELLIPSE
<Axis endpoint 1>/Center: 6,7
Axis endpoint 2:  2,3
<Other axis distance>/Rotation:  4.25,4.25

                        (b)
```

Figure 5–8 Command Sequence for the ELLIPSE Command

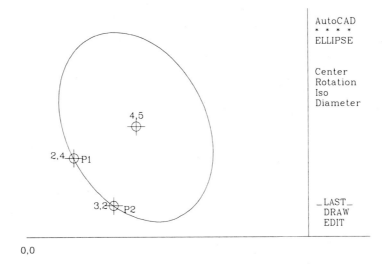

Figure 5–9 Solution to Example 5–3

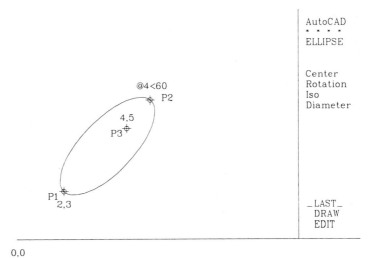

Figure 5–10 Solution to Example 5–4

```
Command:  ELLIPSE
<Axis endpoint 1>/Center:  6,7
Axis endpoint 2:  2,3
<Other axis distance>/Rotation:  R
Rotation  around  major  axis:  45
```

Figure 5–11   Command Sequence for the ELLIPSE Command—Rotational Option

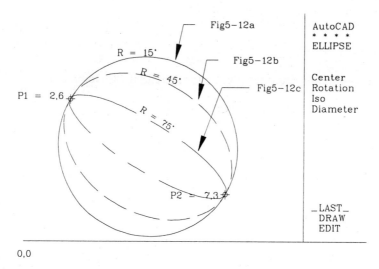

Figure 5–12   Solution to Example 5–5

There is a fourth option called *Isometric Ellipse*. This command is not within the scope of this text.

5.3   OBJECT SNAP Command

The AutoCAD program remembers every command that is used in developing a drawing. This information is placed at the operator's finger tips through the OBJECT SNAP (OSNAP) command.

The OSNAP command has 12 modes:

Nearest	Center	Intersect	Quick
Endpoint	Node	Insert	None
Midpoint	Quadrant	Perpendicular	Tangent

5.3.1   OSNAP Command

The operator has the option of either setting one of the OSNAP modes as a semi-permanent command or for single usage.

5.3.1.1 Semi-Permanent OSNAP Setting

Any of the OSNAP options may be set as a semi-permanent command by using the OSNAP Menu found under the Settings Submenu. The Menu Map for this command is shown in Figure 5–13 and the Command Sequence is listed in Figure 5–14.

The response to the Command Sequence will be one of the 12 options previously listed. The operator must input the option name (via the keyboard or Pointing Device). The current option selection may be turned off by either inputting NONE, OFF, or (R).

NOTE: When selecting the OSNAP option from the keyboard, it is recommended that the first three letters of the option be used as shown in the parentheses () in the list below.

5.3.1.2 OSNAP Object Modes

The OSNAP modes or options operate in a similar fashion as does the SNAP command. In the SNAP command, the Cursor, when activated, moves or snaps to a given grid point. The OSNAP commands also move or snap to a given point located on or near an entity, such as the Midpoint of a line or Center of a circle. The name of the OSNAP mode will define the snapping point of the cursor. These modes are described below:

CENTER (CEN), when activated (by picking the Circle), finds the Center location of an arc or circle.

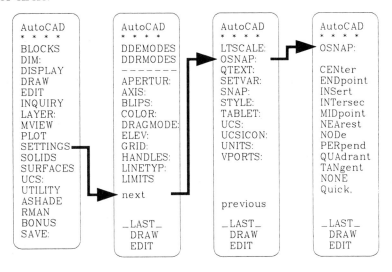

Figure 5–13 Menu Map for the OSNAP Commands

```
Command: OSNAP Object snap modes:
```

Figure 5–14 Command Sequence for the OSNAP Command

ENDPOINT (END), when selected, provides for the exact location of the ENDpoint of a line or arc.

INSERT (INS): This option is used with the advanced editing command, BLOCK/INSERT. This option is discussed in detail in Chapter 11.

INTERSECT (INT) provides for the exact location where two or more entities meet (line, arc, and/or circle or a combination of lines, arcs, and/or circles).

MIDPOINT (MID) provides the location of the midpoint of either a line or an arc.

NEAREST (NEA)* causes the Cursor to snap to the nearest point on a line, arc, or circle.

NODE (NOD) provides the location of a point.

PERPENDIC (PER) locates a point on a line, arc, or circle that would form a line from the last point to a point perpendicular to the current entity selected.

QUADRANT (QUA) snaps to the closest quadrant point (0, 90, 180, or 270) of an arc or circle.

QUICK (QUI) places the Cursor at the nearest point.

TANGENT (TAN) snaps "TO" a point on an arc or circle that, when connected to the last point, forms a tangent line.

NONE turns off the semi-permanent OSNAP command.

NOTE: * means that special care must be used with OSNAP commands to prevent the possiblity of snapping to an incorrect point.

5.3.1.3 *Single Usage of OSNAP Option*

Usually, the OSNAP option is selected on a temporary basis (one command only). The option selection may be input either from the keyboard or the Pointer. If the Pointer is used, either select the **** command from any Screen Menus, press the third button on the Pointer, or select the first column of the Pull Down Menu. Upon selection of the option, an Aperture Box will appear centered over the cross hairs of the cursor. Position the Aperature Box so that the snap point lies inside the box, and pick the point.

Example: If the ENDpoint of a line is required to draw another line, select the LINE command; pick **** Submenu, then ENDpoint; now place the aperture box so that the existing line ends somewhere inside the box; pick the next point and continue the drawing effort. The ENDpoint option has been completed and the same or different OSNAP option may be selected. Try this exercise: Draw a line from 2,2 to 4,5 and a circle whose Center is 5,3 with a Radius of 1.5. Using the single OSNAP usage, connect the MIDpoint of the line to the CENTER of the circle.

5.4 U Option

The U option is part of the UNDO command. The UNDO command is complex and will be discussed in Chapter 7. However, the U option is unique and is located under

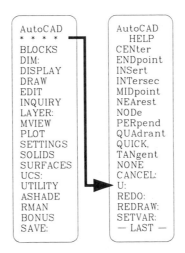

Figure 5–15 Menu Map for the U Command

the **** Submenu and shown in Figure 5–15. The OSNAP Submenu (****) appears on all Screen Menus.

The purpose of the U command is to delete the last command that was entered. When the U command is used, the last sequence to appear on the screen is removed and the drawing on the screen appears as if the drawing sequence never existed. Upon completion of the U command, the command prompt lists the last command. For example: You are asked to draw a box (do not use the POLYGON command) but the third line is accidently drawn incorrectly. You has several choices:

1. Stop the LINE command and erase the third line.
2. Stay in the LINE command but use the U option.

The best approach is to use the U command and continue the drawing. Certain restrictions are placed on the U command. For example, the U command may not be used after the SAVE, PLOT, or PRPLOT commands. If the U command is used, then the OOPS command is negated. The REDO command may be used to undo the U command.

5.5 REDO Command

The REDO command is used to restore one or more commands that have been deleted by the U command. The REDO command is found in the **** Submenu and shown in Figure 5–16.

The REDO command is effective after the U or UNDO commands are used. In operation, the REDO command returns the drawing to the point before the U or UNDO command was used. For example: Draw a box (do not use the POLYGON command) whose lower left corner is located at 3,3 and upper right corner is located at 7,5. When the box is completed, select the U command and the last line drawn will disappear. Now activate the REDO command by selecting REDO from the Screen Menu or typing REDO from the keyboard. The line will reappear.

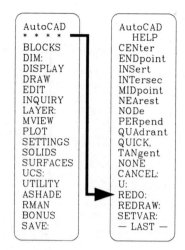

Figure 5–16 Menu Map for the REDO Command

5.6 Pull Down Menu Commands for Chapter 5

All the commands discussed in this chapter appear on the Pull Down Menus and are illustrated in Figure 5–17.

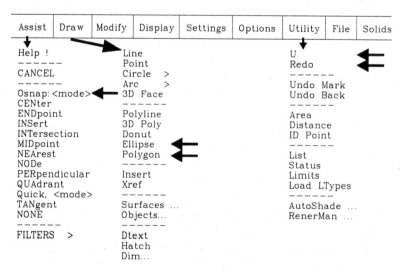

Figure 5–17 Pull Down Menu Commands for Chapter 5

5.7 Template Reference—Chapter 5

Figure 5-18 is the Template Reference for Chapter 5.

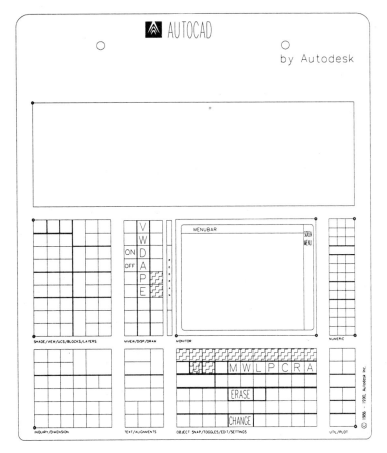

Figure 5–18 Template Reference for Chapter 5

COMMAND SUMMARY

Polygon   Ellipse
OSNAP   U
REDO

GLOSSARY

Polygon: A multi-sided linear figure, whose faces are the same length.

Inscribed mode: A method of drawing a polygon that is inside a circle of a given Radius.

Circumscribed mode: A method of drawing a polygon that is outside a circle of a given Radius.

PROBLEMS

1. Draw a nine-sided polygon using the Inscribed method. The Center is located at 4,5; Radius = 3.
2. Draw an ellipse whose Center is located at 4,6; P1 = 2,4 and P2 = 3,2.
3. Draw an ellipse where P1 = 4,5; P2 = 10,8 and the distance = 2.

6 Display Commands

Instructional Objectives

1. To be able to use the ZOOM command in any of it's eight modes
2. To be able to use the PAN command to move objects on the screen
3. To understand the purpose of the REDRAW command
4. To be able to use the four REGENERATION commands (REGEN, REDRAWALL, REGENALL, and REGENAUTO)
5. To be able to use the VIEW command
6. To be able to set the VIEWRES command for fast zoom and circle/arc resolution

6.1 ZOOM Command

The ZOOM command was first introduced in Chapter 3 to reconfigure or adjust the screen display when new LIMITS are established. This reconfiguration was achieved by using the ZOOM command and All option. There are eight additional operational modes:

ZOOM: Left (L)   ZOOM: Previous (P)
ZOOM: Center (C)   ZOOM: Scale (S)
ZOOM: Dynamic (D)   ZOOM: Window (W)
ZOOM: Extents (E)   ZOOM: Vmax (V)

For demonstration purposes, start a new drawing called ZOOM. Draw the following shapes: Triangle: three-sided polygon, Edge method, First Point O.375,4.25, Second Point 2.54,4.25. Circle: Center at 5,5; Radius of 1.5 units. Square: four-sided polygon, Edge method, First Point 7,4.5, Second Point 7.875,4.5. This drawing is shown in Figure 6-1.

NOTE: This drawing will be used to illustrate the various operational modes of the ZOOM command. The ZOOM command is found under the DISPLAY Submenu, as shown in Figure 6-2.

Figure 6-3 is the Command Sequence for the ZOOM command. The usual response to the command prompts is the first letter of the operational mode that was selected.

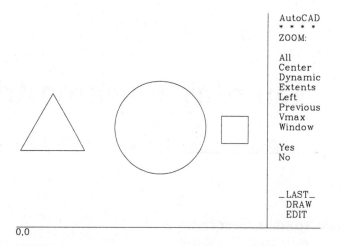

Figure 6-1 Reference Drawing for the ZOOM Command

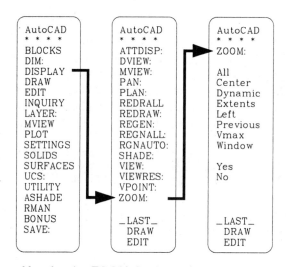

Figure 6-2 Menu Map for the ZOOM Command

```
Command:   'ZOOM
All/Center/Dynamic/Extents/Left/Previous/Vmax/Window/<Scale(X/XP)>:
```

Figure 6-3 Command Sequence for the ZOOM Command

6.1.1 ZOOM Command: All Option

This option is used to reset the screen display when a new set of LIMITS are established for a drawing. In addition, ZOOM All is the equivalent of a multiplication or scale factor of 1. Occasionally, the screen display requires a second regeneration because of a change in drawing extents. When this occurs, the command prompt will show, Second regeneration caused by change in drawing extents. Examples of the ZOOM All option will be highlighted in the other ZOOM modes.

6.1.2 ZOOM Command: Center Option

The purpose of the ZOOM command, Center option, is to place a desired portion of the display in the Center of the screen as shown in Figure 6-4. In addition to centering the display, the size of the display may be changed by one of two methods.

In the first method, when the Center point is inputted, the command prompt lists magnification or height and a number in the default <> brackets. If a number greater than the default value is entered, the display will be changed in proportion to the ratio of the default value divided by the input value. For example: If the default value = 9 and the input value = 4.5, the displayed area of the display will reduced by a factor of 2.

The second method uses the times sign (X). If the input number is 2X, then the drawing entities will be viewed two times larger than the existing image on the screen. If the input number is .5X then the drawing entities will be viewed one half smaller than the entities on the screen. For example: Pick the ZOOM command and Center option. Place the Cursor in the Center of the triangle and depress the ENTER key or (R). The resulting display shows that the triangle has been moved to the Center of the screen but the size remains the same. (Refer to Figure 6-4.) Return figure 6-1 to its original state.

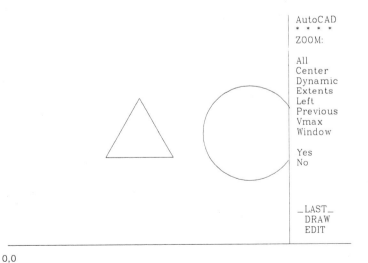

Figure 6-4 Example of ZOOM Command, Center Option

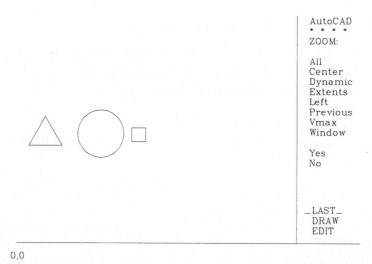

0,0

Figure 6–5 Example of ZOOM Command Center Option, 0.5X

NOTE: To return the drawing to it's original state, use ZOOM All. Repeat the above procedure. (Select ZOOM and Center.) Move the Cursor to the Center of the triangle and input 0.5X and Return (R). The display will be one half the size as shown in Figure 6–5. Return Figure 6–1 to its original state. Move the cursor to the Center of the triangle but this time input 2X and Return (R). The resulting display will be twice the size as shown in Figure 6–6. Return Figure 6–1 to its original state.

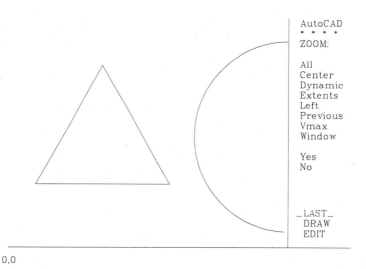

0,0

Figure 6–6 Example of ZOOM Command, Center Option, 2X Size

6.1.3 ZOOM Command: Dynamic Option

The Dynamic option of the ZOOM command provides the operator with a faster regeneration of the display in most applications. Figure 6–7 is the Command Sequence for the ZOOM command, Dynamic option.

```
Command:  'ZOOM
All/Center/Dynamic/Extents/Left/Previous/Vmax/Window/<Scale>:  D
```

Figure 6–7   Command Sequence for the ZOOM Command, Dynamic Option

Before proceeding with this option, we should define several displays that will appear. These displays are: drawing extents (in white); current view (in green); generated area (in red); view box (with the letter X) and view box with the arrow (used to establish the boundaries of the ZOOM portion of the display).

Drawing Extents displays all of the drawing entities.

Current view is like a window outlining what was on the screen prior to the ZOOM Dynamic option.

Generated Area is the display outlined in red that represents the area that can be displayed using the fast regeneration function.

The **View Box** will be the same size as the current view. If another view is required, then depress (R) and the X that was in the box will be replaced by an arrow. The viewing area may now be changed by moving the cursor. Move the cursor so that the area encompassed by the viewing area outlines the desired display. Depress the ENTER key twice to lock in the outlined area and bring the view onto the screen. If you are working outside the drawing limits, a symbol similar to the hourglass will appear in the lower left corner.

Let's try an example. Refering to Figure 6–1, do a Dynamic ZOOM on the triangle. Pick the ZOOM command and select the Dynamic option. Move the Cursor to the screen and unlock the View Box (the X should be replaced with the arrow) by using the pick button. Locate the View Box over the triangle and depress the ENTER key once. The resulting display should show the triangle only. Return the drawing to its original display.

6.1.4 ZOOM Command: Extents Option

The Command Sequence for this option is shown in Figure 6–8. This option displays the current drawing extents, usually providing the largest display of the drawing. Pick ZOOM and select Extents (using Figure 6–1 as the reference). Note that the triangle, circle, and square (drawing extents) fill the screen.

```
Command:  'ZOOM
All/Center/Dynamic/Extents/Left/Previous/Vmax/Window/<Scale>:  E
```

Figure 6–8   Command Sequence for the ZOOM Command, Extents Option

```
Command: 'ZOOM
All/Center/Dynamic/Extents/Left/Previous/Vmax/Window/<Scale>:  L
```

Figure 6–9 Command Sequence for the ZOOM Command, Left Option

6.1.5 ZOOM Command: Left Option

The ZOOM command, Left option, is similar to the Center option procedure. The entities selected are displayed in the lower left corner of the screen. The Command Sequence is shown in Figure 6–9. As we experienced in the operation of the Center option, we have the capability to make the selected display larger or smaller than the original display. The procedure for the use of the Left option is the same as the Center option.

6.1.6 ZOOM Command: Previous Option

This option provides the operator with the capabilities of storing the last 10 sequential views of the drawing. The Command Sequence is listed in Figure 6–10. Examples of the Previous views will be demonstrated during the ZOOM command, Window option.

6.1.7 ZOOM Command: Window Option

The Window option is perhaps the most frequently used option of the ZOOM command. The Command Sequence is shown in Figure 6–11.

The Window option provides the operator with the flexibility of selecting the area to be enlarged (full screen size). The Command Sequence is: Pick the ZOOM command; select the Window option; then place a window around the area to be viewed. The sequence will ask for the location of the first corner, then the second

```
Command: 'ZOOM
All/Center/Dynamic/Extents/Left/Previous/Vmax/Window/<Scale>:  P
```

Figure 6–10 Command Sequence for the ZOOM Command, Previous Option

```
Command: 'ZOOM
All/Center/Dynamic/Extents/Left/Previous/Vmax/Window/<Scale>:  W
```

Figure 6–11 Command Sequence for the ZOOM Command, Window Option

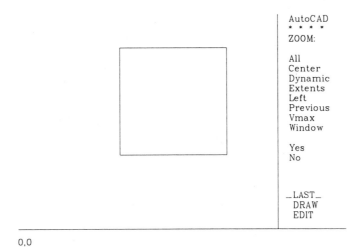

```
                                        AutoCAD
                                        * * * *
                                        ZOOM:

                                        All
                                        Center
                                        Dynamic
                                        Extents
                                        Left
                                        Previous
                                        Vmax
                                        Window

                                        Yes
                                        No


                                        _LAST_
                                        DRAW
                                        EDIT
```

0,0

Figure 6–12 Example of ZOOM Command, Window Option

corner. Try this exercise using Figure 6–1. Using the Window option of the ZOOM command, place the window around the square. The resulting display is shown in Figure 6–12, ZOOM All.

Now repeat the Window procedure, but place the window around the circle of Figure 6–1. Again, ZOOM All. Repeat the last procedure, but place the window around the triangle. Now ZOOM All. This exercise shows the power of the Window option. Now do a ZOOM, Previous option; the display is the triangle. ZOOM, Previous; the display is the normal Figure 6–1 display. ZOOM, Previous; the display is now of the circle. ZOOM, Previous; the display (fourth of the series) is Figure 6–1. For the last display, pick ZOOM, Previous; the display will be of the box. The program remembers the last 10 displays.

6.1.8 ZOOM Command: Scale Option

The Scale option enables the operator to enlarge or reduce the existing view of the entities displayed on the screen display. The Command Sequence is shown in Figure 6–13.

In this option, the overall screen display is changed rather than a limited area as in ZOOM Left or ZOOM Center. To enlarge the display, use the numeric value followed by the X (eg., for a two-time enlargement, input 2X). Try this problem: Using Figure 6–1, select the ZOOM command and input 2X. The entities have doubled in size and some of the drawing entities cannot be seen. Return the drawing to its original size by ZOOM All. Repeat the procedure but use .5X. The display has been reduced by 50%.

```
Command: 'ZOOM
All/Center/Dynamic/Extents/Left/Previous/Vmax/Window/<Scale>:  2X
```

Figure 6–13 Command Sequence for the ZOOM Command, Scale Option

NOTE: Using ZOOM All is the same as using the Scale option and 1X.

6.1.9   ZOOM Command: Vmax Option

The ZOOM command with the Vmax option is a special mode that provides the fastest zoom without regeneration of the screen display. It is very similiar to the ZOOM All option but without the screen regeneration.

6.2   PAN Command

The PAN command is located under the DISPLAY Submenu and is shown in Figure 6–14. It gives the operator the ability to view different portions of the screen without the time consuming ZOOM command. In addition, if any portion of the drawing is off the screen, the use of the PAN command can bring that segment of the drawing to the viewing screen. The Command Sequence (shown in Figure 6–15) calls for the displacement of the drawing.

The displacement may be horizontal, vertical, or at an angle (only if ORTHO is off). In reality, you will be moving the display from one point to another (horizontal, vertical, or angular) point. The Command Sequence asks for the displacement. The displacement may be given in one of three forms: First point, then Second point; a Basepoint, then a Relative displacement followed by a (R); or using the Pointer to locate the First and/or Second point.

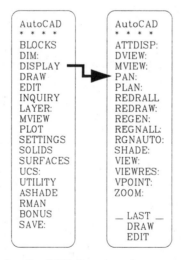

Figure 6–14   Menu Map for the PAN Command

```
Command: 'PAN Displacement: X1,Y1
         Second Point: X2,Y2
```

Figure 6–15   Command Sequence for the PAN Command

Let's try an example. Bring up a new drawing called PAN. Draw a circle with the Center at 6.5,6.5 and a Radius of 1.5.

The circle should be in the upper right corner of the screen. Pick PAN from the DISPLAY Submenu. Answer the prompt with: (Basepoint at) 6.5,6.5; Second point: 3,3. Now pick PAN again and use 3,3 as the basepoint and @3,3 in answer to the Second point, pressing (R). The circle moved 3 units to the right and 3 units up. The (R) signifies (to the program) that the second set of values were relative values.

6.3 REDRAW Command

The REDRAW command acts in the same way that a drafting brush sweeps away the remains of the eraser. This command removes the blips from the screen (from points selected during the drawing sequence) and repairs the GRID display (if the GRID has been activated). The Menu Map for the REDRAW command is shown in Figure 6–16. There is no Command Sequence for this command. The command may be selected from the Screen Menu or Pull Down Menu, or typed from the keyboard. When the command is activated, the screen image disappears and reappears ready for addition work efforts.

6.4 Regeneration Commands

The Regeneration commands (REGEN, REDRAWALL, REGENALL, and REGENAUTO) are listed in the DISPLAY Submenu as shown in Figure 6–17.

The AutoCAD program occasionally requires that the drawing entities (lines, arcs, circles, etc.) displayed on the screen be recomputed. In a large or complex drawing, the recomputation or regeneration takes more time that the REDRAW of the screen display. When AutoCAD requires this regeneration, a message is displayed in the command line area: Regenerating the drawing. . . . However, the operator can limit some of the automatic regeneration effort. It is faster to REDRAW the screen. On your next drawing assignment, note the time it takes to REDRAW and then select REGEN from the DISPLAY Submenu. The more complex the drawing, the greater

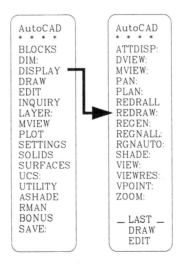

Figure 6–16 Menu Map for the REDRAW Command

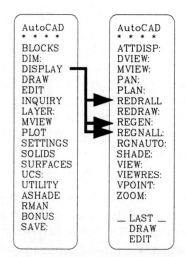

Figure 6–17 Menu Map for the Regeneration Commands

the time it takes to regenerate the screen display. The Regeneration commands, REGEN, REDRAWALL, and REGENALL are available to the operator. Some drawing commands as redefining BLOCK, Changing a LAYER or STYLE automatically require a regeneration. However, the operator can restrict the regeneration by the use of the REGNAUTO command. The Menu Map for the REGNAUTO is shown in Figure 6–18. The Command Sequence is illustrated in Figure 6–19.

Looking at Figure 6–19, if OFF is selected, then the automatic regeneration fea-

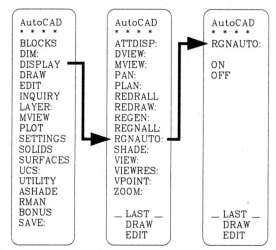

Figure 6–18 Menu Map for the REGNAUTO Command

```
Command: REGENAUTO ON/OFF <ON>:
```

Figure 6–19 Command Sequence for the REGNAUTO Command

tures are turned off. If ON is selected, the screen is automatically regenerated and the automatic feature is re-instated.

6.5 VIEW Command

The VIEW command enables the operator to select a portion of the screen display or view of the drawing and identify this view with a name (maximum of 31 characters). The Menu Map for the VIEW command is shown in Figure 6–20. Figure 6–21 lists the Command Sequence for the VIEW command.

The selections of the Command Sequence options are defined below:

? = Display of all view names

D (Delete) = Used to delete a view. Respond with the view name.

R (Restore) = Used when a specific view is requested. Respond with R and the view name.

S (Save) = Used to save an identified view. Respond with view name.

W (Window) = Typical window operation to select a portion of the drawing to be an identified view

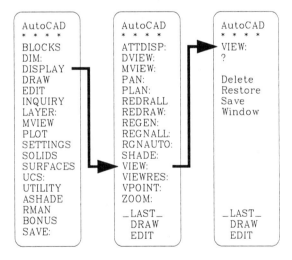

Figure 6–20 Menu Map for the VIEW Command

```
Command: ?/Delete/Restore/Save/Window:

D = View name to delete
R = View name to restore
S = View name to save
W = View name to save
```

Figure 6–21 Command Sequence for the VIEW Command

The VIEW command is usually used when detailing a section of the drawing. After the view has been saved, editing of the drawing automatically updates the view. Bring up a new drawing called VIEW. Draw a circle whose Center is located at 3,3, with a Radius of 3". Draw a square whose sides are 2' long and whose Center is located at 3,3. Select the VIEW command (DISPLAY Submenu), Window option, and window the square (called the View SQUARE). Using the POLYGON command, draw an equalateral triangle, using the Inscribed option, whose Center is at 3,3, and with Radius = 1". Now erase the square. Pick VIEW command, Restore option; View Name SQUARE. The screen will show the triangle only. Quit the drawing.

6.6 VIEWRES Command

The VIEWRES command controls the FAST ZOOM mode and the resolution for the circle, arc and linetype. The LINETYPE command is discussed in Chapter 16. The VIEWRES command is listed in the DISPLAY Submenu. The Menu Map is illustrated in Figure 6–22 and the Command Sequence in Figure 6–23.

This command provides the operator with two options: FAST ZOOM and arc/circle resolution. The FAST ZOOM option is activated by answering Y, or Yes, to the FAST ZOOM question. This makes the regeneration speed for ZOOMs, PANs, and VIEWs the same as that of the REDRAW. An N, or No, requires additional time to perform the regeneration.

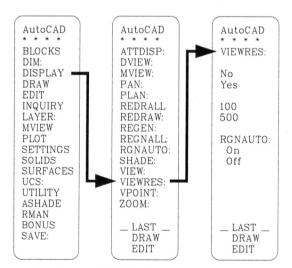

Figure 6–22 Menu Map for the VIEWRES Command

```
Command: VIEWRES
Do you want fast zooms? <Y>: Y
Enter circle zoom persent (1–20000) <100>: 100
```

Figure 6–23 Command Sequence for the VIEWRES Command

The second option is the display resolution of an arc or circle. The program draws a circle or arc as a series of line segments. The use of larger line segments means a shorter time to display the entity on the screen. Sometimes, due to size, the circle or arc appears round, but it is not the case. Using the ZOOM command Window option, window a section of the circle. You will see that the circle is made of line segments. The operator has the option to decrease or increase the size of the segment. In answer to the Circle ZOOM, a percentage of 10 produces a larger segment than that of 1000. The default value is 100. This is illustrated in the following example. Bring up a drawing called VIEWRES. Draw a circle whose Center is 5,5 and whose Radius is 2'. Using ZOOM Window, select the first quadrant (from 0 to 90°) of the circle. Note the length of the line segment. Select VIEWRES command, with Circle ZOOM percent of 1000. This requires an automatic regeneration. The resulting circle segment is smaller than the default. Repeat the VIEWRES command but use 10 as the Circle ZOOM percentage. The line segment is longer. Now, ZOOM All. The circle appears to be round. Quit the drawing.

6.7 Pull Down Menu Commands for Chapter 6

Figure 6-24 displays the Pull Down Menu for Chapter 6.

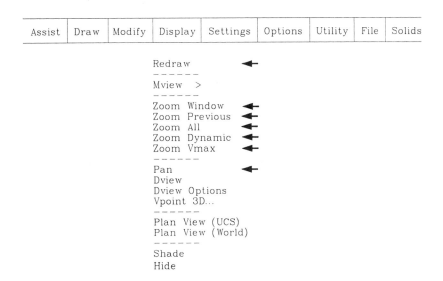

Figure 6–24 Pull Down Menu Commands for Chapter 6

6.8 Template Reference—Chapter 6

Figure 6-25 is the Template Reference for Chapter 6.

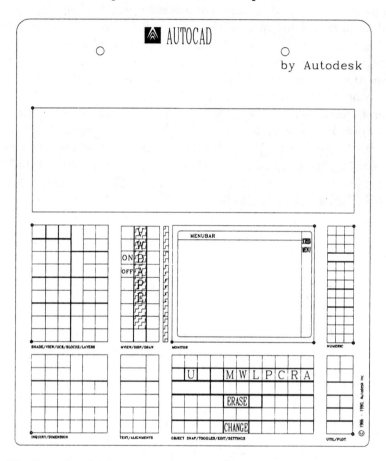

Figure 6–25 Template References for Chapter 6

COMMAND SUMMARY

PAN	REGENALL
REDRAW	REGENAUTO
REGEN	VIEW
REDRAWALL	VIEWRES

ZOOM:		
	All	Previous
	Center	Scale
	Dynamic	Vmax
	Extents	Window

7

Text Commands

Instructional Objectives

1. To understand the difference between TEXT, STYLE, and style commands
2. To be able to select any one of four proportional spacing fonts or the monotext font
3. To be able to place two or more different fonts on the same drawing
4. To be able to use the DTEXT command
5. To understand the use of the QTEXT command and how to apply the command
6. To be able to use special control codes for underlining, overscoring, and the like

7.1 Introduction

The TEXT command is divided into three commands: TEXT, STYLE, and style as shown in Figure 4–43. The Menu command TEXT is described in Chapter 4, paragraph 4.8 TEXT command.

NOTE: There are two types of "STYLE". The first command is capitalized while the second is in lowercase. In general, AutoCAD is *not* case sensitive.

7.2 STYLE Command

The STYLE command is used to establish the specifications for a specified type of font. These specifications are: Font type, Height and Width of the letters, Oblique Angle of the letters, and the orientation of text (Backward, Upside down, and/or Vertical). The STYLE command is found under the Settings Submenu and is shown in Figure 7–1.

The Command Sequence asks for seven answers (Font, Height, Width, Oblique Angle, Backwards, Upside down, and Vertical) to form the STYLE of a textstring. Figure 7–2 shows the Command Sequence for the STYLE command.

The default name for the STYLE filename is STANDARD. However, the operator may select up to eight characters for the STYLE name.

REMEMBER: A drawing may have many STYLEs but each STYLE must have a unique name.

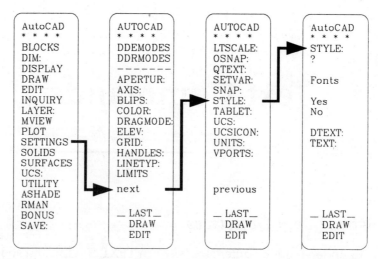

Figure 7–1   Menu Map for the STYLE command

```
Command:   STYLE   Text style name (or ?) <STANDARD>:

Existing style.
Font file <txt>: Simplex (R)
  Height <0.0000>: (R)
  Width factor  <1.00>: (R)

Obliquing angle <0>: (R)
Backwards? <N> (R)
Upside-down? <N> (R)
Vertical? <N> (R)
```

Figure 7–2   Command Sequence for the STYLE command

7.2.1 Fonts

The Font names are divided into three categories. Category A includes those fonts (Txt, Simplex, Complex, Italic, and Monotxt) used before Release 9. Category B includes those fonts to be used in current drawings (Roman, Script, Greek, Italic, Cyrillic, Cyriltic, and Gothic) since all but the Monotxt Font will be removed from the program. Category C is comprised of special symbol fonts designed for Astronomy, Mapping, Mathematics, Music, Meteorology, and TXT. Figure 7–3 illustrates the Category A fonts. All fonts, except for the Monotxt Font, provide text or symbols with proportional spacing but Monotxt provides uniformly spaced lettering.

There are seven new fonts, each font (except for the Gothic fonts) has a number of modes. These are shown in Table 7–1.

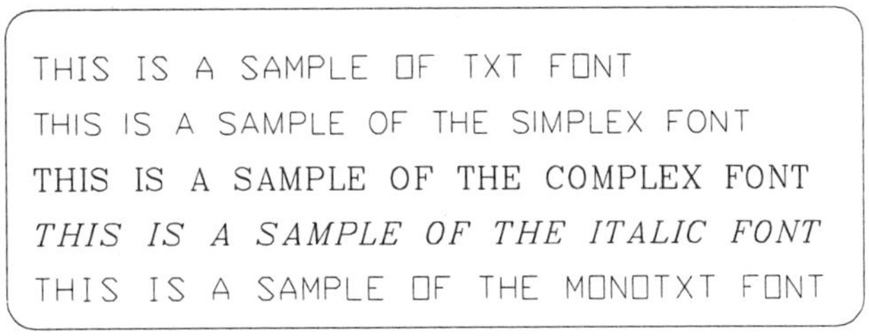

THIS IS A SAMPLE OF TXT FONT
THIS IS A SAMPLE OF THE SIMPLEX FONT
THIS IS A SAMPLE OF THE COMPLEX FONT
THIS IS A SAMPLE OF THE ITALIC FONT
THIS IS A SAMPLE OF THE MONOTXT FONT

Figure 7–3   Category A Text Fonts

Three Dialogue Boxes are used to illustrate and select one of the current and symbol fonts. These are shown in Figures 7–4, 7–5, and 7–6.

The operator may select any one of 17 different Font modes (including Category A) plus six Symbol fonts. Figure 7–7 illustrates the Font correlation between the Font mode and the uppercase keyboard letter. Figure 7–8 illustrates the Font correlation between the Font mode and the lowercase keyboard letter.

The remaining STYLE command selections are the following:

Height: If the drawing calls for all text to be the same height, then input the height value at this point. If the textstrings are to be of different heights, then the Height value for this command is 0.000.

> **NOTE:** If a nonzero value is used, then all letter heights will be the same. This includes the letter/number heights used in the DIMENSIONING command. HINT: In general practice, if the drawing calls for two or more letter heights, set the STYLE Height equal to zero. The letter height should be specified in the Text sequence.

Width: The nominal character width is 1.0000. For wider characters, use a value greater than 1.0000. For narrower characters, use a value less than 1.0000. Figure 7–9 shows the difference between a width factor of 1.25, 1, and .5.

Oblique Angle: This is the angle at which the character will lean. Positive values of angle produce a forward slant, while negative values produce a backward slant.

TABLE 7–1

Current Font Modes

Font Name	Simplex	Duplex	Complex	Triplex	Gothic
Roman	X	X	X	X	
Script	X		X		
Greek	X		X		
Italic				X	
Cyrillic			X		
Cyriltic			X		
Gothic					X

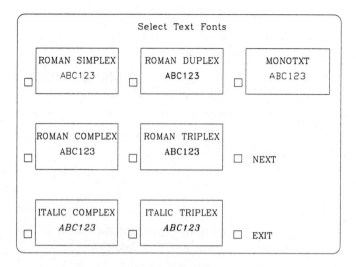

Figure 7–4   First Dialogue Box for Fonts

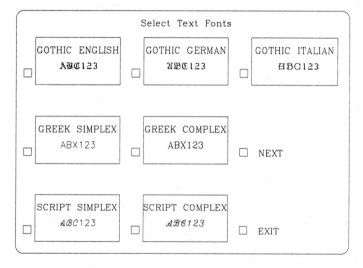

Figure 7–5   Second Dialogue Box for Fonts

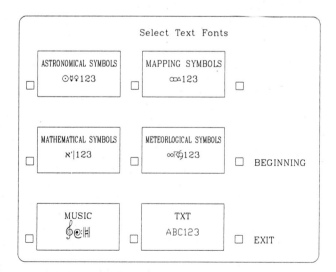

Figure 7–6   Third Dialogue Box for Fonts

KEYBOARD INPUT

A B C D E F G H I J K L M N O P Q R S T U V W X Y Z [\ ] ^ _ '

cyrillic	А Б В Г Д Е Ж З И Й К Л М Н О П Р С Т У Ф Х Ц Ч Ш Щ Ъ Ы Ь Э Ю '
cyriltlc	А Б Ч Д Е Ф Г Х И Щ К Л М Н О П Ц Р С Т У В Ш Ж Й З Ь Ы Ъ Ю Э '
greekc	A B X Δ E Φ Γ H I ϑ K Λ M N O Π Θ P Σ T Υ ∇ Ω Ξ Ψ Z [\ ] ^ _ '
greeks	A B X Δ E Φ Γ H I ϑ K Λ M N O Π Θ P Σ T Υ ∇ Ω Ξ Ψ Z [\ ] ^ _ '
syastro	⊙ ☿ ♀ ⊕ ♂ ♃ ♄ ♅ Ψ ♇ ☾ ⚹ ✳ ♌ ♉ ♈ ♊ ♋ ♎ ♍ ♏ ♑ ♐ ♒ ♓ [\ ] ^ _ '
symap	○ □ △ ◇ ☆ + × ∗ ● ■ ▲ ◀ ▼ ▶ ★ ⌐ ⊥ ⊤ × ☥ ⚓ ⚐ ✠ © ✿ △ [\ ] ^ _ '
symath	ℵ ' | ‖ ± ∓ × · ÷ = ≠ ≡ < > ≦ ≧ ∝ ~ √ ∪ ∩ ⊃ ∈ → ↑ [\ ] ^ _ '
symeteo	· ⌁ ▪ ▴ ▪ ◤ ⌒ ⌒ ⌣ ⌣ ⌒ ' ` ʃ ∾ ∞ ℞ ℔ — | \ ⌐⌐⌐ / [\ ] ^ _ '
symusic	· ⌐ ♩ ♩ ○ ○ ● ♯ ♮ ♭ ━ - ⌐ ⌐ 𝄞 𝄢 𝄐 ⌐ · · ⌐⌐⌐^ ≍ ▽ [\ ] ^ _ '

Figure 7–7 Uppercase Font Correlation

KEYBOARD INPUT

a b c d e f g h i j k l m n o p q r s t u v w x y z ⟨ \| ⟩ ⌐ ⟨ ⟩

cyrillic	а б в г д е ж з и й к л м н о п р с т у ф х ц ч ш щ ъ ы ь э ю я
cyriltlc	а б ч д е ф г х и щ к л м н о п ц р с т у в ш ж й з ь ы ъ э ю я
greekc	α β χ δ ε φ γ η ι ∂ κ λ μ ν ο π ϑ ρ σ τ υ ∈ ω ξ ψ ζ } | { ~ < >
greeks	α β χ δ ε φ γ η ι ∂ κ λ μ ν ο π ϑ ρ σ τ υ ∈ ω ξ ψ ζ } | { ~ < >
syastro	⚹ ' ` ∪ ∩ ∈ → ↑ ← ↓ ∂ ∇ © ⌒ ∂ ˘ ℵ § † ‡ Ǝ ℒ ® © } | { ~ < >
symap	☥ ⚓ ⚐ ♀ ⚘ · · ○ ○ ○ ○ ○ ⊂ ⊃ ☐ ⊥ ∠ ∴ ♀ ♡ ◇ ♣ ❀ ✿ } | { ~ < >
symath	← ↓ ∂ ∇ √ ∫ ∮ ∞ § † ‡ Ǝ ∏ ∑ ( ) [ ] } } { { √ √ ≈ ≅ } | { ' < >
symeteo	| \ ⌐ ⌐ ⌁ \ ⌒ ⌒ ⌣ ( ) ∾ ∿ ∿ ⌐ ℓ α σ ▷ φ ♂ · } | { ~ < >
symusic	· ⌐ ♩ ○ ○ ● ♯ ♮ ♭ ━ - ⅃ ⌐ 𝄞 𝄢 𝄐 ⊙ ☿ ♀ ⊕ ♂ ♃ ♄ ♅ Ψ ♇ } | { ~ < >

Figure 7–8 Lowercase Correlation

THIS TEXT STRING HAS A WIDTH FACTOR OF .5000

THIS TEXT STRING HAS A WIDTH FACTOR OF 1.0000

THIS TEXT STRING HAS A WIDTH FACTOR OF 1.25

Figure 7–9 Character Width

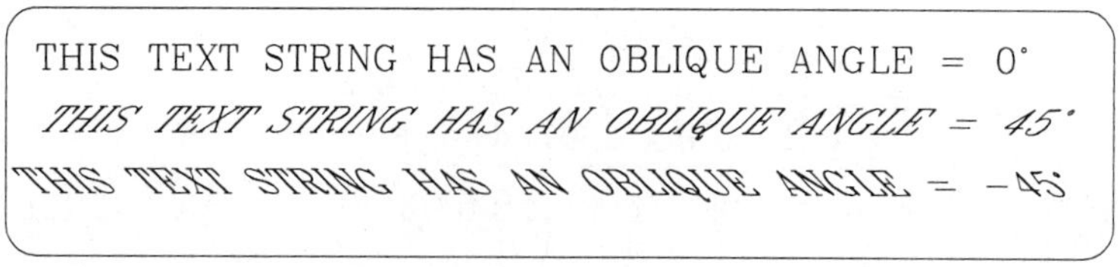

THIS TEXT STRING HAS AN OBLIQUE ANGLE = 0°

THIS TEXT STRING HAS AN OBLIQUE ANGLE = 45°

THIS TEXT STRING HAS AN OBLIQUE ANGLE = -45

Figure 7-10   The Effects of the Oblique Angle

Figure 7-10 illustrates the differences between 45°, 0°, and -45°. The maximum positive Oblique Angle is 80° while the maximum negative angle is 85°.

Backwards: If the answer to this prompt is Y or YES, then the textstring will be backwards as shown in Figure 7-11.

Upside Down: An affirmative answer to this prompt makes the textstring upside down in appearance as shown in Figure 7-12.

NOTE: When selecting the text Start point for this option, remember that the text will be placed from right to left.

Vertical: If the operator wants to place the characters in a vertical display, answer Y or YES to this prompt. An example of this mode is shown in Figure 7-13. The rotation angle (part of the TEXT command) will automatically be set at 270°.

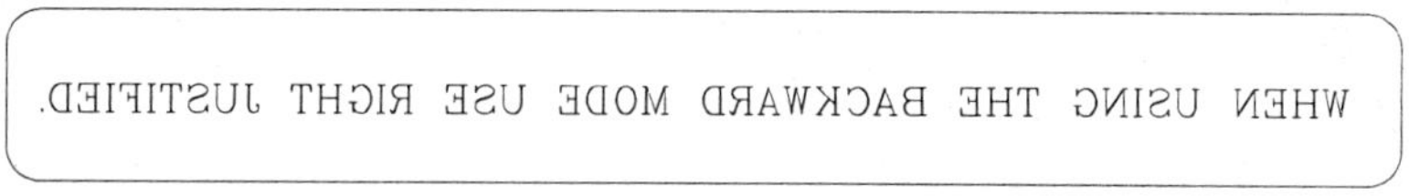

WHEN USING THE BACKWARD MODE USE RIGHT JUSTIFIED.

Figure 7-11   Textstring Using the Backwards Option

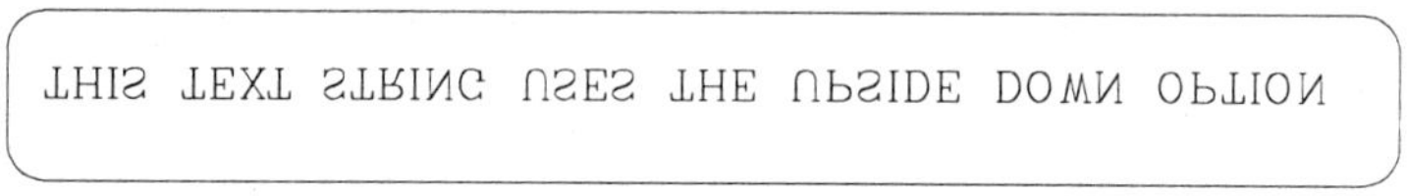

THIS TEXT STRING USES THE UPSIDE DOWN OPTION

Figure 7-12   Illustration of the Upside-down Mode

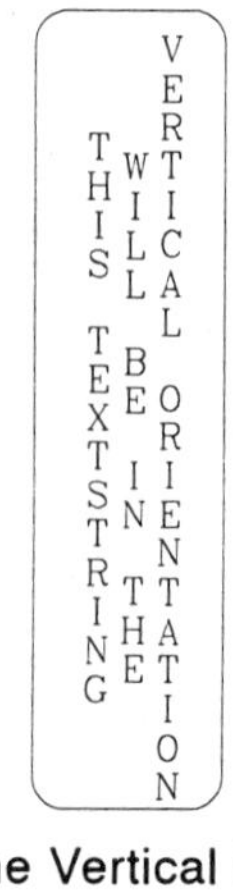

```
            V
            E
            R
  T W       T
  H I       I
  I L       C
  S L       A
            L
  T B       O
  E E       R
  X I       I
  T N       E
  S T       N
  T         T
  R H       A
  I E       T
  N         I
  G         O
            N
```

Figure 7-13   An Example of the Vertical Mode

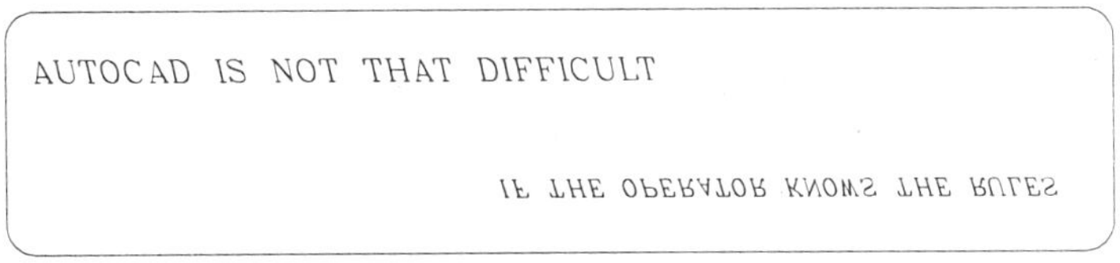

AUTOCAD IS NOT THAT DIFFICULT

It THE OPERATOR KNOWS THE RULES

Figure 7–14 Solution to Example 7–1

One or more of the above modes may be combined. Only one font may be specified for a given STYLE name. However, it is possible to have more than one STYLE for any drawing. For example, STYLE:STANDARD may be configured as: Font: TXT; Height = 0.00; Oblique Angle = 15°; and Backwards. A second STYLE (STYLE1) using Italic font; Height = 0.0; Oblique Angle = 0°; and Vertical orientation may also be placed on the drawing. Both STYLEs may be used on the same drawing.

Example 7–1: The assignment calls for two font files to be used on the same drawing. One STYLE will be called STANDARD and the second will be called STYLE1. The STANDARD STYLE will be: TXT; Height = 0.2"; and Oblique Angle set for -12.5°. STYLE1 calls for: Italic font; Height 0.15"; and Upside down. Figure 7–14 reflects the two styles. The textstring for the STANDARD STYLE is, "AutoCAD is not that difficult"; start at 1,5. The second textstring is "If the operator knows the rules" start at 10,6 and right justified.

NOTE: If the same STYLE name is used for two textstrings, the last STYLE specified will appear on the screen. All other textstrings will automatically revert to the last STYLE.

7.2.2 STYLE Command

The style command is located in the TEXT Submenu as shown in Figure 7–15. This command permits the operator to select any of the STYLE names that have been

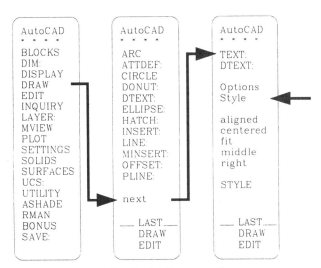

Figure 7–15 Menu Map for the Style Command

```
Command: TEXT Start point or Align/Center/Fit/Middle/Style: style
Style name (or ?) <STANDARD>: STANDARD
```

Figure 7–16   Command Sequence for the Style Command

developed. The Command Sequence for this command is shown in Figure 7–16. A listing of STYLE filenames is displayed if the ? is used, followed by (R).

7.2.3   Special Character Commands

Currently, there are six special character commands or codes that provide special symbols: underscoring, overscoring, degree symbol, plus/minus symbol, circle diameter symbol, and a special symbol reserved for future programming.

%%o toggles the overscore line. This symbol is placed at the start and end of the overscore line.

%%u toggles the underscore line. As with the overscore line, the symbol must be at the start and end of the line.

%%d draws the degree symbol.

%%p draws the plus and minus tolerance symbol.

%%c draws the symbol for circle diameter.

%%nnn is reserved for future programming.

Figure 7–17 illustrates each symbol.

Example 7–2:   Place the following text on the screen: "The limits of temperature shall not exceed 100° Centigrade." Figure 7–18a shows the text input and Figure 7–18b shows the result of the text input.

7.3   DTEXT Command

This command, DYNAMIC TEXT, permits the operator to see the text (on the video screen) as the data is typed (at the keyboard). The *initial* placement of the characters

```
%%o  =  OVERSCORE LINE       OVERSCORE LINE
%%u  =  UNDERSCORE LINE        UNDERSCORE LINE
%%d  =  DEGREE SYMBOL         35°C
%%p  =  PLUS/MINUS SYMBOL     2'6"±.25"
%%C  =  CIRCLE DIAMETER       ø
%=  %  SYMBOL                 94%
```

Figure 7–17   Special Character Symbols

```
The % %u limits %%u shall not
% %u exceed%%u 100 %%d Centigrade   ⌐ (a)

The limits shall not
exceed 100 ˚Centigrade   ⌐ (b)
```

Figure 7–18 Solution to Example 7–2

is in accordance with the Left Justified mode of operation regardless of the text mode selected. After the textstring (one or more lines) has been typed, the complete textstring is removed from the screen and placed in the specified location. The DTEXT command is listed under the DRAW Submenu and shown in Figure 7–19.

The Command Sequence for this command is listed in Figure 7–20.

In a multi-line text, the DTEXT command prompts are different from those of the TEXT command. After the first line of text has been input, the command prompt asks for the second line of text instead of TEXT command and location. Upon completion of the input, a (R) is required to instruct the program that the task has been completed. All of the text disappears from the screen for a few moments and then

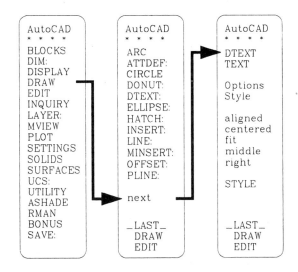

Figure 7–19 Menu Map for the DTEXT Command

```
Command: DTEXT Justify/Style/<Start point>: 2,5
Height <0.2000>: (R)
Rotation angle <0>: (R)
Text:
```

Figure 7–20 Command Sequence for the DTEXT Command

reappears in its proper location. Figure 4–52 (see Chapter 4) illustrates the Pull Down Menu for the DTEXT options. You are now ready to do further work on the drawing.

NOTE: In the DTEXT command, the Align mode will properly place the text automatically for succeeding textstrings.

7.4   QTEXT Command

The QTEXT command improves the regeneration time for those drawings that have text information. The QTEXT command is listed under the Setting Submenu and is shown in Figure 7–21. The Command Sequence is illustrated in Figure 7–22.

When the QTEXT command is activated, all lines of text are replaced with a rectangle whose length is equal to the textstring and whose height is equal to the height of the characters. The regeneration time is reduced and the text data is held in memory until QTEXT command is turned OFF. When turned OFF, the rectangles are replaced by the text data. Figure 7–23(a) shows a drawing with all the textstrings present. Figure 7–23(b) shows the same drawing with the QTEXT activated and the rectangle boxes replacing the textstrings.

CAUTION: The QTEXT command effects the entire drawing and not just a section of the drawing.

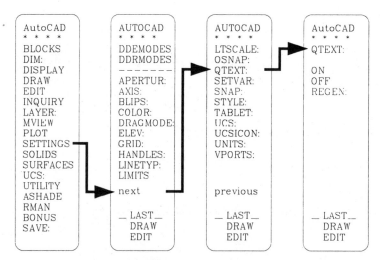

Figure 7–21   Menu Map for the QTEXT Command

```
Command:  QTEXT ON/OFF <off>:  on
```

Figure 7–22   Command Sequence for the QTEXT Command

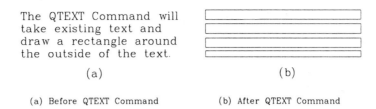

The QTEXT Command will
take existing text and
draw a rectangle around
the outside of the text.

(a)   (b)

(a) Before QTEXT Command   (b) After QTEXT Command

Figure 7–23   The Effect of the QTEXT Command

7.5   Pull Down Menu for Chapter 7

Figure 7-24 is the Pull Down Menu for Chapter 7.

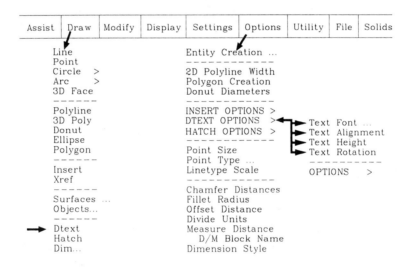

Figure 7–24   Pull Down Menu for Chapter 7

7.6   Template Reference—Chapter 7

See Figure 7-25 on page 104.

COMMAND SUMMARY

STYLE   style
DTEXT   QTEXT

PROBLEMS

1. Name the seven independent style modes or options.
2. True or False: The default name of the STYLE file is STANDARD.
3. Name at least four of the five font options.

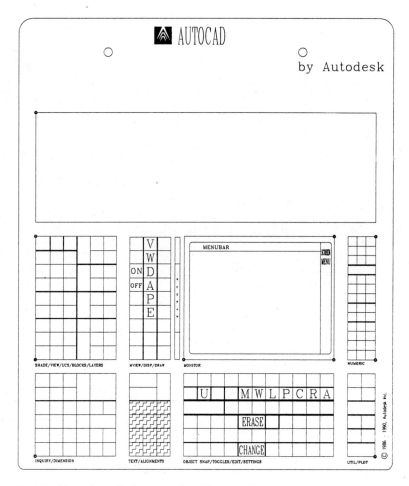

Figure 7–25 Template Reference for Chapter 7

4. Using the STANDARD style, establish a text style in accordance with Height = .65; Oblique Angle = -10; and Vertical option. The text to be used is, "Good CAD operators will", the second line will be "permit the CAD equipment", and the third line will be "to do the job."

5. Your drawing calls for text having two different fonts. Drawing notes will require Italic font; 0.25" high; and width of character = 0.9. The parts list will use Simplex font; Height = 0.2"; character width = 1.0; and Oblique Angle = 10°. The note is located at 0.25,7 and reads, "All plastic material must be inspected before use." The parts list is located at 0.5,3 and reads, "0.25" plastic sheet per ABC spec 10923." Do a PRPLOT at half scale.

8 Obtaining Hard Copy

Instructional Objectives

1. To understand the Printer or Plotter Screen Menu items
2. To be able to program the necessary line items in order to obtain a Printer plot of a drawing
3. To be able to program the necessary line items to obtain a Plotted copy of the drawing

8.1 Hard Copy

AutoCAD provides the operator with two independent methods of obtaining a copy of the drawing displayed on the screen: A Printer plot (accomplished by a dot matrix Printer) or a Plotted output (accomplished by using a Plotter with either a felt tip pen or liquid ink). The Printer plot is used as a check print to determine if the drawing is satisfactory. The Plotted plot of the drawing is considered suitable as a final drawing.

8.2 Common Printer and Plotter Commands

Figures 8-1 and 8-2 show the Command Sequence for the Plotter and Printer, respectively.

```
Specify the part of the drawing to be plotted by entering:
Display, Extents, Limits, View, or Window <D>:

Plot will NOT be written to a selected file
Sizes are in inches
Plot origin is at (0.00,0.00)
Plotting area is 16.00 wide by 10.00 high (B size):
Rotate plot 0/90/180/270 <0>
Pen width is 0.010
Area fill will NOT be adjusted for pen width
Hidden lines will NOT be removed
Plot will be scaled to fit available area

Do you want to change anything? <N>:
Effective plotting area: 14.24 by 10.00 high
Position paper in plotter.
Press RETURN to continue or S to Stop for hardware setup
Processing vector; 752
```

Figure 8-1 Command Sequence for the Plotter Command

```
Specify the part of the drawing to be plotted by entering:
Display, Extents, Limits, View, or Window <D>:

Plot will NOT be written to a selected file
Sizes are in Inches
Plot origin is at (0.00,0.00)
Plotting area is 8.00 wide by 10.50 high (A size):
Rotate plot 0/90/180/270 <0>
Hidden lines will NOT be removed
Scale is 1=4

Do you want to change anything? <N>
Effective plotting area:   1.37 wide by 2.27 high
Position paper in printer.
Press RETURN to continue:
Processing vector: 2343
Printer plot complete.
Press RETURN to continue
```

Figure 8–2   Command Sequence for the Printer Command

A review of the Command Sequence for both Plotter and Printer lists eight Command prompts that are the same. These prompts are:

Prompt: Specify the part of the drawing to be Plotted by entering: Display (D), Extents (E), Limits (L), View (V), or Window (W):

The program is asking for the section of the screen area to be copied. (AutoCAD assumes that the drawing output will be in a rectangular configuration.) The available selections are:

Display (D): AutoCAD plots the entities presently displayed on the screen.

Extents (E): This selection restricts the Plotted area to be copied to the drawing entities as show on the screen. Figure 8–3 shows the difference between the Display

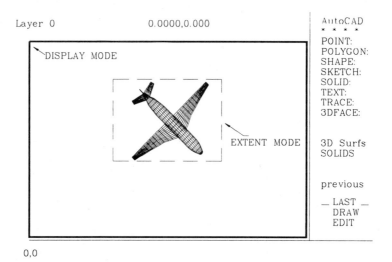

Figure 8–3   Differences Between Display and Extents Modes

and Extents. The Area within the dashed lines represent the Extents, whereas the area enclosed by the wide lines represents the Display option.

Limits (L): A response of L or Limits informs the program to plot all information that is contained within the limits of the drawing whether or not displayed.

View: This prompt calls for a specific area of the drawing that has been specified as a named View during the drawing effort.

Window: A reply of W or Window is used when a specified area is to be Plotted. The W procedure is identical to other Window options.

Prompt: Plot will *NOT* be written to a select file: The operator may select to write the drawing file to a file and not to the Plotter or Printer. If this is true, the operator responds with Y or YES. The prompt then asks for the filename. When the new filename is given, the extension of the file is changed automatically from .DWG to either .PLT for the Plotter function or .LST for the Printer function. A prompt response of N or NO sends the drawing file to either the Printer or Plotter program.

Prompt: Sizes are in Inches: This prompt is used to specify the units of the drawing. The operator may select either drawing inches (I) or millimeters (M). The default value is in inches.

Prompt: Plot origin is at (0.00,0.00): The origin represents the Printer or Plotter's home point. The origin is located differently for the Plotter and Printer. Figures 8–4 (a) and 8–4(b) illustrate the location of the origin for A-size paper. Figure 8–4(a) represents the origin for the Printer application, while Figure 8–4(b) shows the origin point for the Plotter. The origin is located in the lower left corner of the drawing. However, because of the physical arrangement of the Plotter, the origin used for the Plotter is the upper left corner of the paper. The key word is *paper*. It appears that the paper is rotated by 90°. This is true. For most Plotters, the origin is located in the lower left corner and a change in the X value moves the point to the right or left and a change in the Y value moves the origin up or down. This is reversed for the Printer system.

Prompt: Plotting area: The workstation configuration calls for a specific Plotter and/or Printer. Within the software specifications of the selected Printer or Plotter is the maximum drawing size that either unit can accommodate. The operator must inform the program as to the size of paper that will be used to make the hard copy.

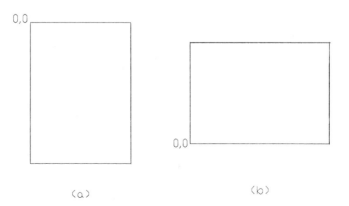

(a)   (b)

Figure 8–4 Paper Orientation for Printer and Plotter

Table 8–1

Size notation	Paper size	Plot/print size*
A	8.5″ × 11″	8″ × 10.5″
B	11″ × 17″	10.5″ × 16.5″
C	17″ × 22″	16.5″ × 21.5″
D	22″ × 34″	21.5″ × 33.5″
E	greater than D	
MAX	Maximum size that the device can use.	
USER	Used for nonstandard paper	

* The actual plotting/printing size is smaller than the paper size, due to the space needed to transport the paper. The rule of thumb is .25″ on each side.

The paper sizes have been standardized by the American National Standard Institute (ANSI). Table 8–1 reflects the standardized paper sizes.

Prompt: One of two prompts will appear. The first prompt, **Plot not rotated**, appears when the initial Command Sequence appears. The second prompt, **Rotate plot: 0/90/180/270**, appears if the answer to the question "Do you want to change anything?" is Y or YES. The operator may select any one of the four degree values or answer the prompt with a Y or YES. The Y or YES instructs the program to rotate the plot by 270°. With any other rotation, answer with a numerical value.

Prompt: Hidden lines will *not* be removed. This prompt is used for 3D drawings only. Hard copy of 3D drawings may require hidden lines to be removed prior to the copying of the drawing. An affirmative reply activates this prompt. However, if this prompt is activated, the removal of hidden lines from a complex drawing may take a considerable length of time. The time period is usually measured in hours.

Prompt: Specify scale by entering: Plotted inches = Drawing Units or Fit or ? <F>: There are two possible answers: (1) the actual scale to be used in copying the drawing [i.e. 3 plotted inches for 1 inch on the screen (3=1)]; and (2) answer by typing F for fit. The F answer instructs the program to scale the drawing so that it fits on the paper. The resulting drawing should not be scaled.

8.3 PLOT Command

The operator has the facilities to plot the drawing either from the Main Menu (refer to Chapter 2 Figure 2–1) item 3 or from the drawing editor (while in the drawing mode). The PLOT command is found under the Plot Submenu as shown in Figure 8–5. The Command Sequences for both plotting methods are identical and shown in Figure 8–1 and Figure 8–2.

AutoCAD provides a checklist of the current prompt status. The operator should review each line item and make any changes needed to produce the drawing as desired. If changes are necessary, then answer the prompt, "Do you want to change anything <N>" with Y or YES. AutoCAD then displays each line item for modification. Upon completion of this review, the program automatically goes into its plotting mode. The display will read "Effective plotting area:,". Place the plotting

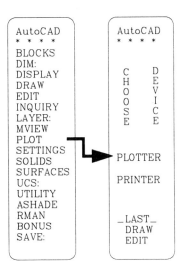

Figure 8–5 Menu Map for the PLOT Command

paper into the Plotter and press the ENTER key to continue the plotting procedure. The drawing file is then fed into the Plotter buffer (memory). You will notice on the Monitor that the number of processing vectors will increase. At the end of the plotting mode, "Return to continue" is displayed. Answer this prompt with (R).

8.3.1 Pen and Linetype Selection

The selection of the Plotter depends on a number of factors. Some Plotters have a single pen capability and other units have software-controlled multiple-pen capability (up to 15 colors). The writing tips are available in several different configurations, namely, fiber tip, ball tip, and liquid ink. Each pen type is designed for different applications. The color of each pen, when used in a multiple-pen carrier, must be selected from the Command Sequence Menu (second page) as shown in Figure 8–6.

Entity Color	Pen No.	Line Type	Pen Speed	Entity Color	Pen No.	Line Type	Pen Speed
1 (red)	1	0	36	9	1	0	36
2 (yellow)	2	0	36	10	2	0	36
3 (green)	3	0	36	11	3	0	36
4 (cyan)	4	0	36	12	4	0	36
5 (blue)	5	0	36	13	5	0	36
6 (magenta)	6	0	36	14	6	0	36
7 (white)	7	0	36	15	7	0	36
8	8	0	36		8	0	36

```
Line  types    0  =  continuous line
               1  =  __ __ __ __
               2  =  __ __ __ __
               3  =  ___ ___ ___ ___
               4  =  ____ ____ ____
               5  =  __ . __ . __ -
               6  =  __ . . __ . . __ . .
```

Figure 8–6 Command Sequence (Second Page) Pen and Linetype Menu

The operator should review the color assigned to each pen holder and make sure that the pen color assigned to that pen holder (during the LAYER procedure) is the same as shown on the screen. The pen speed assignment is made by the operator in accordance with the Configuration of the Plotter. Usually the operator selects the fastest speed. If the line work is not satisfactory, however, he or she will reduce the pen speed.

CAUTION: Prior to the initial use of the Plotter for that day, make sure that the pens are working (the pen tips sometimes dry out) and that the pen color matches the pen assignment. This review may be implemented by answering Y or YES to the prompt, "Do you want to change any of these parameters? <N>:". This prompt is displayed immediately after the Linetype Menu.

A number of CAD systems do not support a linetype program. The Plotter manufacturers include a linetype program within the Plotter software and these are displayed at this time. AutoCAD has its own linetype program, therefore the plotter linetype Program is *not* needed. The answer to this prompt is zero (0).

8.4   PRINTER PLOT (PRPLOT) Command

As in the case of the PLOT command, two methods can activate the Printer plot process. The first method is to select item 4 from the Main Menu. (See Chapter 2 Figure 2–1.) The second method is used during the normal drawing effort. The selection of the PRINTER command is listed in the Plot Submenu and shown in Figure 8–7. The initial Command Sequence is shown in Figure 8–2. Except for the pen and linetype selection, the Command Sequence for both the Plotter and Printer is the same.

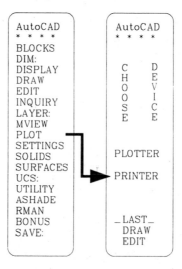

Figure 8–7   Menu Map for the Printer Command

8.5 Pull Down Menu for Chapter 8

The Pull Down Menu for Chapter 8 is shown in Figure 8-8.

Figure 8-8 Pull Down Menu for Chapter 8

8.6 Template Reference—Chapter 8

The Template Reference for Chapter 8 is shown in Figure 8-9.

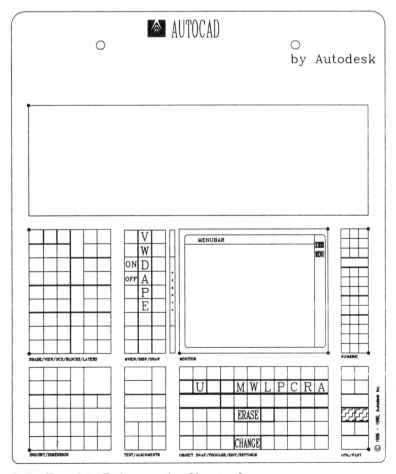

Figure 8-9 Template Reference for Chapter 8

COMMAND SUMMARY

PLOT
PRPLOT

GLOSSARY

View: A specific view of a drawing that is saved under a specific name.

Linetype: A series of dashes and dots to give the operator the ability to draw different lines.

Extents: A term that deals with any entities of the drawing.

ANSI: American National Standards Institute.

Limits: The limits established at the start of the drawing.

PROBLEMS

1. What command would be used to restrict the Plotter or Printer to print all data contained in a specific area of the drawing?
2. If an A-sized (8.5″ × 11″) sheet is used for plotting, what are the usable dimensions?

9 Auxiliary Drawing Commands

Instructional Objectives

1. To understand when and how the FILLET command may be useful
2. To be able to implement the FILLET command
3. To understand how and when to use the CHAMFER command
4. To be able to implement the CHAMFER command
5. To understand the limitations of each command
6. To be able to use either command in conjunction with the Polyline entities
7. To use the FILLET or CHAMFER command to complete a corner

9.1 FILLET Command

The purpose of the FILLET command is to relieve the stress caused by sharp corners of sheet metal or other materials with an arc of a given Radius. The FILLET command is located in the EDIT Submenu as shown in Figure 9–1.

There are four possible applications for the FILLET command:

1. Filleting two nonparallel straight lines
2. Filleting a polyline segment

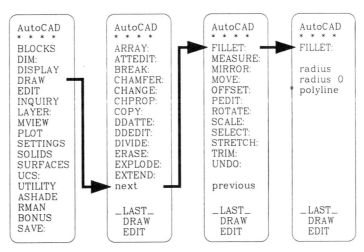

Figure 9–1 Menu Map for the FILLET Command

113

3. Filleting arcs
4. Automatic filleting of an entire polyline

9.1.1 FILLET Command as Applied to Non-Straight Lines

The AutoCAD program assumes that the Fillet (suitable Radius) will be applied to two lines that will intersect. Where necessary, the FILLET command will automatically extend the lines (so that the lines may meet), place the Fillet, and remove any extraneous lines. If the lines do not meet or the Radius is too large, the command prompt states that the FILLET command was rejected. The Command Sequence is shown in Figure 9–2 and is used for any of the four FILLET options.

The Fillet Radius must be specified first by picking the FILLET command and then either (1) picking the Radius from the Screen Menu or (2) typing R (Radius), (R), and inputting the value of the Radius from the keyboard. The Radius must be in the same units as the current drawing. The next prompt calls for the selection of two lines. If the lines meet within the limits of the drawing, a Fillet of the specified Radius will be drawn and any line excess will be removed. If the specified Radius is either too big or small, no Fillets will be drawn but the prompt line will indicate why the FILLET command was not completed.

Example 9–1: Draw two lines (line 1: 2,3 to 8,7; and line 2: 10,5 to 5,3.6); Radius = 0.50 units. The lines will be automatically extended until the Fillet can be drawn. The Fillet for this example is located approximately at 3.83, 3.71. Try another example using the existing lines. (Use the U command to remove or undo the Fillet.)

Set the Radius to 0.0. Both lines will be extended until they meet. Since the Radius is zero, the Fillet is not drawn. Repeat the U command procedure. Now set the Radius to 2.0. Pick the two lines. The screen display will remain unchanged. The prompt line will read Radius too large, *invalid*.

NOTE: The FILLET command with Radius = 0 may be used at any time to extend lines for corners. The FILLET command may be used to reduce the keystrokes to bring two nonparallel lines together.

9.1.2 Filleting a Polyline (PLINE)

The Polyline option of the FILLET command covers two different types of polylines: PLINES and POLYLINES (similar to the POLYGON). The definition of PLINE and POLYLINE is given in Chapter 11. For the moment, a polyline is a single entity with

```
Command:
FILLET Polyline/Radius?<Select two objects>:  R
Enter fillet radius <0.0000>:  .25
Command:
FILLET Polyline/Radius/<Select two objects>:  (pick the two adjacent lines)
```

Figure 9–2 Command Sequence for the FILLET Command

3 or more sides. Filleting polylines becomes an easy task because of the automatic filleting feature built into the AutoCAD program. After the polyline is drawn, pick the FILLET command and specify the Radius. Then pick POLYLINES from the Screen Menu or input P from the keyboard. Pick one line. The program knows: (1) that the drawing is a polyline and (2) the Radius. (The program will automatically fillet all corners without any additional input.)

Example 9–2: Draw a four-sided polygon using the Edge method. (Edge is located at 7,3 and 10.1,4.75.) Select the FILLET command; Radius = 0.5. Select polyline from the Screen Menu or input P from the keyboard. Place the pointing device on any line and pick the line. The program will then automatically fillet all four corners. Figure 9–3 is the solution to this example. If the Radius is too large, the AutoCAD program fillets whatever lines it can and leaves a message in the prompt area. Repeat the polygon constructed in the prior example. This time use a Radius of 2. Figure 9–4 illustrates the resultant polygon. In addition to the drawing, the prompt line will state, 2 lines were filleted, 2 were too short.

If a Pline is used, the Close command must be used to obtain complete Filleting.

9.1.3 Filleting Arcs and Circles

Arcs and circles can be filleted but the placement of the fillet is more difficult. In this filleting application, it is possible to have more than one location to place a fillet. The operator must show the program the approximate location of the fillet. The Window, Crossing, or Last options may not be used. AutoCAD will choose the location of the fillet whose endpoints are nearest the location selected by the operator. If the resulting fillet is not located correctly, use the U command to undo the fillet action and try it again. Try the following examples:

Example 9–3: Draw a line from 1,2 to 7,3. Draw a 3P arc: pt 1 = 3.6,4; pt 2 = 4.4,3.3; and pt 3 = 6,3.8. Draw a second arc: pt 1 = 5.8,2.3; pt 2 = 6.5,1.6; and pt 3 = 8.4,2.1.

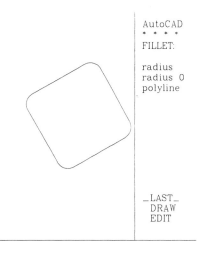

```
AutoCAD
*  *  *  *
FILLET:

radius
radius 0
polyline




_LAST_
DRAW
EDIT
```

0,0

Figure 9-3 Solution to Example 9–2

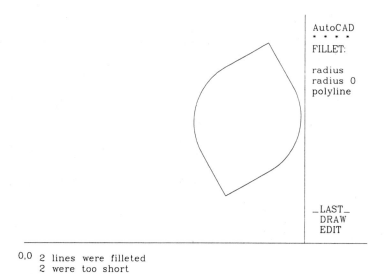

Figure 9–4   Fillet with a Polygon

Call the first arc Arc A and the second Arc B. Pick the FILLET command and a Radius = 0.3. Pick the point (4.75,2.625) on the line and 4.75,3.25 on Arc A. Repeat the fillet on the line and the Start point of Arc B. Notice that the excess lines are trimmed automatically. The solution is shown in Figure 9–5.

Example 9–4:   Draw a line from 2,2 to 4.6,7.8; Arc A (SCA): Start pt = 3,6; Center = 2,6; Angle = 110; Arc B (SCA): Start pt = 6.3,6; Center = 6.6,7.8; Angle = -60. Select FILLET command; Radius = 0.5; select end of line (4.6,7.8) and a point on Arc B (4.96,7.0). Repeat the FILLET command using the same Radius. Pick the last point

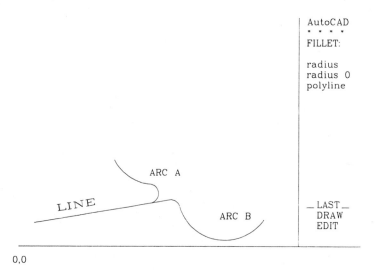

Figure 9–5   Solution to Eample 9–3

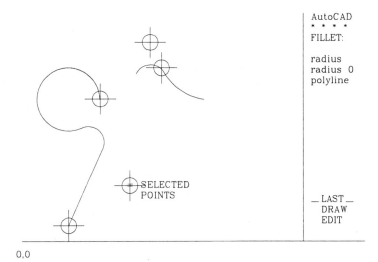

Figure 9–6   Solution to Example 9–4

on Arc A and First point on line (2,2). Figure 9–6 shows the final drawing of this example. The same technique applies to a circle, a line, or an arc.

NOTE: The fillet points must be picked by the Pointer and *not* input from the keyboard. (Make sure F8 is ON.)

9.2   CHAMFER Command

A Chamfer (straight line segment) is another alternative to relieve the stress in a sharp corner (in a similar fashion as the fillet). The CHAMFER command is listed under the EDIT Submenu and is shown in Figure 9–7.

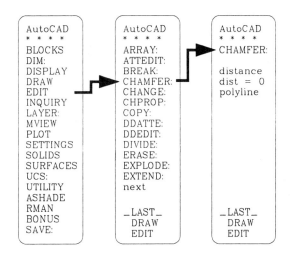

Figure 9–7   Menu Map for the Chamfer Command

```
Command:  CHAMFER  Polyline/Distances/<Select  first  line>:  D
Enter  first  chamfer  distance  <0.0000>:  0.2
Enter  second  chamfer  distance  <0.2000>:0.5

Command:  Polyline/Distances/<Select  first  line>:  PICK  FIRST  LINE
Select  second  line:  PICK  SECOND  LINE
```

Figure 9–8   Command Sequence for the CHAMFER Command

AutoCAD expects the operator to specify the chamfer distance from the corner of the first line and a second chamfer distance (if necessary) for the second line. If the distance to the second corner is the same as that to the first corner depress the ENTER key to use the default value for the second distance. The distances may either be actual values or pointed out using the Pointing device. The Command Sequence is shown in Figure 9–8. A distance of zero for both lines will automatically extend the two lines until they meet. If a chamfer cannot be drawn, the prompt indicates that the command is rejected.

Example 9–5:   Draw four lines: line 1 = 2,2, to 4,2; line 2 = 4,2.25 to 4,5; line 3 = 3.75,5 to 2.25,5; and line 4 = 2,5 to 2,2.25. Pick the CHAMFER command with the distance for both lines set to zero. Pick the two lines forming the lower right corner. The lines will be extended until the lines meet. Set the chamfer distance for the first line as 0.5 units and the second line for 1 unit. Pick the top point of line 2 and the right point of line 3. A chamfer will be drawn. Reset the distance for the first and second lines to 0.75 units. Pick the left end of line 3 and the top of line 4. Repeat the chamfer for lines 4 and 1. The solution is shown in Figure 9–9.

NOTE: As in the FILLET command, the chamfer points must be picked by the Pointer and *not* input by keyboard.

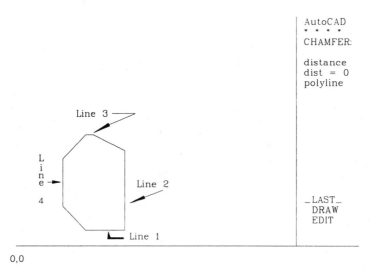

Figure 9–9   Solution to Example 9–5

9.3 Pull Down Menu for Chapter 9

Figure 9-10 is the Pull Down Menu for Chapter 9.

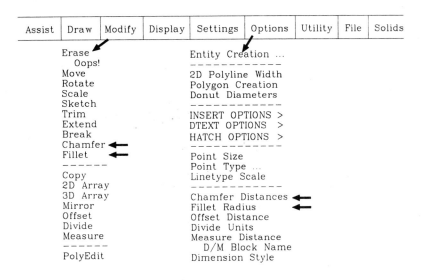

Figure 9-10 Pull Down Menu for Chapter 9

9.4 Template Reference—Chapter 9

See Figure 9-11 on page 120.

COMMAND SUMMARY

FILLET
CHAMFER

GLOSSARY

Fillet: The procedure used to round corners to relieve a stress point.

Chamfer: A procedure similiar to the fillet with the exception that straight lines are used to relieve the stress.

PROBLEMS

1. Draw two lines: line 1: 1,7 to 7,7; line 2: 6,7 to 7,1. Fillet the corners with a .5 Radius.
2. What command would be used to close two lines (1,1 to 4,1 and 4,8 to 4,2)?

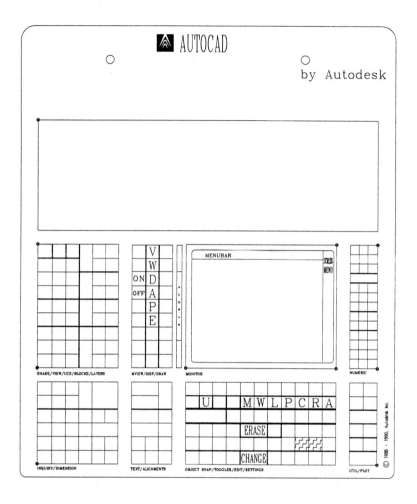

Figure 9–11 Template Reference for Chapter 9

3. Draw a seven-sided polygon using the Edge method. The Start point is 3,6; Second edge point at 3,4. Fillet all corners with a Radius of 0.5.
4. Chamfer the four corners of a square whose sides are 3 units long. The Starting point is 2,2. The chamfer distance is .375 from each edge.

10 First Level Edit Commands

Instructional Objectives

1. To be able to effectively use the BREAK command
2. To understand the use of the REMOVE and ADD command options listed in the EDIT Submenu
3. To be able to use the MOVE command
4. To implement the COPY command, either in the single or multiple mode
5. To be able to use the MIRROR command for drawings, except for text
6. To be able to find and use the SETVAR command
7. To be able to use the MIRROR TEXT command

10.1 BREAK Command

The purpose of the BREAK command is to remove a segment of a Line, Trace, Polyline, Pline, Arc, or Circle as compared to erasing the complete entity and starting over again. The BREAK command may be found in the EDIT Submenu as shown in Figure 10–1.

The Command Sequence, shown in Figure 10–2, may be confusing the first time it is used. It calls for the selection of the object that is to be broken; then the operator

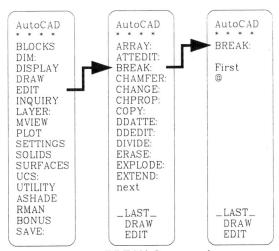

Figure 10–1 Menu Map for the BREAK Command

```
Command: BREAK Select object:
Enter second point (or F for first point): F
Enter first point:3,5
Enter second point:4,5
```

Figure 10-2 Command Sequence for the BREAK Command

is to input the first point where the break will start (called First point) and the location where the break will end (called Second point). However, if the First point is the same point used to select the object, the program will use this data (that the selection point and the first point are the same) and the letter F (F for first point) is not to be used. If the First point is not the same point used to select the object, then the operator, by using the letter F, informs the program that a First point has not been selected. The operator then inputs the location of the First point and Second point either from the keyboard or by use of the Pointer.

Example 10-1: Start a new drawing called BREAK. Draw a line from 2,5 to 8,5. Now remove the line segment 3,5 to 4,5. There are two possibilities: (1) Erase the line and replace it with two lines (the first line 2,5 to 3,5 and the second line 4,5 to 8,5); or (2) use the BREAK command. Pick the EDIT Submenu and then select the BREAK command. Pick the object by placing the cursor anywhere on the line. The line will change from a solid line to a dotted line to show the operator the selected line for this operation. Confirm the selection of the line by depressing the ENTER key (R). Input the letter F (thereby instructing the program that the location of the First point has not been made); input 3,5 (either from the keyboard or by use of the Pointer) then (R) and the location fo the Second point 4,5 (R). The line between 3,5 and 4,5 will disappear. The next break will be located from 5,5 to 6.25,5. Pick the BREAK command and combine the functions of object selection and the First point by inputting (from the keyboard or the Pointer) either 5,5 or 6.25,5. If you are using the Pointer, use a Grid of 0.25 units and a Snap of 0.125, to aid you in finding the correct location. If the 5,5 location is used for the object selection and First point, then use the 6.25,5 to complete the command.

Example 10-2: Draw a line from 3,3 to 8,8. Break the line so that the upper half of the line is removed. Select the BREAK command and combine the object selection with the first point by using OSNAP (MID). Complete the command by picking the end of the line at 8,8 by either using OSNAP (ENDpoint) or inputting 8,8. The upper portion will be removed.

10.1.1 BREAK Command for Arcs and Circles

The Menu Map and the Command Sequence (Figures 10-1 and 10-2) remain the same for all entities. The major problem of breaking arcs and circles is the location of the First point. Remember that AutoCAD draws arcs and circles in a counterclockwise (CCW) direction. Therefore, the selection of the First point becomes critical. The

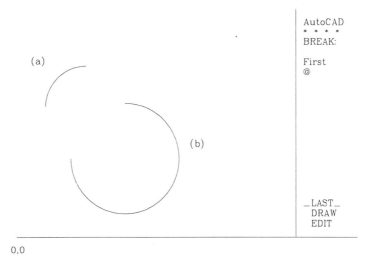

0,0

Figure 10–3 Solution to Example 10–3

First point will be the start of the break in the CCW direction. The Second point is at the end of the break.

Example 10–3: Start a new drawing called BREAK1. Draw a circle whose Center is located at 4,4 and whose Radius is 1.75 units. You need to remove the segment of the circle from the 90° location (top of the circle) to the 180° point (left edge of the circle). Select the EDIT Submenu and the BREAK command. Combine the object selection and the First point by picking the 180° point. Now pick the second point (90°). The remaining arc, from 90° to 180° [Figure 10–3(a)], shows us that the First point selected was incorrect since we need to eliminate the segment of the circle from the 90° point to the 180° point. Using the U command, undo the break. Repeat the break procedure but first select the 90° point and then the 180° point. The resulting drawing will appear as shown in Figure 10–3(b).

REMEMBER: AutoCAD draws circles or arcs in a CCW direction.

NOTE: The @ symbol (shift 2) provides the operator with the ability to split an object into two parts by deleting a small portion of the object. The @ symbol is used as the second point location.

10.2 Remove and Add Option

The Remove and Add options are found in many EDIT Submenu listings, such as MOVE, ERASE, or COPY. These options enable the operator to either remove or add an object from the selected entities. These options are activated after selecting the object(s), but *before they are confirmed*. Examples of these options are presented in the following section.

10.3 MOVE Command

The MOVE command enables the operator to change the location of one or more entities without the loss of entity information. The MOVE command is listed on the flip side of the EDIT Submenu, as illustrated in Figure 10–4.

The Command Sequence is similar to other commands listed under the EDIT Submenu as is shown in Figure 10–5.

The MOVE command is the first of many commands that include the Remove and Add options as part of the object selection process. These two options enable the operator either to remove an object from those selected for MOVE or to add an object to the overall object selections prior to completing the command.

Example 10–4: Bring up a new drawing called MOVE. Draw a five-sided polygon (Edge method, First point 2,3; Second point 5,3); a circle (Center at 3.477,5.072, Radius 2.09) and a four-sided polygon (Edge method, First point 2.04,3.61; Second point 4.94,3.61); a three-sided polygon (Edge method, First point 8,3; Second point 9,3). We want to move the three objects (all but the Triangle) from their present position (basepoint 4,5) to a new basepoint location at 5,5. Select the EDIT Submenu and the MOVE command. Using the Window option, draw a window that encloses the three objects on the screen. Notice that the solid lines of each object have been changed to show the objects that will be moved.

Before we confirm the object selection, remove the circle by picking Remove from the Screen Menu and pick the circle. Note that the line forming the circle has now changed back to a solid line. Now the triangle has to be moved with the other selected objects. Pick Add from the Screen Menu and pick the triangle. The line forming the triangle is now changed to show that the triangle is part of the selected objects. Confirm the selection by depressing the ENTER key (R). The basepoint is the reference location that the MOVE will use (4,5). The second point is 5,5.

All selected items will be moved one unit to the right. The original drawing is shown in Figure 10–6 and Figure 10–7 shows the drawing after the MOVE command has been completed.

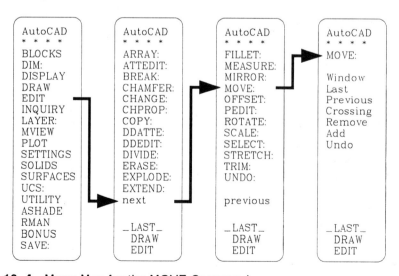

Figure 10–4 Menu Map for the MOVE Command

```
Command: Move
Select objects: 1 selected, 1 found.
Select object: (R)
Base point or displacement: Second point of displacement:
```

Figure 10–5   Command Sequence for the MOVE Command

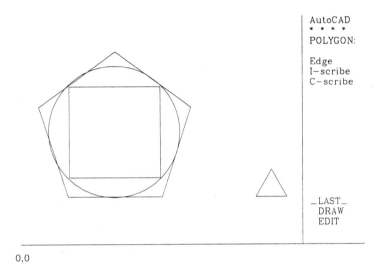

Figure 10–6   Initial Drawing for Example 10–4

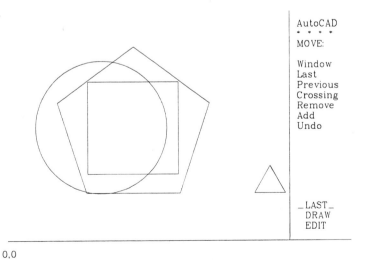

Figure 10–7   Solution to Example 10–4

Movement or displacement of selected objects may be specified by Relative Co-ordinates or by picking the points with the Pointer.

10.4 COPY Command

The COPY command is listed in the EDIT Submenu as shown in Figure 10–8. The COPY command makes it possible to make one or more (multiple) copies of a draw-ing or sections of a drawing.

This command is located in the EDIT Submenu; the objects must first be se-lected and confirmed (similar to the MOVE command). The Command Sequence is shown in Figure 10–9.

After the selection of the object(s) has been completed and confirmed, the com-mand prompt asks, "<Basepoint or displacement>/Multiple." If two or more copies are required, then input M (for Multiple copies) then the basepoint. If only one copy is required, then give the basepoint or displacement.

Example 10–5: Start a new drawing called COPY. Draw an inscribed Polygon of six sides, with the Center at 3,2 and a Radius of 2. Pick the EDIT Submemu and the COPY command. One copy of this drawing must be located at 9.5,6.8. The resulting display will look like Figure 10–10.

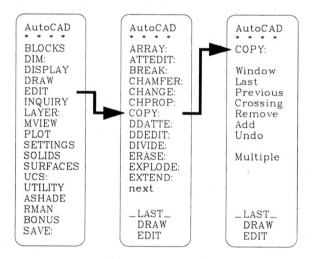

Figure 10–8   Menu Map for the COPY Command

```
Command: COPY
Select objects: 1 selected, 1 found.
<Base point or displacement>/Multiple:  M
Base point: Second point of displacement:
```

Figure 10–9   Command Sequence for the COPY Command

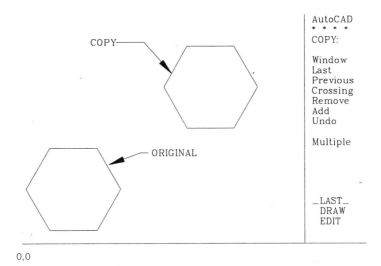

Figure 10–10 Solution to Example 10–5

Now try this multiple copy problem. Using the existing drawing, we want to make two additional copies of the polygon to be located at 3,6 and 8,3. Select the COPY command and the original polygon and confirm the selection. Answer the next prompt, "<Basepoint or displacement>/Multiple with M". Now pick the Center of the polygon (3,2) for the basepoint, 3,6 for the first copy, and 8,3 for the second copy. The use of the (R) will inform the program that additional copies are not wanted.

10.5 MIRROR Command

We have discussed the moving and copying of selected objects. The MIRROR command provides the operator with the ability to make mirror images of existing objects on the screen. In addition, the MIRROR command gives us the opportunity to delete the old objects prior to the completion of the MIRROR command. The MIRROR command is located in the EDIT Submenu as shown in Figure 10–11.

The Command Sequence for this command is shown in Figure 10–12.

The Command Sequence is similar to that of the MOVE and COPY commands in that the object(s) must be selected and confirmed prior to the command. After the selection of the object(s) has been completed, an invisible line is drawn, which represents the mirror line. The mirror line may be located at any angle to the selected objects. After the First point of the mirror line has been established, it is possible to use either Absolute Coordinates, Relative Coordinates, or the DRAG feature to establish the second point. After the mirror line has been completed, the command prompt will ask, "Delete old objects?<N>." The answer is either Y for YES or N for NO.

Example 10–6: Bring up a new drawing called MIRROR. Draw an eight-sided polygon, whose edges are 1 unit long, starting at 1.5,2. Make a mirror image of the polygon using the following points for the mirror line: locate the first mirror line point

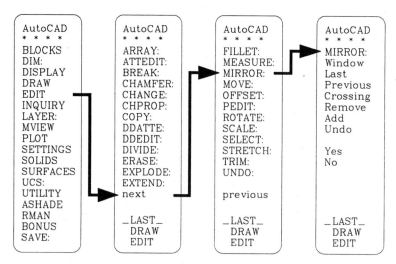

Figure 10–11 Menu Map for the MIRROR Command

```
Command: MIRROR
Select objects: 1 selected, 1 found.
Select objects: (R)
First point of mirror line:   Second point:
Delete old objects? <N> (R)
```

Figure 10–12 Command Sequence for the MIRROR Command

at 3.5,2 and the second point at 3.5,3. Do *not* delete the old object. The resulting draw-ing is shown in Figure 10–13.

Example 10–7: Repeat the assignment but this time make the mirror line at an angle of 40°. Draw the mirror line. Start at 3,4.625; the Second point is located at @1<-40. The mirror line does not have to be the height or width of the objects. Delete the old objects. The screen display should look like Figure 10–14. Erase the drawing on the screen.

Example 10–8: Draw the following: circle at 2,7; Radius of 1.5 units. Place your name inside the circle using Complex font, Text Middle option at 2,7; height = .2 units. Mirror the circle and text with the MIRROR command. The Mirror line is to be located at 1,5 to 2,5. Do not delete old objects. Your drawing should look like Figure 10–15. Note that the text is also mirrored and is difficult to read.

10.5.1 MIRROR TEXT Command

The MIRROR command works very well with the one exception that the text will also be mirrored. AutoCAD has a specific remedy for this condition if reversed text becomes a problem. AutoCAD makes use of default values in its initial drawing vari-ables (SETVAR) of the ACAD drawing. These default settings establish certain con-

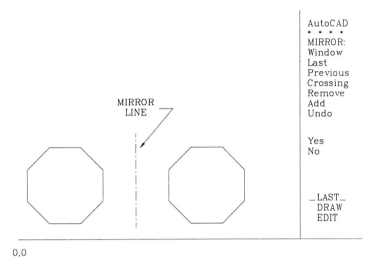

Figure 10–13 Solution to Example 10–6

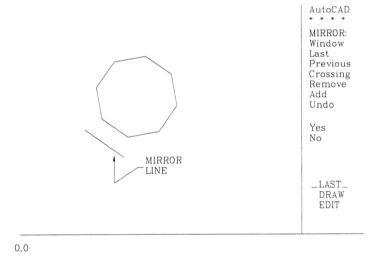

Figure 10–14 Solution to Example 10–7

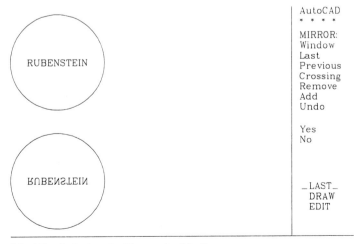

Figure 10–15 Solution to Example 10–8

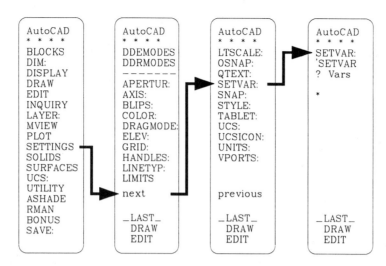

Figure 10–16   Menu Map for the SETVAR Command

ditions as the SNAP ON/OFF and increment, GRID ON/OFF and its spacing, and so on. One of the system variables is called MIRRTEXT. The default value is set to 1. If this value is set to zero, then the textstring will not be reversed. The SETVAR (SET VARIABLES) command is located under the SETTINGS Submenu, as shown in Figure 10–16.

Select the SETTINGS Submenu and the SETVAR command. The command prompt asks for the variable name: type MIRRTEXT. Then set the value of the variable to zero. Return to the drawing on the screen.

Example 10–9: Pick the original circle and place the mirror line from 4,8 to 4,6. Do *not* delete the old objects. Note that the text appears normal but the remaining drawing is reversed.

10.6   Pull Down Menu for Chapter 10

See Figure 10-17 on page 131.

10.7   Template Reference—Chapter 10

See Figure 10-18 on page 131.

COMMAND SUMMARY

BREAK	MOVE
COPY	MIRROR

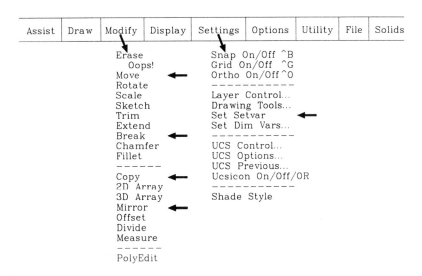

Figure 10–17   Pull Down Menu for Chapter 10

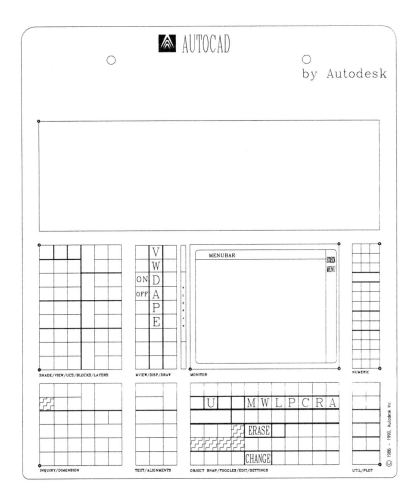

Figure 10–18   Template Reference for Chapter 10

GLOSSARY

MIRRTEXT: A system variable that enables the operator to mirror a drawing but leave any text unchanged.

Multiple mode: A command modifier that permits more than one copy of a drawing.

PROBLEMS

1. True or False: It is possible to use the BREAK command on a polyline entity.
2. Name one command that gives the operator a chance to delete the old drawing.
3. What value of MIRRTEXT will permit the mirroring of text so that the text appears in a normal fashion?
4. Name three types of entities where the BREAK command is effective.

11 Additional First Level Edit Commands

Instructional Objectives

1. To understand and apply the CHANGE command for lines, circles, and poly-lines
2. To understand and be able to use the BLOCK command
3. To be able to make suitable changes to a blocked drawing and Reblock using the same BLOCK name
4. To understand the differences between the BLOCK command and the WBLOCK command
5. To be able to use the INSERT command
6. To be able to make changes to a BLOCK or WBLOCK through the use of the INSERT* command
7. To be able to use the EXPLODE command
8. To understand the difference between the INSERT* and EXPLODE command
9. To understand the difference between the MINSERT ARRAY and the RECTAN-GULAR ARRAY
10. To be able to use the MINSERT command
11. To be able to develop either a rectangular or polar array by means of the ARRAY command

11.1 CHANGE Command

The CHANGE command has been divided into two distinct areas of operation: Part A CHANGES work on changes to lines, circles, and text; Part B CHANGES deal with changes to the *properties* of the entities such as, color, elevation, layer, Ltype, or thickness. CHANGE Part B, or CHPROP command, is discussed in Chapter 14.

11.1.1 CHANGE Command for Lines

The CHANGE command change the endpoint of a line to another location. The endpoint that changes will be the closest endpoint to the new location. The CHANGE command is found under the EDIT Submenus as shown in Figure 11–1.

Figure 11–2 shows the Command Sequence used to change the location of the line's ENDpoint.

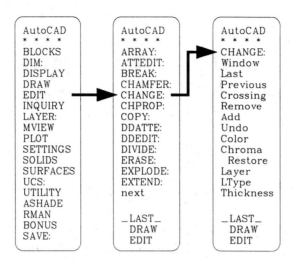

```
AutoCAD          AutoCAD          AutoCAD
* * * *          * * * *          * * * *
BLOCKS           ARRAY:           CHANGE:
DIM:             ATTEDIT:         Window
DISPLAY          BREAK:           Last
DRAW             CHAMFER:         Previous
EDIT             CHANGE:          Crossing
INQUIRY          CHPROP:          Remove
LAYER:           COPY:            Add
MVIEW            DDATTE:          Undo
PLOT             DDEDIT:          Color
SETTINGS         DIVIDE:          Chroma
SOLIDS           ERASE:            Restore
SURFACES         EXPLODE:         Layer
UCS:             EXTEND:          LType
UTILITY          next             Thickness
ASHADE
RMAN
BONUS            _LAST_           _LAST_
SAVE:            DRAW             DRAW
                 EDIT             EDIT
```

Figure 11–1   Menu Map for the CHANGE Command

```
Command: CHANGE
Select objects:    Select objects: 1 selected, 1 found.
Properties/<Change point>: 3,3
```

Figure 11–2   Command Sequence for the CHANGE Command, Line Option

The CHANGE command is designed to change the length of the line as well as the direction of the line.

CAUTION: If the ORTHO Mode is ON (F8), the resulting change will either be in the horizontal or vertical orientation. If the ORTHO Mode is OFF (F8), then any changes made will respond correctly. The following example will help.

Example 11–1(a): Bring up a new drawing, using the name CHANLINE. Set ORTHO to OFF. Draw a line from 1,3 to 7,4 (Line A). Now use the CHANGE command to change Line A's ENDpoint (7,4) to a new ENDpoint at 5,2. Select CHANGE command from the EDIT Submenu (Figure 11–1). Now select Line A as the object. Notice that the line from 1,3 to 7,4 becomes dotted until the object selection has been completed. Input the new line ENDpoint of 5,2 and (R). The original ENDpoint (7,4) of Line A will change location to 5,2. Now, let's try the same command with the ORTHO Mode ON. Using the U command, undo the last CHANGE. Repeat the problem but turn ORTHO ON before proceeding. Notice the difference in location between Line A's ENDpoint with and without the ORTHO Mode turned ON.

Example 11–1(b): Now using the U command, undo Example 11–1(a) until the right ENDpoint of Line A is located at 7,4. Next draw two additional lines: Line B,

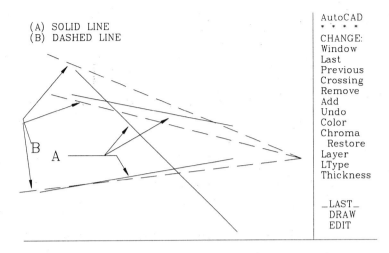

(A) SOLID LINE
(B) DASHED LINE

```
AutoCAD
* * * *
CHANGE:
Window
Last
Previous
Crossing
Remove
Add
Undo
Color
Chroma
  Restore
Layer
LType
Thickness

_LAST_
DRAW
EDIT
```

Figure 11-3   Example 11-1(a) and Solution to Example 11-1(b)

7,5 to 2,6; and Line C, 3,6 to 8,1. These lines are shown in Figure 11-3(a). Use the CHANGE command to change the ENDpoints nearest to 9.75,4. Use either Window or individual selection and pick the three lines. Then input 9.75,4. the three lines will meet at 9.75,4. This solution is shown in Figure 11-3(b).

11.1.2 CHANGE Command for Circles

The CHANGE command, as used for circles, changes the Radius of the circle. Erase the three lines from the screen. Draw a circle with a Center of 4,5 and a Radius of 2. Select the CHANGE command (from the EDIT Submenu) and pick the circle. Confirm the selection.

NOTE: The confirmation of the object selection is routine for most of the edit commands. Therefore, for further examples, the object selection is automatic.

Input the change point of 5,5. The circle will retain its original Center location but the Radius will change to 1 unit. In addition to the use of Absolute Coordinates, the new location can be specified by using the Relative Coordinate System or the Pointer. Repeat the CHANGE command and input @3.2,2.

NOTE: The use of this portion of the CHANGE command is restricted to lines and circles but will not apply to ARC, TRACE, PLINE or Polyline.

11.1.3 CHANGE Command for Use with the TEXT Command

The CHANGE command may be used on a textstring to change either: Start point, STYLE, rotation angle, textstring, or a combination of the above. The change point

```
Command: CHANGE
Select objects: 1 selected, 1 found
Select objects:
Properties/<Change point>: (R)
Enter text insertion point: (R)
Text style: STANDARD
New style or Return for no change: (R)
New height <0.2000>: 0.2500
New rotation angle <0>: (R)
New text <>: (R)
```

Figure 11-4 Command Sequence for the CHANGE Command, Text Option

becomes the new location of the textstring. Figure 11-4 shows the Command Sequence for the CHANGE command for the Text option.

The command prompts (Figure 11-4) ask for the change to the text, starting with the Insertion or Starting point. If the location is not to be changed, then (R). The prompt will change and if a change is not required (as called out in the prompt), then (R). In summary, the CHANGE commands for the textstring are listed in sequence as follows:

1. Insert point (Start point)
2. New Text STYLE
3. New Height
4. New Rotation angle
5. New textstring

11.2 BLOCK Command

The BLOCK command, listed in the BLOCK Submenu, will place either drawing entities, textstrings, or both into the drawing data base as a single entity, listed under a specific name. The operator develops a drawing and then BLOCKS that drawing. Once blocked, the drawing may be recalled from the *drawing memory* at any time by using the INSERT command. However, there is a restriction in that the blocked drawing must be the current drawing. The blocked drawing may be recalled and used in its original configuration or modified (scale factor or rotation) prior to the insertion of the BLOCK. Figure 11-5 presents the Menu Map for the BLOCK command.

Figure 11-6 shows the Command Sequence for the BLOCK command. The BLOCK command is used after the drawing or a section of the drawing has been completed and there is a good possibility that the drawing will be used again. There are advantages and disadvantages in using the BLOCK command: One advantage is that it converts all drawing and textstring entities into one entity; One disadvantage is that if a change of the blocked drawing is made, then another command must be used to return the blocked drawing to the screen for modification.

Although there is a Screen Menu item called BLOCKS, this name does *not* represent the BLOCK command. (The name does not have a colon (:) after the name.) The BLOCK command is listed in the BLOCKS Submenu as shown in Figure 11-5.

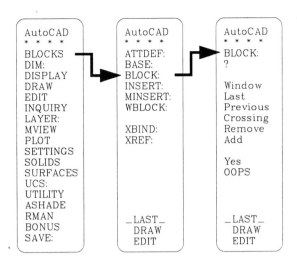

Figure 11–5 Menu Map for the BLOCK Command

Identification of the block is as important as the identification of the drawings. The block name may have a maximum of 31 characters. The key to the successful use of the block is to keep the block name simple for ease of memory recall. If a block exists with the name you have assigned, the command prompt will state Block (name) already exists. Redefine it? <N>:. At this point, you may input another name or redefine the block.

After the name has been assigned, the command prompt calls for the Insertion Point of the block. A good rule to follow for the Insertion point of the block is to use the Center of the block (if a circle or arc is involved) or the lower left corner (for a rectangle). There are no hard and fast rules. The problem in the past has been that so many exceptions exist, there can be no rules. Be consistent.

The last part of the blocking procedure is to select the object(s) that makes up the block. The selection can be by individual objects or by Window. After the selection has been made and confirmed, the drawing will disappear from the screen. This disappearance shows that the BLOCK was successful. If the drawing remains on the screen, then the BLOCK was not successful. The entities used to make up the BLOCK may be brought back to the screen by using the OOPS command.

CAUTION: The drawing brought back to the screen does *not* have the *blocked* characteristics.

```
Command: BLOCK Block name (or ?): filename
Insertion base point: X,Y
Select objects: 1 selected, 1 found.
Select objects
```

Figure 11–6 Command Sequence for the BLOCK Command

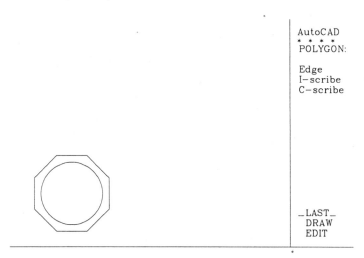

Figure 11-7 Solution to Example 11-2

Example 11-2: Start a new drawing called BLOCK. Draw an eight-sided polygon using the Edge option; Starting at 2,2; each side 1 unit long. Erase one side of the polygon. You can erase the entire polygon but not a part of it. The polygon is a *block*. Now place a circle, whose Center is the Center of the polygon and whose Radius is 1 unit (as shown in Figure 11-7).

Now BLOCK the polygon and circle and name the block CONFIG1 with the Insertion point at the Center of the circle. If you are successful, the drawing will disappear. Now locate and pick the INSERT command. (There are four places to select the INSERT command: BLOCK Submenu, OSNAP Submenu, DRAW Submenu, or typed from the keyboard.) The block name is CONFIG1, and the Insertion point is 4.5,4.5. (The Center of the circle is located at 4.5,4.5.) After the Insertion point has been input, depress the ENTER key three times. The exact procedure for the INSERT command is detailed in the next section (11.3). The screen display should show the polygon and circle. The blocked drawing may be moved, copied, or mirrored with the same ease as a line.

Example 11-3: Let's move the blocked drawing from its present location to a new location, 3,7. Select the MOVE command from the EDIT Submenu. When the prompt asks for the object selection, pick any part of the CONFIG1 drawing, since this is a block. Figure 11-8 (solution to Example 11-3) shows the MOVE command before (A) and after (B).

Example 11-4: Make a copy of the original CONFIG1 drawing and locate the copy at 3,3. This is shown in Figure 11-9.

Example 11-5: Make a mirror copy of the two copies shown in Figure 11-9. Save the drawing using FIG11-9 as the filename. Locate a vertical mirror line at 5,7 and 5,3. Do not delete the old drawing. Figure 11-10 demonstrates the MIRROR command on a blocked drawing.

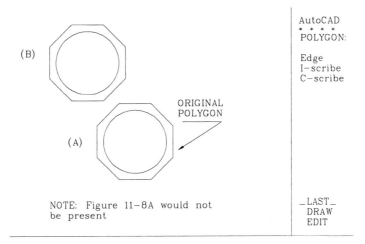

Figure 11-8   Solution to Example 11-3

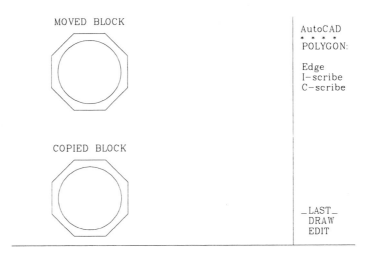

Figure 11-9   Solution to Example 11-4

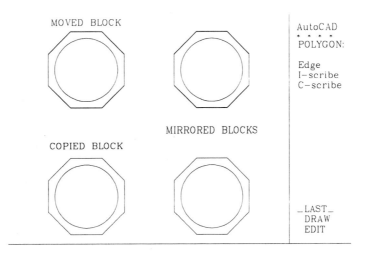

Figure 11-10   Solution to Example 11-5

```
Command:  BLOCK Block name (or ?):  filename
Block filename already exists.
Redine it?  <N> Y
Insertion base point: X,Y
Selected objects: 1 selected 1 found
Select objects (R)
```

Figure 11–11 Command Sequence for Reblocking Procedure

11.2.1 Reblock

Reblock is *not* an AutoCAD command, rather it is a procedure that can be used to modify a blocked drawing. Since the blocked drawing is a single entity, the block must be "unblocked." (The blocked drawing must be returned to the original entities that were present prior to the time of the block.) Two commands may be used to unblock: INSERT* or EXPLODE. These commands are discussed in sections 11.4 and 11.5 of this chapter. Assuming that all changes have been made to the unblocked drawing, we may either block the revised drawing using a different name or use the current name ("reblocking"). Reblocking enables the operator to make whatever changes are necessary to the unblocked drawing and use the same name. See Figure 11–11 for the procedure.

The command prompt will ask for the block name. Reply with the existing name. The AutoCAD program then searches for that name and the prompt states, BLOCK filename already exists Redefine it? <N>: An N or NO answer will keep the block as originally drawn. A Y or YES answer will process the revised drawing, make a new BLOCK (original drawing plus changes) with the existing name, and automatically change any existing blocked drawing to the updated drawing.

NOTE: It is important to unblock the drawing before making any changes. If this is not done, it will appear that a successful block was made, but when inserted into a drawing, nothing will happen and the command line will state Block references itself and the block will not appear.

11.2.2 WBLOCK Command

When a drawing is blocked, the blocked data will be part of the drawing file and not available for insertion in any other drawings. AutoCAD developed the WBLOCK command (WRITE BLOCK information to drawing files) so that the blocked drawing may be used in other drawings. Figure 11–12 shows the WBLOCK command in the BLOCKS Submenu.

The WBLOCK filename is usually the same as the BLOCK filename. There are four responses that are acceptable to the AutoCAD program.

1. Actual name
2. The Use of the equal sign (=) when the BLOCK and WBLOCK names are the same

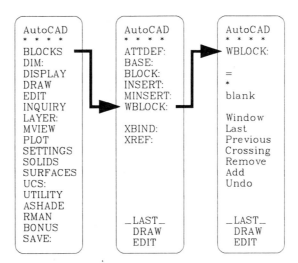

Figure 11–12   Menu Map for the WBLOCK Command

3. The Asterisk (*). The entire drawing file is written and any unreferenced BLOCKED names are deleted
4. (R): Generaly used when the BLOCK command is *not* used. Additional data will be required.

Figure 11–13 is the Command Sequence for the WBLOCK command.

As a drawing is wblocked, that drawing is placed in the hard disk and may be inserted into any drawing.

11.3 INSERT Command

The INSERT command enables the operator to place or INSERT the blocked drawing into the current drawing on the screen. In addition, any wblocked drawing may also be inserted into the current file. The third application of the INSERT command is to be able to unblock any blocked/wblocked drawing.

```
Command: WBLOCK File Name:
Block name:
Insertion point:
Select objects:
```

```
Note: If a Block name is used, then
      the Insertion point and selection
      of objects are not required
```

Figure 11–13   Command Sequence for the WBLOCK Command

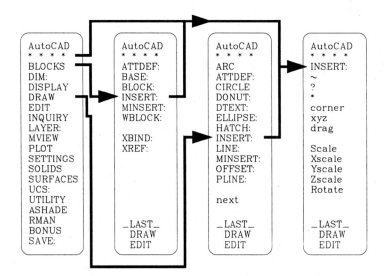

Figure 11–14   Menu Maps for the INSERT Command

11.3.1   Inserting a Drawing

The same procedure used for the blocked drawing is used for the wblocked drawing. Figure 11–14 shows the INSERT command located in one of four places: OSNAP Submenu, BLOCKS Submenu, DRAW Submenu, or typed in at the keyboard.

The Command Sequence for the INSERT command is the same for the four locations and is shown in Figure 11–15.

The Command Sequence provides the operator with the capability of: (1) presetting the scale factors (X, Y, Z, or rotation angle) of a block prior to the insertion of that block or (2) changing the scale factors of the block during the insertion of the block. The preselection is accomplished by selecting the Scale, Xscale, Yscale, Zscale, or Rotation from the Screen Menu prior to inputting the Insertion point. If one or more Preset values is used, then that value will be omitted from the Command Sequence after the Insertion point has been input. After calling up the block by name, the next question is the location of the Insertion point. The Insertion point location (Center of a circle or the lower left corner of the drawing) will be placed at the specified Absolute Coordinates or at a location by the Pointer. The next prompt or question asks for the X scale factor followed by the Y scale factor. The X scale factor is the default value for the Y scale factor. The operator may change the X dimension, or

```
Command: INSERT Block name (or?): filename
Insertion point:
X scale factor <1> / Corner / XYZ:
Y scale factor (default = X):
Rotation angle:
```

Figure 11–15   Command Sequence for the INSERT Command

the Y dimension, or a (R) will make the drawing the same size as it was when blocked. The X and Y scale factors are independent of each other (except for the default value of Y). The next prompt calls for a Rotation angle. The default value is 0°. Remember that the angle is usually drawn in a CCW direction. Perhaps an example will help.

Example 11–6: Bring up a new drawing called CONFIG2. Draw a six-sided polygon, with the Edge method, Starting at 2,1; length of Edge is 3″. Inscribe a circle using the 3P method. Block the drawing using the name XEH1, with Insertion point at the Center of the circle. If the block is successful, the drawing should disappear from the screen. Bring back the drawing by using the OOPS command. Try to erase the circle only. The circle can be erased but the polygon remains. This proves that a drawing has been blocked but the drawing brought back to the screen by the OOPS command is not a blocked drawing. Erase the complete drawing. Now INSERT block XEH1 at 3.5,3.5. Answer the X and Y scale factor with the default value (1). Rotation angle is 0°. The block should be on the screen. Now try to erase either the polygon or the circle. If you erase one part of the drawing the remaining drawing will also be erased. We now have a blocked drawing. Now insert the same block but this time use: 3.5,6.5 as the Insertion point; X scale factor = 0.5 ; Y scale factor = 0.25; and rotation angle = 45°. Figure 11–16 shows both inserted drawings.

Now insert Figure 11–9 (filename FIG11–9) using the same procedure as outlined above. Use the following values: Insertion point (IP) = 6,2; scale factors of .5 for X and Y; Rotation angle = 0. The first two insertions (Examples 11–4 and 11–5) made use of a blocked drawing and the last insertion made use of a drawing in the drawing file (or a wblock). Therefore, any file drawing may be inserted into a drawing. AutoCAD has a special file which lists the blocked drawings that are available. Call up the INSERT or BLOCK command and reply with a question mark (?) instead of a name. The screen will shift to the Text Screen mode and list the blocks that have been made, if any. Use the function key F1 to return to the graphical screen.

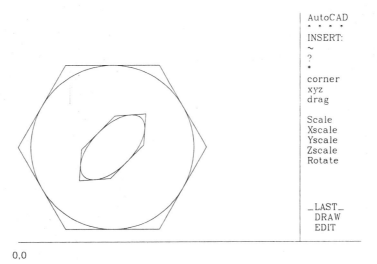

Figure 11–16 Solution to Example 11–6

11.3.2 INSERT* Command

The placement of the asterisk (*) before a block name instructs the AutoCAD program to release all the entities within the blocked drawing, so that the drawing may be modified.

Example 11–7: Erase the screen. Insert the block XEH1, but use the * before the name (*XEH1). Insertion point at 8,3; scale factor = .75 (for X and Y); rotation angle = 0. Try to erase the circle. The circle or the polygon may now be erased individually. Exit the drawing by using the QUIT command. (See Chapter 3 section 3.8.2 of this text.)

Another application of the INSERT* command is to modify existing drawings by using the reblocking technique. For example, place four copies of an existing block on the screen and modify these drawings with a minimum number of keystrokes. This modification is accomplished placing a fifth block on the drawing but the block name is preceeded by the *. Place this *block on the drawing (location is not important), with scale factor = 1 and Rotation = 0, and make the necessary changes to the *block. After the changes have been completed, REBLOCK the *block drawing using the original block name. When the block prompt asks you if you want the block redefined, answer YES. Select and confirm the objects. The *block will disappear from the screen and a few moments later, the four blocked drawings will also disappear and then reappear. Please note that the changes made to the fifth drawing (using INSERT*) were carried over to the four other blocks.

Example 11–8: Insert block XEH1 at 3,3 using a scale factor of 0.5, Rotation angle = 0. Copy, Insert, or Mirror three additional XEH1 and place them at the following locations: 3,6.7; 7,8; and 7.8,3. The change that is required is to place a message inside the circle that reads, CAD IS PRODUCTIVE (Complex font, Middle option located at the Center of the circle; letter Height = .1 unit). To change these first four XEH1s, insert another XEH1, but place an * before the name (*XEH1). The Insertion point is 5.3,4.9, and the scale factor is 0.5. Place the text in the Center of the *XEH1. Reblock XEH1. We want to redefine the block to include the textstring, the Insertion point remains the same. Complete the blocking procedure. The *XEH1 drawing will disappear from the screen, followed by the other four drawings. Within a few moments, the four original blocks will return to the screen with the textstring in place. The message and the size of the individual drawings will be reduce by a factor of .5 (because the INSERT*ed drawing was inserted at a scale factor of .5). Figure 11–17 is the solution to Example 11–8.

11.4 EXPLODE Command

The EXPLODE command is similar to the INSERT* command in that the command releases the entities of a block. If a block contains another block, then the EXPLODE command releases the first block but not the second block. The INSERT* removes all the blocked entities of the drawing. The EXPLODE command removes the first level of block references, and certain polylines and dimensions. In addition to these limitations, problems may develop in ARRAY commands, ATTRIBUTE commands, and

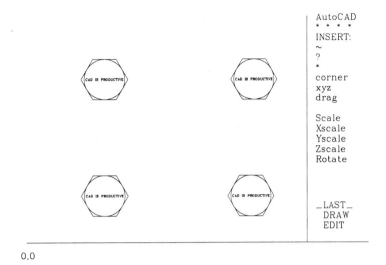

0,0

Figure 11-17 Solution to Example 11-8

with certain polylines. (The ARRAY and ATTRIBUTE commands are covered later in this text.)

The EXPLODE command is located in the EDIT Submenu as shown in Figure 11-18 and the Command Sequence for the EXPLODE command is shown in Figure 11-19.

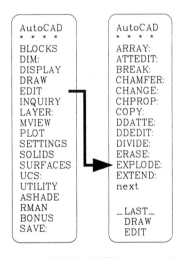

Figure 11-18 Menu Map for the EXPLODE Command

```
Command: EXPLODE
Select block reference, polyline, dimension, or mesh:
```

Figure 11-19 Command Sequence for the EXPLODE Command

As in the INSERT command, there is no way to tell if a drawing was Inserted* or Exploded. Clear the screen and insert XEH1 with Insertion point 4,4 and scale factor of 1. Pick the EXPLODE command and pick or point to any drawing entity. Notice the dotted lines informing you that these entities will be exploded. When the object selection has been completed, the drawing will leave the screen for a few moments before returning. Now, using the ERASE command, erase the bottom line of the polyline. The ERASE procedure is working because the EXPLODE command has unblocked the drawing. In the event that the drawing cannot be EXPLODED, the command prompt will state, NOT a block reference, polyline or dimension.

11.5 ARRAY Commands

One of three commands may be used to create an Array [either Rectangular (R) or Polar (P) configurations]: MINSERT, Rectangular Array, and Polar Array options. The MINSERT command (MINI INSERT) is listed under the DRAW Submenu, while the RECTANGULAR and POLAR ARRAY commands are listed under the EDIT Submenu, ARRAY command.

11.5.1 MINSERT Command

The MINSERT command provides for a rectangular array configuration with specific limitations as compared to the Rectangular Array option which is part of the ARRAY Submenu. The MINSERT command acts as a modified INSERT command, and the inserted drawing must be in block form. The MINSERT command is found either in the DRAW Submenu as shown in Figure 11–20 or in the BLOCKS Submenu as the alternative route.

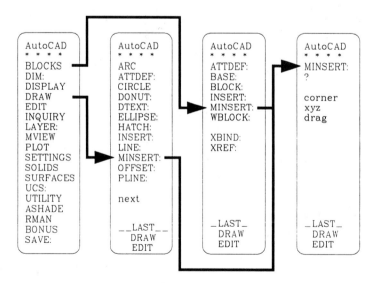

Figure 11–20 Menu Maps for the MINSERT Command

```
Command:  MINSERT Block name (or ?): XEH1
 Insertion point: 9,8,7
 X scale factor <1> / Corner / XYZ:  0.5
 Y scale factor (default=X):  0.5
 Rotation angle <0>:  (R)

Number of rows (– – –) <1>:  2
Number of columns (|||) <1>:  3
Unit cell or distance between rows (– – –):  2.85
Distance between columns (||||):  4.000
```

Figure 11–21   Command Sequence for the MINSERT Command

Figure 11–21 is the Command Sequence for the MINSERT command. The initial prompts (Figure 11–21) are similar to the INSERT command prompts (Figure 11–15). After the block has been called up, the Insertion point input, and the X and Y scale factors have been specified, the prompt will ask for the number of rows (vertical spacing) and columns (horizontal spacing). The distance between the rows and columns becomes important. Figure 11–25 defines the following terms: rows, columns, distance between rows, and distance between columns. The Unit Cell distance combines the information for distances between rows and columns by showing the two points that make up Unit Cell [lower left point and upper right point (similar to a Window)].

If the answer to the distance between rows is a number (not a Unit Cell), then the prompt for the distance between columns must also be a number. If the Unit Cell is specified, then there is no need for additional information. When specifying the distance between rows, care must be taken to include the spacing between rows and the height of the object. When specfying the distance between columns, the actual width of the object must be added to the distance between columns. In either case, if a scale factor is used on the initial insertion, the actual value of width and height (as shown

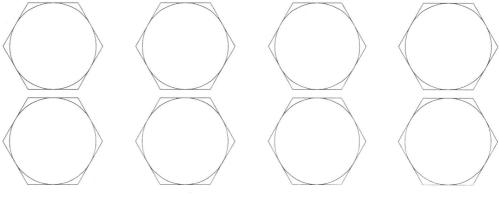

Note: Distance between rows = 2.85
       Distance between columns = 4

Figure 11–22   Sample MINSERT Array

on the screen) must be used. If the drawing is a box (whose width is 2″ and height is 1.5″) and the distance between rows is 1″ and the distance between columns is .75″, determine the actual distance between rows and columns. The distance between rows equals the height of the object (1.5″) plus 1″ for a total distance of 2.5″. Similarly, the distance between columns equals the width of the object (2″) plus the distance of .75″ for a total distance of 2.75″. Bring up a new drawing called ARRAY1. Make an array using the MINSERT command, and the XEH1 block: have 2 rows and 3 columns; distance between rows is .25 units; scale factor = .5; and the distance between columns is 1 unit. Insertion point is 9.8,7. (Remember to go to the left or below a given point, using a negative (-) sign in front of the distance value.) Quit the drawing.

11.5.2   ARRAY Command

The ARRAY command is listed in the EDIT Submenu and the Menu Map is shown in Figure 11–23.

The Command Sequences used for the Rectangular and Polar Arrays are different. Figure 11–24 provides the Command Sequence for the Rectangular Array, and Figure 11–26 provides the Command Sequence for the Polar Array.

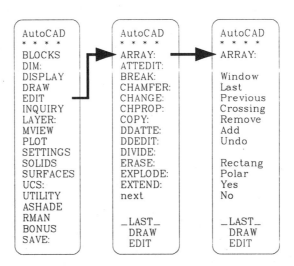

Figure 11–23   Menu Map for the ARRAY Command

```
Command: ARRAY
 Select objects: 1 selected, 1 found
 Select objects: (R)
Rectangular or Polar array (R/P): Rectangular
Number of rows (---) <1>: 3
Number of Columns (||||) <1>: 4
Unit cell or distance between rows (---): 2.000
Distance between columns (||||): 1.500
```

Figure 11–24   Command Sequence for the RECTANGULAR ARRAY

11.5.2.1 RECTANGULAR ARRAY Command

The RECTANGULAR ARRAY command looks identical to the MINSERT command. The differences are not in the appearance but in the program. Table 11.1 shows the major differences.

Table 11.1

Drawing requirement	Rectangular Array	MINSERT
Object present on screen prior to command	Yes	No
EXPLODE command operational	Yes	No
Distance calculations for rows and columns	Same	Same

The first prompt in the Command Sequence for the ARRAY command (either Rectangular or Polar options) is to select the object(s) and then confirm the selection by (R). This follows the standard procedure for the COPY, MOVE, MIRROR, and many other commands listed in the EDIT Submenu. After the object(s) has been selected and confirmed, the prompt asks "Rectangular/Polar Array?" Either respond with R for Rectangular or P for Polar. Input R or P from the keyboard or pick Rectangular or Polar from the Screen Menu. If the Rectangular Array is required, input R, and the next prompt will ask for the number of rows and columns, followed by the distance between rows and columns (similar to that requested in the MINSERT command). Remember the distance to the left of the object is specified by using the negative sign (-) prior to the X value and (-) for the Y value for a location below the object.

Example 11–9: Bring up a new drawing whose name is RECTANG. Draw a four-sided polygon with each side 1 unit long and the Initial point 1,1. We need a Rectangular Array of 3 rows and 4 columns. Distance between rows (Dr) is 1 unit and the distance between columns is .5 units (Dc). Therefore the total distance between the rows = 2 units (1 + 1) and between columns = 1.5 units (1 + .5). The solution is shown in Figure 11–25.

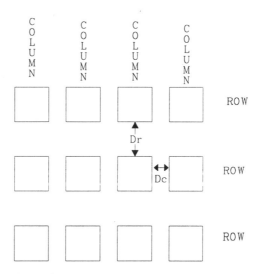

Figure 11–25 Solution to Example 11–9

11.5.2.2 POLAR ARRAY Command

Figure 11–26 lists the Command Sequence for the Polar Array. Please notice that the object selection procedure is exactly the same as the one used by the RECTANGULAR ARRAY command. However, different information is required for Polar Array: Center point of the array and the number of items to be placed on the screen. The operator has a choice in the design of the Array. Choice 1: Inform the program of the total angular displacement (the computer will determine the angle between items); or Choice 2: Tell the program the angle between each item. To select Choice 2, the answer to Choice 1 must be 0. The last prompt, "Do you want the objects rotated?", completes the Command Sequence.

Example 11–10: Bring up a new drawing called POLAR. Draw a square whose sides are 1 unit and whose Starting point is 6,5. Now draw a triangle whose base is the bottom of the square and whose apex meets at the midpoint of the top line of the box. Pick the ARRAY command and the square and triangle drawing as the objects; select Polar (either from the Screen Menu or input P from the keyboard). Center of the Array is 6.5,3.6. Our assignment calls for seven objects in a Polar Array spaced evenly over a 360° circle. Do not rotate the objects. The resulting Array is shown in Figure 11–27.

```
Command: ARRAY
 Select objects: 1 selected, 1 found
 Select objects: (R)
Rectangular or Polar (R/P): Polar
Center point of array: 4,3
Number of items: 5
Angle to fill (+=CCW, -=CW) <360>: 0
Angle between items: 30
Rotate objects as they are copied? <Y>: (R)
```

Figure 11–26   Command Sequence for the POLAR Array

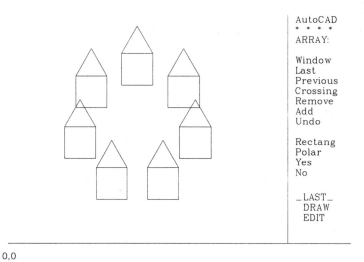

AutoCAD
* * * *
ARRAY:

Window
Last
Previous
Crossing
Remove
Add
Undo

Rectang
Polar
Yes
No

LAST
DRAW
EDIT

0,0

Figure 11–27   Solution to Example 11–10

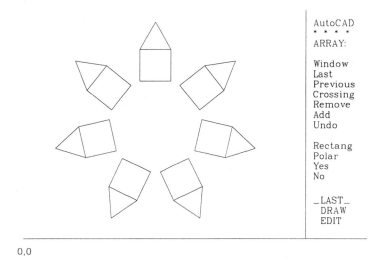

Figure 11–28 Solution to Example 11–11

Example 11–11: Erase all the objects shown in Example 11–10 with the exception of the objects located at 6,5. Repeat the above prompts but answer the last prompt "Do you want the objects rotated" with YES. Figure 11–28 shows the Array in its final form.

11.6 Pull Down Menu for Chapter 11

Figure 11-29 illustrates the Pull Down Menu for Chapter 11.

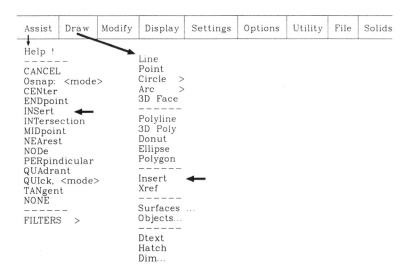

Figure 11–29 Pull Down Menu for Chapter 11

11.7 Template Reference—Chapter 11

The Template Reference for Chapter 11 is shown in Figure 11–30.

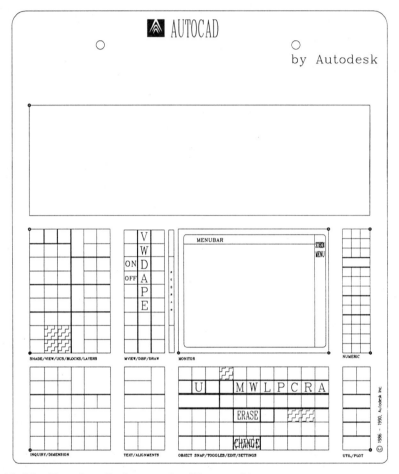

Figure 11–30 Template Reference for Chapter 11

COMMAND SUMMARY

CHANGE	BLOCK	WBLOCK	INSERT
MINSERT	EXPLODE	ARRAY	INSERT*

GLOSSARY

MINSERT: An abbreviation for multiple insert; similar to the INSERT command. Creates a Rectangular Array with rows and columns.

Rectangular Array: A grouping of objects that takes the form of rows and columns. Similar to the Minsert command without the blocked drawing requirement.

Polar Array: A grouping of objects in a circular pattern.

Row: The horizontal component of a Rectangular Array.

Column: The vertical component of a Rectangular Array.

PROBLEMS

1. Draw three lines. Line 1: 2,3 to 6,3.5; Line 2: 1,1 to 7,7; Line 3: 2.6,1.3 to 8.6,4.4. Use the CHANGE command so that the three lines have a common point located at 8.4,5.9. Use the U command, to undo the change. Now change the lines so that they meet at 1.4,5.

2. Erase the screen. Draw a circle that is inscribed in an equilateral triangle that is located inside a box. The triangle's sides are 7 units long. The lower left corner of the triangle and box is located at 2,2. The base of the box and triangle is the same. Assume that the box is a square. Block the drawing using the block name CBT. Insertion point is the Center of the circle. Bring back the drawing and do a PRPLOT at .5 scale. Wblock CBT.

3. Bring up a new drawing (M1). Using the MINSERT command, draw a Rectangular Array, with 3 rows and 3 columns. Use the CBT block at .25 scale factor and a rotation of 30°; Insertion point at 7,2. Use the value of 2 for the total distance between rows and columns. PRPLOT with EXTENTS and .5 scale.

4. Bring up a new drawing (MM1). Draw a circle whose Radius is 3". Draw an equilateral triangle whose sides are 2" long. Move the triangle to the circle so that the Center of the triangle is at the Center of the circle. The exact location of either the circle or triangle is not important. Erase any construction lines. Block the drawing using the block name CIRCLE1. Insert the block CIRCLE1 at 7",7"; scale factor = 0.25; Rotation angle set at 10°. Using the ARRAY command, draw a Rectangular Array of 4 rows and 3 columns. Distance between rows and columns is 2". Do a PRPLOT at .75 scale. Wblock CIRCLE1.

5. Bring up a new drawing (1A1). Insert the block CIRCLE1 using the INSERT* method. Insertion point = 1.5,4; scale factor = .5; Rotational angle = 30°. Erase the triangle. Draw a circle whose Center is the same as that of the large circle; Radius = 0.5". Reblock the changed drawing using the same name (CIRCLE1). Bring drawing back to the screen by using the OOPS command. PRPLOT at .5 scale.

6. Bring up a new drawing (A2Q). Draw a 10–sided polygon using the Inscribed method, Center at 4.5",4.5"; Radius = 3". Erase any *one* face of the polygon. It *cannot* be done. Now use the EXPLODE command on the polygon. Now erase any one side of the polygon. PRPLOT at half scale.

7. Explain the differences between the MINSERT command and the ARRAY command for Rectangular option.

8. What is the difference between the INSERT* method to make a change to a block and the use of the EXPLODE command to make the block change.

12 Polyline Commands

Instructional Objectives

1. To be able to understand the limitations of the TRACE command
2. To understand the differences between the TRACE command and the PLINE command
3. To be able to apply the TRACE command successfully
4. To be able to turn the FILL command ON or OFF as required for the TRACE, PLINE, SOLID, and DONUT commands
5. To be able to use the PLINE command for either linear or tapered segment, arcs or filled circles
6. To be able to FILL a polygon and understand the limitations of the SOLID command
7. To be able to draw a filled ring or circle without the use of the PLINE command
8. To be able to delete a portion of a polyline segment by using the BREAK command

12.1 Definition of a POLYLINE / TRACE / PLINE

A POLYLINE (such as a polygon), a TRACE (a linear segment with a defined width) and a PLINE (a segment drawn with the use of the PLINE command) are considered a single entity. In addition, the POLYLINE/TRACE/PLINE may have the following characteristics.

- The PLINE may be used to form a filled circle or donut.
- The sequence of lines and arcs may form a closed polygon.
- The trace has a limited capability (linear segments of constant width only).
- Plines are effected by INSERT and the commands resident in the DRAW and EDIT Submenus.
- The area, circumference, and/or the perimeter of objects are automatically determined by the commands listed in the INQUIRY Submenu.

12.2 TRACE Command

The TRACE command provides the operator with the ability to change the width of a line to any width required for a drawing. After a trace has been drawn, it will

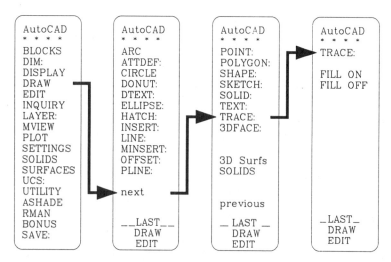

Figure 12–1 Menu Map for the TRACE Command

remain constant until changed. A trace segment is similar to a polyline of specified width, located between two specified points. The TRACE command is limited to a linear segment of any constant width. A TRACE cannot be used for arcs, circles, or tapered linear segments. (The operator must use the PLINE command, detailed in section 11.4 of this chapter.)

The TRACE command is located on the flip side of the DRAW Submenu and is shown in Figure 12–1. The Command Sequence is listed in Figure 12–2.

The first prompt of the TRACE command is the width of the trace or segment. A width that is equal to zero is considered the thinnest line on the screen. The width of a segment may be specified by either a numerical value from the keyboard or two points selected by the Pointer on the screen. The specified width will automatically appear as the default value in succeeding TRACE commands.

The remainder of the prompts are similar to the LINE commands. (Refer to Chapter 2.) After the width is specified, AutoCAD wants to know the location of the From point and the To point. The location of the From Point is established by either Absolute Coordinates or by use of the Pointer to pick a location on the Monitor. The To location(s) may be specified by either: Absolute Coordinates, Pointer Pick, or use of one of the two relative location commands. The width of the line segment may be changed after each line segment is drawn. The actual drawing of the TRACE (on the screen) is delayed until the next location is specified or (R) has been made.

```
Command: TRACE
Trace width <0.0000>: 0.075
From point: X1,Y1
To point: X2,Y2
```

Figure 12–2 Command Sequence for the TRACE Command

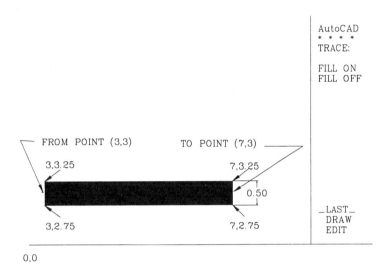

Figure 12–3 Solution to Example 12–1

CAUTION: The TRACE width will be centered on a drawn line between the From and To locations.

Example 12–1: Draw a TRACE segment from 3,3 to 7,3 and a width of .5 units, the screen display will show a filled rectangle whose corner locations are 3,3.25; 7,3.25; 7,2.75; and 3,2.75. The solution to Example 12–1 is shown in Figure 12–3. The width is centered on the line from 3,3 to 7,3.

Example 12–2: Draw two traces as described below:
TRACE A: Trace width = 0.5 units located from 1.75,5.5 to 7,4.375.
TRACE B: Trace width of 0.1 units located from 7,4.375 to 10.75,7.875.

Refer to Figure 12–4 for the solution.

　　Do not forget to use either the space bar or ENTER key at the end of each segment. (This will indicate to the program that the command has been completed.) Now try another example.

Example 12–3: Draw four continuous trace segments, whose widths are 0.4 units for all segments; Start point is 2,2 then 4,2; 4,4; 2,4; and 2,2. You will observe that the last location (2,2) leaves a notch in the trace drawing.

NOTE: The Close option *cannot* be used with the TRACE command.

The operator must compensate (in this example) by adding half of the trace width (in the Y direction). The endpoint for the last trace should be 2,1.8. The solution to this example is shown in Figure 12–5. Except on rare occasions, the PLINE command provides a linear segment with fewer problems. The PLINE command is described in paragraph 12.4 of this chapter.

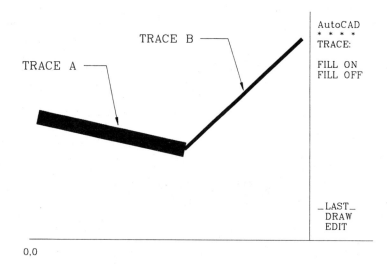

Figure 12–4   Solution to Example 12–2

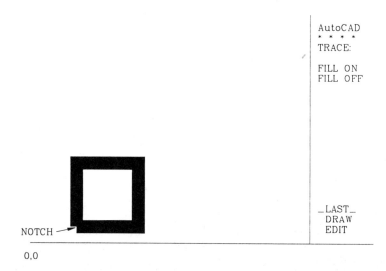

Figure 12–5   Solution to Example 12–3

12.3   FILL Command

The FILL command is actually a toggle switch (ON/OFF) where the outline of the drawing using the TRACE, PLINE, DONUT, and SOLID commands are either filled in or remain as an outline. The purpose of this command is to reduce the plotting time for a filled section of the drawing. The FILL command is part of the polyline subcommands (TRACE, PLINE, SOLID, and DONUT and the SETVAR options). The FILL command is located in the last Menu Map for the TRACE, PLINE, DONUT, and SOLID commands. (See Figure 12–1.)

When the SETVAR command is used, the SETVAR variable name is FILLMODE (1 = the FILL ON condition; 0 = the Fill OFF condition). After the FILL command has been set (ON/OFF), future commands use the new FILL command

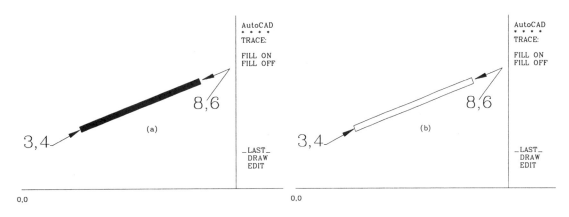

Figure 12-6 Solution to Example 12-4

status. However, when the drawing is regenerated, all polylines are changed to match the current FILL setting.

Example 12-4: Start a new drawing by the name of FILL. Select the TRACE command and set the FILL command to ON. Trace width = .25 units. The endpoints are 3,4 and 8,6. The solution to Example 12-4 is shown in Figure 12-6(a).

Now return to the TRACE command and set the FILL mode to OFF. Type or pick from the DISPLAY Submenu, REGEN. The trace will remain, but the fill will not be seen. See Figure 12-6(b).

12.4 PLINE Command

The PLINE (POLYLINE) is used to draw a filled segment for lines, arcs, and circles. The PLINE command is listed under the DRAW Submenu as illustrated in Figure 12-7.

The Command Sequence for this command is divided into two major areas, covering linear segments and arc segments. The initial prompts are the same for both segments: they ask for the location of the From point and display the default value of the width. (Refer to Figure 12-8.) If the default value of the width is not acceptable, input either W from the keyboard or pick the width from the Screen Menu.

12.4.1 Linear Segments

After the From point has been specified and the width of the segment established, another set of prompts is displayed for the linear segments of the PLINE command. (See Figure 12-9.)

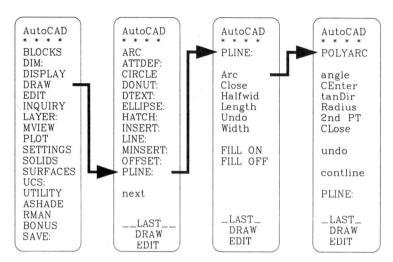

Figure 12-7 Menu Map for the PLINE Command

```
Command: PLINE
From point: 2,2
Current line width is 0.0000
```

Figure 12-8 Initial Command Sequence for the PLINE Command

```
Current line width is 0.0000
Arc/CLose/Halfwidth/Length/Undo/Width/<Endpoint of line>: W
Starting width <0,0000>: 0.25
Ending width <0.0000>: 0.25
Arc/Close/Halfwidth/Length/Undo/Width/<Endpoint of line>: 4,7
Arc/Close/Halfwidth/Length/Undo/Width/<Endpoint of line>: 4,4
```

Figure 12-9 Command Sequence for the PLINE Command, Linear Option

The terms listed in Figure 12-9 are defined below:

Arc: A word that acts as a switch to change from the linear Segment PLINE option to the arc segment PLINE option.

Close: Same as the CLOSE option used in the LINE command. When the CLOSE option is used, AutoCAD draws a segment from the last point to the first point. In addition, this option will make certain that the corners are squared and not notched as in the TRACE command.

Halfwidth: Similar to the Width option. It permits the operator to specify the width from the Center of the segment to the outer edge. The resulting segment width is twice the Halfwidth value.

Length: An option that permits the operator to draw a line using a numerical value. AutoCAD assumes that the direction of the prior line segment will be the same for the new segment. If a change in direction (angle) is required, then input the length and angle using the Relative Coordinate notation.

Undo: Is the same function as in other commands.

Width: Enables the operator to change the starting width, ending width, or both widths. When the starting width is not the same as the ending width, the resulting segment will be a taper.

After the initial location and width have been determined the next line segment may be specified by inputting the location of the endpoint. The width of the segment remains constant.

Example 12–5: Start a new drawing called PLINE. The Start or From point will be 1,7; starting width = .25 units; ending width = .25 units; segment Endpoint is 4,7. Continue the segment to 4,4. Now change the width of the next segment (either pick Width from the Screen Menu or input W from the keyboard) to 0.25 for the starting width and 0 for the end width. The third segment has an Endpoint of 1,4. The fourth segment will have a starting width of 0 and an end width of .25. Use the Close option. Notice that the corners are square. The result of this example is shown in Figure 12–10.

Note that the corners are irregular as the segments are input, but will be changed automatically to square corners when the Close option is used.

12.4.2 ARC Segments

To draw a filled arc segment, the initial prompts (refer to Figure 12–9) must be answered. Then input A for Arc or pick Arc from the Screen Menu. This will automat-

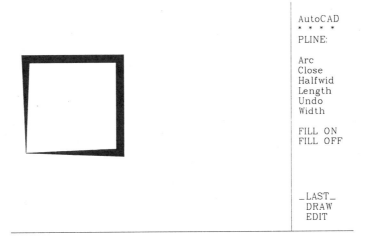

Figure 12–10 Solution to Example 12–5

```
Arc/Close/Halfwidth/Length/Undo/Width/<Endpoint of line>:  Arc
Angle/CEnter/CLose/Direction/Halfwidth/Line/Radius /
     Second pt/Undo/Width/<Endpoint of arc>:
```

Figure 12–11 Command Sequence for the PLINE Command, ARC Option

ically bring up the Command Sequence for the Arc segment as shown in Figure 12–11. The Arc options are also listed in Figure 12–7.

The new terms used in Figure 12–11 are defined below:

Angle: Permits the operator to input the specified angle. (Remember that AutoCAD draws its arcs and circles CCW.) AutoCAD will respond with "Included Angle".

Center: Permits the operator to specify the Center of the Arc. AutoCAD will respond with "Angle/Length/<Endpoint>:" (where L is the length of the Chord).

Close: Same as Close Option listed for the linear segment.

Direction: The AutoCAD program normally draws the next arc tangent to the prior arc. If this is not satisfactory, then specify the new direction with a single point. AutoCAD will respond with "Endpoint:".

Line: A word that acts as a toggle switch to change from the Arc Segment mode to the Line Segment mode. The LINE command is the reverse of the ARC command used in the linear segment. Another feature of the LINE option is the continue function. When the switch to linear segments is complete, then the line segment will continue from the last arc endpoint.

Radius: Is used to specify the Radius of the arc. AutoCAD responds with "ANGLE/<Endpoint>:".

Second: An option used when a 3P arc segment is required. AutoCAD responds with "Second point:" then "Endpoint:".

Example 12–6: Erase the drawing on the screen. Draw a series of arc segments using the PLINE command. Start from 7,4; width (starting and ending) = 0.3; pick Arc; Endpoint = @0,2.25; next Endpoint = @1.25<200; pick an angle = 60; Center = 4.75,5.625; Endpoint = 6,5.5; and close. The solution is shown in Figure 12–12.

Example 12–7: This example will include linear segments, arc segments, and tapered segments. Erase the drawing on the screen. Start point: 5,3; Width (Start and Ending) = 0.25; Endpoint = 7,3; change to arc by inputting Arc; Endpoint = 7,5; change the Ending width to .4; Endpoint = 7,6.6; change the end width to 0; angle = 95; Center = 5.5,5.5; pick Contline (for linear segment); Endpoint = 2,5; change widths: Starting width = 0, Ending width = 0.4; and close. Refer to Figure 12–13 for the solution to this example.

For those individuals who have difficulty in making arrows, the PLINE command is the solution. Erase the screen; Start point = 6,1.25; Starting width = 0, End width = .5; Endpoint = 4.75,1.25; Width change: Starting and Ending width = .1; Endpoint = 2.5,1.25.

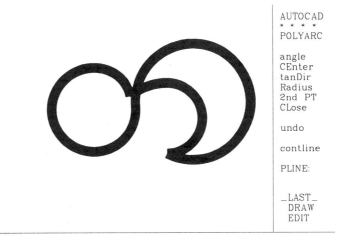

Figure 12–12   Solution to Example 12–6

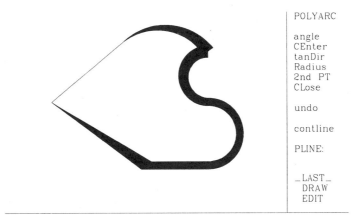

Figure 12–13   Solution to Example 12–7

12.5   FILLED Circle and DONUTS

Prior to AutoCAD Program version 2.5, the operator had to use the PLINE command to draw filled circles or filled rings (DONUT). AutoCAD developed the DONUT command for version 2.5, and called it DONUT (sometimes listed as Doughnut). This command is listed under the DRAW Submenu as shown in Figure 12–14. The Command Sequence is described in Figure 12–15.

The DONUT prompt calls for the value of the Inside diameter (ID) first and then the Outside diameter (OD). This forms the Donut. If the Inside diameter is zero, then we have the filled circle. The last prompt asks for the Center of the Doughnut. This is a repetitive command so that any number of identical donuts may be drawn. A null reply [space bar, or (R)] cancels the command. The inside and outside diameter values remain the same until changed by the operator.

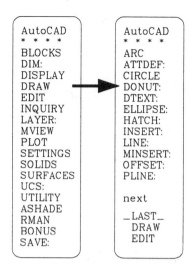

```
AutoCAD              AutoCAD
* * * *              * * * *
BLOCKS               ARC
DIM:                 ATTDEF:
DISPLAY              CIRCLE
DRAW         ──────▶ DONUT:
EDIT                 DTEXT:
INQUIRY              ELLIPSE:
LAYER:               HATCH:
MVIEW                INSERT:
PLOT                 LINE:
SETTINGS             MINSERT:
SOLIDS               OFFSET:
SURFACES             PLINE:
UCS:
UTILITY              next
ASHADE
RMAN                 _LAST_
BONUS                DRAW
SAVE:                EDIT
```

Figure 12–14   Menu Map for the DONUT Command

```
Command: DONUT
Inside diameter <0.5000>:(R)
Outside diameter <1.0000>:(R)
Center of doughnut: 1,2
```

Figure 12–15   Command Sequence for the DONUT Command

Example 12–8: Start a new drawing called DONUT. Pick the DONUT command from the DRAW Submenu; ID = .25; OD = 1.75; place the Center of the Donut at 3,6 and 3,3; null response. Set the FILL command to OFF; pick the DONUT command; do not change the ID or OD values; place the filled rings at 7,6 and 7,3. You should have four rings: two rings filled and 2 rings showing the outline of the outer and inner circles. Pick the REGEN command from the DISPLAY Submenu or input REGEN from the keyboard. Notice that the two rings that were filled are now the same as the "unfilled" rings. The REGEN command will regenerate the drawing to the latest fill configuration (in this example, FILL OFF). Change the FILL command to ON. Pick DONUT; ID = 0, OD = 1.75; Center of the circle is 5,4.625. This will give us a filled circle.

12.5.1 Using the BREAK Command on Polyline Entities

The BREAK command may be used to delete a portion of any polyline (Plines and donuts). The procedure is similar to that described in paragraph 10.3.

A polyline may be broken (or deleted) by first selecting the object, and then picking the First and Second points. The point used to select the object may also serve as the First point. As in the other Break applications, if the select point is not to be used as the first point, then the letter F must be input prior to the First and

Second points. When the BREAK command is used, the AutoCAD program will scan forward from the polyline vertex and delete the section of the polyline that lies between the two BREAK points.

If a Pline segment is broken, the cut ends will be cut square. When a filled circle or donut is broken, the break lines will go through the Center.

12.6 SOLID Command

The SOLID command will fill any rectangular object but can not be used for the arc or circle. The SOLID command, shown in Figure 12–16, is located on the flip side of the DRAW Submenu.

The Command Sequence is listed in Figure 12–17.

There is a *cardinal rule* that must be followed when using the SOLID command. AutoCAD must know the location of the Starting edge (two points) and the location of the Ending edge (two points). If a triangle is used, select the three points and use the null response for the fourth point. If the sequence of points (the location of the starting edge and the location of the finished edge) is not followed, the resulting drawing will appear as a bow tie instead of a filled rectangle.

Example 12–9: Start a new drawing called SOLID. Draw a rectangle using the points listed: Point A: 3,2; Point B: 3,5; Point C: 5,5; and Point D: 5,2. The Starting

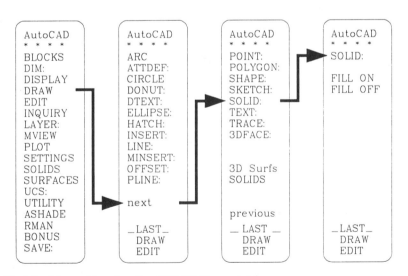

Figure 12–16 Menu Map for the SOLID Command

```
Command: SOLID First point: 3,2
Second point: 3,5
Third point: 5,2
Fourth point: 5,5
```

Figure 12–17 Command Sequence for the SOLID Command

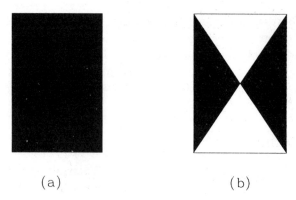

(a)   (b)

Figure 12–18   Solution to Example 12–9

edge is defined by 3,2 and 3,5; the Ending edge is defined by 5,2 and 5,5. Pick the SOLID command from the DRAW Submenu. Use the OSNAP command for INTersection, or input the point location (3,2; 3,5; 5,2; and 5,5). The rectangle is filled to the edge of the drawing. This is shown in Figure 12–18(a). Erase the filled rectangle. Pick the SOLID command. Input the rectangle points as follows: 3,2; 3,5; 5,5; and 5,2. The resulting drawing will be a bow tie as shown in Figure 12–18(b).

Several additional sequences may be used to obtain a filled rectangle (3,5; 5,5; 3,2; and 5,2) or (3,2; 5,2; 3,5; and 5,5).

12.7   Pull Down Menu for Chapter 12

Figure 12-19 illustrates the Pull Down Menu for Chapter 12.

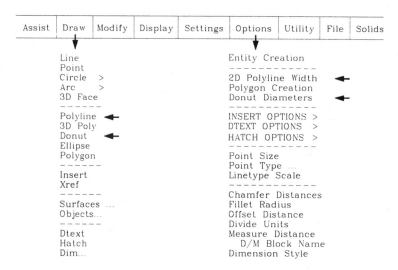

Figure 12–19   Pull Down Menu for Chapter 12

12.8   Template Reference—Chapter 12

Figure 12-20 illustrates the Template Reference for Chapter 12.

NOTE: The Template is not programmed for the TRACE, FILL, or SOLID commands.

COMMAND SUMMARY

TRACE   FILL   PLINE
DONUT   SOLID

GLOSSARY

Arc segment: The width may be constant or variable but in the form of an arc.

Linear segment: The width of the Pline or Trace is constant.

Tapered segment: The width of the Pline may be changed.

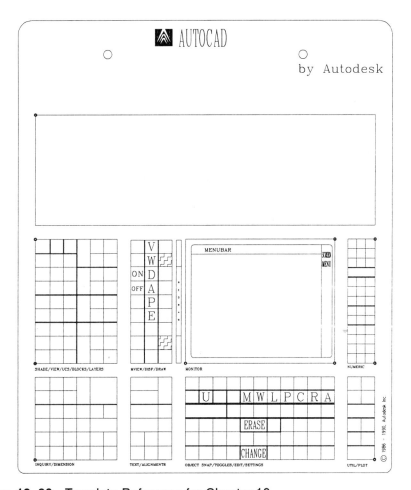

Figure 12–20   Templete Reference for Chapter 12

PROBLEMS

1. What are the limitations of the TRACE?
2. Can the PLINE command be used in forming a filled circle?
3. Set the drawing limits to 48′, 36′. The front of the house is 40′ wide by 12′ high. A door (3′ wide by 6′ high) is centered in the front of the house. The roof is peaked at 10′ in line with the Center of the door. Use the TRACE Command (width = 1′) to outline the front of the house. Outline the door with a PLINE (width = 6″). Place the door so that the Center of the bottom of the door (Pline) is 1′ above the Center of the Trace for the bottom of the house. Make sure all corners are square.
4. True or False: It is possible to use the Close option while using the TRACE command.

13 Second Level Edit Commands

Instructional Objectives

1. To be able to preselect an object(s) for the commands listed in the EDIT Submenu
2. To be able to TRIM a line, an arc, and polylines to an exact boundary location
3. To be able to EXTEND an entity to a given boundary location
4. To understand and be able to change, when necessary, the AutoCAD variables as listed in the SETVAR Submenu
5. To understand the differences between the DIVIDE and MEASURE commands
6. To be able to DIVIDE an entity into equal segments
7. To be able to use the MEASURE command
8. To be able to STRETCH an entity to a new endpoint

13.1 SELECT Command

The purpose of the SELECT command is to pick the object(s) that will be changed prior to activating the commands in the EDIT Submenu. This will improve the efficiency of the drafter as well as relieve the operator of some of the routine tasks. Once the object(s) is picked (under the SELECT command) the operator may use a number of the commands (listed under the EDIT Submenu) by picking the command and then the "Previous" selection mode. Figure 13–1 shows that the SELECT command

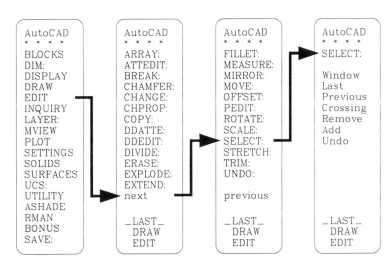

Figure 13–1 Menu Map for the SELECT Command

```
Command: SELECT
Select objects: 1 selected, 1 found

Select objects: (R)
```

Figure 13-2 Command Sequence for the SELECT Command

is listed on the flip side of the EDIT submenu. Figure 13–2 lists the Command Sequence or prompts for the SELECT command.

Example 13–1: Start a new drawing called SELECT. Draw a five-sided polygon using the Edge method, Starting point = 2,2; each side is 2 units long. Draw a triangle, Starting at 2,2, whose sides are 2 units long. Draw a circle that is inscribed in the triangle. Pick the SELECT command; identify the three objects (polygon, triangle, and circle) and confirm the selection. Now the location of the objects has to be moved to 8,.75. Select the MOVE command, pick Previous from the Screen Menu or input from the keyboard. Again, the operator must confirm the selection of the objects, prior to inputting the numerical values of the new basepoint. Repeat the exercise, but this time use the COPY command and place a copy of the drawing at 4.5,.75 and .875,.75. The solution is shown in Figure 13–3.

If a change is made to the selection of the objects, then the SELECT command must be reapplied.

Example 13–2: The drawing assignment calls for a copy of the circle (drawn in Example 13–1) to be placed at 5.5,4.75. Use the COPY command and pick the circle as the revised object selection. Pick the MIRROR command and MIRROR the complete drawing, using the "Previous" mode for the selection of the objects. Note that the only object in the "Previous" selection is the circle. Therefore, diligent care must be exercised in the object selection portion of the SELECT command.

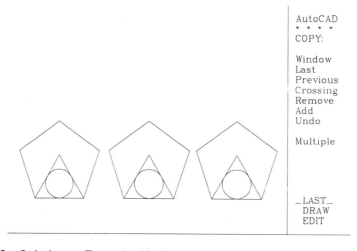

Figure 13–3 Solution to Example 13–1

13.2   TRIM Command

The TRIM command removes a segment of a line, arc, circle, or polyline. The BREAK command provides a similar function but is limited to a single entity. The TRIM command is listed under the EDIT Submenu and is shown in Figure 13–4.

> **NOTE:** When a polyline is trimmed, the width of the polyline (Pline) is ignored and the trim line will pass through the Center of the entity.

The Command Sequence for this command is listed in Figure 13–5.

The TRIM Command Sequence calls for the identification of two entities. The first identification is the boundary or cutting edge. The second identification is the object that is to be trimmed to the cutting edge. Unlike the BREAK command, the cutting edge could include one or more objects.

Example 13–3: Erase the screen. Draw a five-sided polygon, start at 3,1.875; use the Edge method; make each side 2 units long. Now draw a 3P arc using the following locations: 3.25,3.75; 4,6; and 4.25,4. Draw a circle whose Center is 5,3 and whose Radius is 1 unit. Select the TRIM command from the EDIT Submenu. Trim the arc so that all points lie outside the polygon. Trim the circle so that a portion of it remains

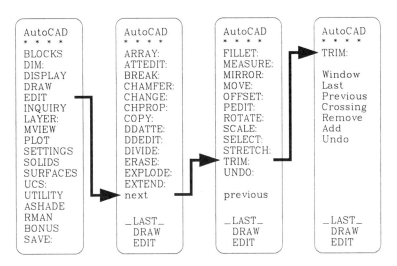

Figure 13–4   Menu Map for the TRIM Command

```
Command: TRIM
Select cutting edge(s)...
Select objects: 1 selected, 1 found
Select objects: (R)
Select object to trim:
```

Figure 13–5   Command Sequence for the TRIM Command

inside the polygon. Try this exercise on your own. If you have any trouble, use the procedure listed below:

1. Pick the polygon as the cutting edge.
2. Trim the right side of the arc. (The cutting edge is the upper right polygon face.)
3. Trim the left side of the arc.
4. Trim the circle so that the remaining arc is located inside the polygon.

The resulting solution is shown in Figure 13–6. Let's do one more example before going to the next command.

Example 13–4: Start a new drawing called TRIM. Using the PLINE command, 0.15 units wide, redraw the polygon (use OSNAP) and the 3P arc. Use the DONUT command (ID = .5; OD = 2); Center at 5,2. Select the Pline polygon as the cutting edge and trim the arc and donut. The solution is shown in Figure 13–7.

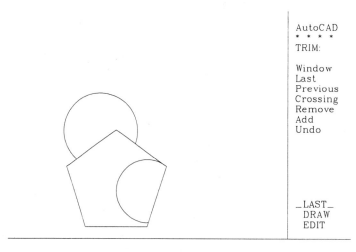

Figure 13–6   Solution to Example 13–3

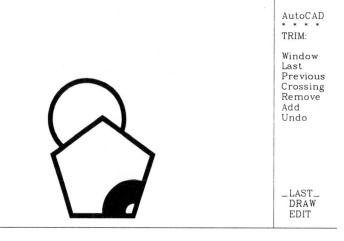

Figure 13–7   Solution to Example 13–4

REMEMBER:

1. A Trace cannot be trimmed.
2. One section of the cutting edge should be picked for each trim. A multiple trim may result in the loss of a portion of the drawing.
3. If AutoCAD cannot trim the object, then the prompt will read "Entity does not intersect at the edge" or "Cannot trim this entity."

13.3 EXTEND Command

The EXTEND command is the opposite of the TRIM command. The operator must select the boundary to which a selected entity will be extended. The EXTEND command is located in the EDIT Submenu and is shown in Figure 13–8. The Command Sequence for this command is listed in Figure 13–9.

As in the TRIM command, the boundary must be selected first, then the object(s) that is to be extended or lengthened is specified.

Example 13–5: Erase the screen. Draw the following items: Draw an equilateral triangle; Start point = 2.75,2.5; 6.75 units per side. Draw Arc A (3P arc): 7.25,8.125; 9.5,6.5; 9.75,4.25. Draw Arc B (3P arc): 5.25,8.125; 1,6.125; 2,3.5. Draw a line from

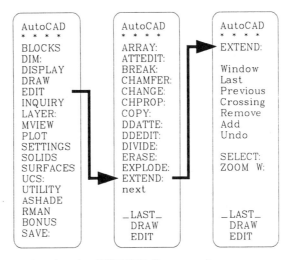

Figure 13–8 Menu Map for the EXTEND Command

```
Command: EXTEND
Select boundary edge(s)
Select objects: 1 selected, 1 found
Select objects:
Select object to extend
```

Figure 13–9 Command Sequence for the EXTEND Command

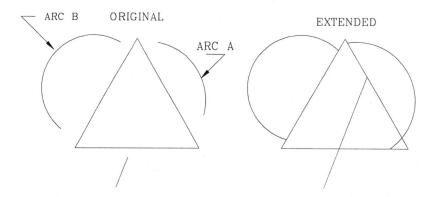

Figure 13–10   Solution to Example 13–5

5,.375 to 5.625,2. Select the EXTEND command from the EDIT Submenu. Pick the triangle base as the boundary; extend the line to the base; now pick the triangle's right face as the boundary and extend the line to meet that side. Extend Arc A to the right face. Pick the triangle base as the boundary and extend the bottom end of Arc A to the base. Pick the top point of Arc A and extend the arc to the triangle. Pick the left face of the triangle as the boundary, then extend both ends of Arc B to the left face. The solution to this example is shown in Figure 13–10.

13.4 SETVAR Command

The AutoCAD program contains 161 system variables such as COORDS, FILLMODE, GRID UNIT, etc. The operator can change 111 variables. The remaining variables are considered "read only" but are listed in this command for information only. The SETVAR command is found in the flip side of the SETTINGS Submenu and is shown in Figure 13–11. The Command Sequence is listed in Figure 13–12.

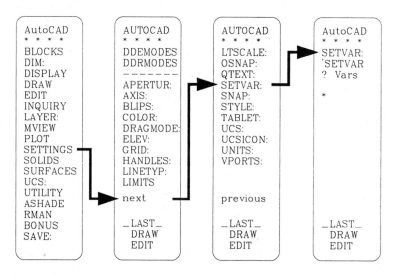

Figure 13–11   Menu Map for the SETVAR Command

```
Command: SETVAR Variable name or ?: PDMODE
New value for PDMODE <0>: 3
```

Figure 13–12   Command Sequence for the SETVAR Command

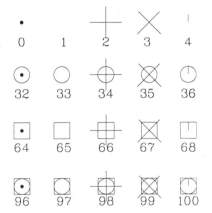

Figure 13–13   PDMODE Symbol Chart

The command prompt will ask for the name of the variable or ?. If the ? is input, the list of system variables will be placed on the Monitor screen. Once the variable name is input a new value for the variable (usually 0 for OFF and 1 for ON) is selected.

The SETVAR variables PDMODE and PDSIZE will be used as two examples. The PDMODE controls the shape of the Point Symbol. There are 20 Point Symbols as shown in Figure 13–13.

To establish a Point Symbol, select SETTINGS, then SETVAR and PDMODE, and then the numerical value of the Point Symbol. (Value is listed under the selected symbol.) The size of the symbol is a function of the system variable called PDSIZE. If the size is positive, then the numerical value is the absolute size of the symbol. If the size is negative, then the size of the symbol is a percentage of the screen size. Therefore during a ZOOM command, the size of the symbol does not change. There is no automatic change in the Point Symbol or size when a new symbol or size is selected. However, the first time that the drawing is regenerated, the existing symbols will be changed to the latest symbol selection and size. Examples of PDMODE and PDSIZE will be demonstrated in the DIVIDE and MEASURE command examples.

13.5   DIVIDE Command

The DIVIDE command divides a selected object into a number of equal parts. The DIVIDE command uses the Endpoint nearest the point of object selection. The operator has the option of selecting any integer from 2 to 32,767. Any of the Point Symbols (listed in Figure 13–13) may be used. If the PDMODE is set to 1, a blank space will

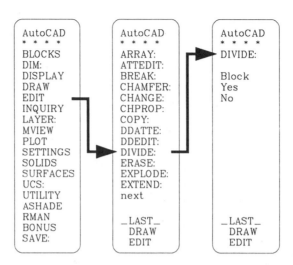

Figure 13–14 Menu Map for the DIVIDE Command

```
Command: DIVIDE
<Number of segments>/Block: 4
```

Figure 13–15 Command Sequence for the DIVIDE Command

appear on the screen. The DIVIDE command is found in the EDIT Submenu and shown in Figure 13-14. The Screen Menu for the POINT command (see Chapter 4, Figure 4–10) also calls out the PDMODE and PDSIZE variables and may be used to set these variables.

The Command Sequence for the DIVIDE command is shown in Figure 13-15.

The object to be divided is selected at the first prompt. (No confirmation is required.) The second prompt asks for the number of segments. An integer is the proper answer. The DIVIDE command will use the current PDMODE and PDSIZE values. Lines, arcs, circles, or polylines may be divided. If an object cannot be divided by this program, the command prompt will reply with "Cannot divide this entity".

Example 13–6: Erase or clear the screen and draw the following entities:
Pline from 2,2; width = 0.2; arc: @2<90; @2<90; l (line) @3<0; arc: @2<-90; @2<-90; ^C

Line from 4.5,7.25 to 8.5,7.25

Circle with Center = 9,4.75; Radius = 1.25

(1) Divide the Pline into 15 segments using PDMODE = 66; PDSIZE = 1 unit. (2) Divide the circle into 5 segments. (3) Change PDMODE to 99 and PDSIZE to .5 units and divide the line into 4 segments. Notice that the first two divide symbols are different. Now type in REGEN or pick this command from the DISPLAY Submenu. The symbol and size (for the first two examples) are now the same as those of Part 3 (the line divide symbol). The solution to this example is shown in Figure 13–16.

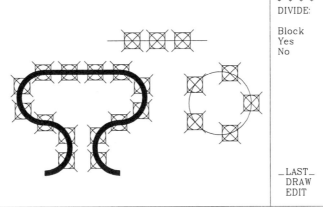

Figure 13–16 Solution to Example 13–6

13.6 MEASURE Command

The MEASURE command is similar to the DIVIDE command. The MEASURE command places a marker (PDMODE and PDSIZE) at a given segment length. The MEASURE command is listed in the EDIT Submenu and shown in Figure 13–17. The Command Sequence is listed in Figure 13–18.

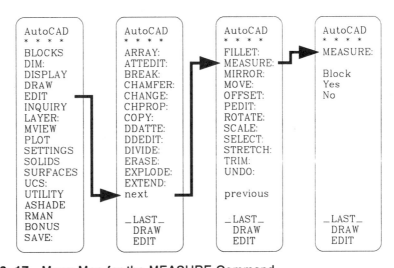

Figure 13–17 Menu Map for the MEASURE Command

```
Command: MEASURE
Select object to measure:
<Segment length>/Block:
```

Figure 13–18 Command Sequence for the MEASURE Command

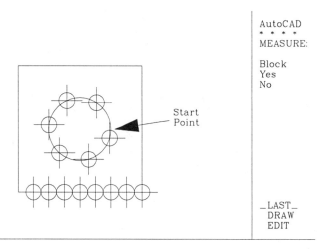

Figure 13-19   Solution to Example 13-7

Example 13-7:   Clear the screen. Draw a rectangle whose lower left corner is located at 2,3 and whose upper right corner is located at 6,7. Place a circle in the Center of the rectangle with a diameter of 2. Set PDMODE = 62 and PDSIZE = 0.5 units. Measure the rectangle (pick the lower left corner) for a segment of 0.5 units. Measure the circle (pick the point that is 0°) for a segment length of 1 unit. The solution is shown in Figure 13-19.

NOTE: The Starting point for the measurement of the segment length is the endpoint nearest the point that was used to pick the object. This is similar to the DIVIDE command.

13.7   STRETCH Command

The STRETCH command enables the operator to select a portion of the drawing to be moved or stretched while being connected to the remaining part of the drawing. This command is extremely helpful when the operator dimensions a drawing. If the dimensioning variables (DIMVAR) are set correctly, the dimension value will change as that part of the drawing is stretched. The DIMVARs are discussed in Chapter 16. The STRETCH command is located on the flip side of the EDIT Submenu and is shown in Figure 13-20.

The Command Sequence for this command is listed in Figure 13-21.

The command prompts call for the object selection procedure. This command requires that the *Crossing Window* be used for object selection. The lines, circles, arcs, and polylines that are "cut" by the Crossing Window rectangle, will be stretched. Once the object(s) is selected, then a basepoint must be picked and a New point specified. As in all the other drawing options, if the DRAGMODE is ON and ORTHO is OFF, it is possible to drag the drawing into place.

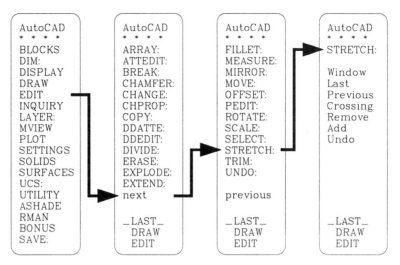

Figure 13–20   Menu Map for the STRETCH Command

```
Command: STRETCH
Select objects to stretch by window...
Select objects: C
First corner:        Other corner:
Select objects:
Base point:
New point:
```

Figure 13–21   Command Sequence for the STRETCH Command

NOTE: To stretch an arc, one endpoint must be included in the Crossing Window. When the STRETCH command is used on a circle, the circle remains the same size but the Center of the circle is moved.

Example 13–8: Quit the existing drawing and start a new drawing called STRETCH. Draw a hexagon, using the POLYGON command; Inscribed mode; Center = 3,4 and; a Radius of 2 units. Pick the STRETCH command and Crossing Window option. Place the window so that it cuts through the upper and lower right side (intersection). The Basepoint is equal to the intersection, and the New point is 7,3. The solution is shown in Figure 13–22.

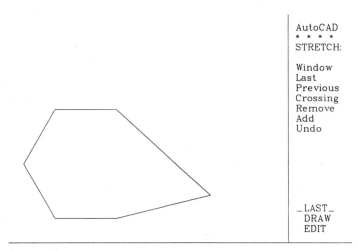

Figure 13–22   Solution to Example 13–8

13.8   Pull Down Menu for Chapter 13

Figure 13–23 represents the Pull Down Menu for Chapter 13.

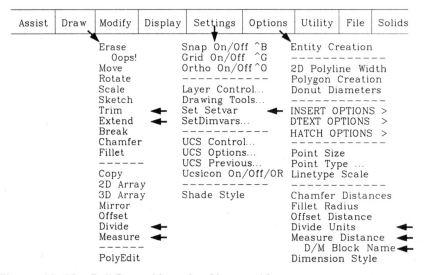

Figure 13–23   Pull Down Menu for Chapter 13

13.9 Template Reference—Chapter 13

Figure 13–24 shows the Template location (highlighted by a crosshatch) for the commands discussed in this chapter. The SELECT and SETVAR commands are not on the Template.

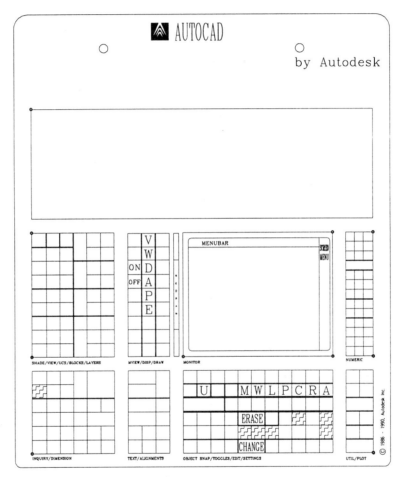

Figure 13–24 Template Reference for Chapter 13

COMMAND SUMMARY

SELECT	TRIM	EXTEND	SETVAR
DIVIDE	MEASURE	STRETCH	

GLOSSARY

Boundary: Used in TRIM and EXTEND commands to designate the end of an entity or a cutting edge.

PDMODE: A collection of 20 symbols designating a point.

PDSIZE: The size of the PDMODE symbols.

SETVAR: An abbreviation for System Variables.

Trim edge: The actual edge of the entity to be trimmed.

PROBLEMS

1. True or False: It is possible to extend a Trace.
2. True or False: It is possible to extend a Pline Segment.
3. Can two different point symbols appear on the screen at the same time? Explain your answer.
4. Define the terms (as used in AutoCAD):
   a. Cutting edge
   b. PDMODE

14 Second Level Commands Continued

Instructional Objectives

1. To be able to expand or reduce the size of an entity with the use of the SCALE command
2. To be able to make parallel or OFFSET copies of lines, circle, arcs, and Plines
3. To be able to rotate an entity by means of the ROTATE command
4. To understand what is meant by TRANSPARENT commands
5. To understand the limitations of the TRANSPARENT commands
6. To be able to input the TRANSPARENT command by the use of the " ' " keystroke

14.1 SCALE Command

The operator may change the size of the entity or complete drawing by means of the SCALE command. This command is listed on the flip side of the EDIT Submenu and is shown in Figure 14-1.

The Command Sequence is listed in Figure 14-2.

Once the SCALE command has been selected, the Command Sequence prompt calls for the selection and confirmation of the entities to be scaled. The operator may use any of the standard selection options. After the selection has been confirmed, the

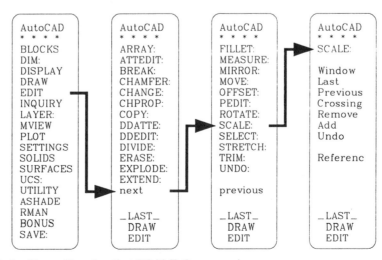

Figure 14–1 Menu Map for the SCALE Command

```
Command: SCALE
Select objects: 1 selected, 1 found
Select objects: (R)
Base point:
<Scale factor>/Reference: R

   If R is used, the following prompts are displayed
Reference length <1>:
New length:
```

Figure 14-2 Command Sequence for the SCALE Command

prompt will call for the location of the Basepoint. This Basepoint may be anywhere on the screen. If the Basepoint is on the drawing, the scaling process uses this location as its Center. The last prompt will call for either a Scale Factor or Reference. The Scale Factor is numeric (if less than one, the resulting drawing becomes smaller; if greater than one, the resulting drawing becomes bigger). The numeric value is not limited to an integer. The other response to this prompt is the letter R (R stands for Reference). If the Reference is used, the operator will be able to show the current dimension and then the new dimension.

NOTE:
1. When a polygon (using the Edge method) is used in any example, the Second point will always be to the right of the Basepoint. For example, draw a five-sided polygon using the Edge method; the Basepoint is 4,3. Each edge is 2 units. The Second point will be located at 6,3.
2. The statement "Clear the Screen" means that the current drawing should be erased.

Example 14-1: Bring up a new drawing called SCALE. Draw a six-sided polygon using the Edge method, starting at 3,3 with an edge length of 3 units (the location of the Second point is 6,3). Reduce the polygon by a factor of 2. Pick the SCALE command from the flip side of the EDIT Submenu. Identify and confirm that the polygon is the object to be scaled. The Basepoint will be the Center of the polygon (4.5000,5.5981) and the Scale Factor is 0.5. After the SCALE command has been completed, measure any edge length. (The edge length should be 1.5 units.) Confirm this value by using the Coordinate display (in the Status Line). Repeat the command, but use the Reference option for the second prompt. Show the existing length with the use of the Pointer (Start and End of one edge). The new length uses the last point of the Reference length, therefore show the new length. The Second point will inform the program as to the Scale Factor you are looking for. If the Second point of the new length is between points 1 and 2 or the Reference length, the Scale Factor is less than 1. If the new point exceeds the distance, between reference points 1 and 2, the Scale Factor is greater than one. In general practice, the Scale Factor is specified as a numeric value.

Example 14-2: Clear the screen. Draw a square (four-sided polygon) using the Edge method; 2 units per side; Start at 3,3. Make the square larger by using a Scale Factor

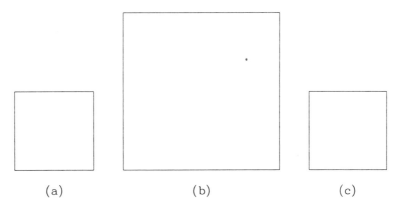

Figure 14–3 Solution to Example 14–2

of 2. Pick and confirm the selection of the box. Basepoint is at 3,3. Watch the screen. The scaling process starts at the Basepoint. Let's repeat the SCALE command, but this time use the Reference option. The Basepoint is at 3,3; Reference length goes from 3,3 to 7,3 (4 units); and the new length to the midpoint of the edge or 5,3 (scale factor of .5). The polygon was scaled to its original dimensions. Figure 14-3(a) shows the original polygon; Figure 14-3(b) shows the 4 unit edge; and Figure 14-3(c) represents the last scale change.

14.2 OFFSET Command

When the OFFSET command is used, it draws a parallel line/arc/circle/polyline to the selected object at a specified distance and direction. The distance may be specified as a numeric distance or a given point location. The OFFSET command is located either in the DRAW or EDIT Submenu and is shown in Figure 14-4. Figure 14-5 represents the Command Sequence for this command. The OFFSET command is similar to the LINE command since the prompt requests the next datum point.

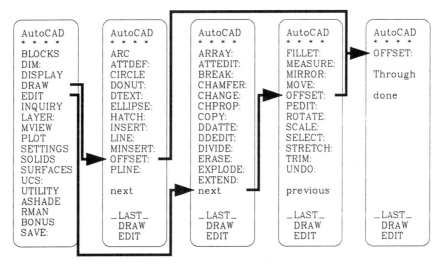

Figure 14–4 Menu Map for the OFFSET Command

```
Command: OFFSET

Figure 14-5a
IF DISTANCE OPTION IS USED
Offset distance or Through <Through>: 0.5
Select object to offset:
Side to offset:

Figure 14-5b
IF THROUGH POINT OPTION IS USED
Offset distance or Through <Through>: T
Side to offset:
Through point:
```

Figure 14–5   Command Sequence for the OFFSET Command

Figure 14-5(a) describes the prompts when the OFFSET is a given distance. Figure 14-5(b) lists the prompts for the Through option.

Example 14-3(a): Bring up a new drawing called OFFSET. Draw two lines: Line A from 2,2 to 5,4 and Line B from 5,4 to 2,7. Draw a 3P arc using the following points: 6.5,6; 8,5; 7,2. Pick the OFFSET command from the EDIT Submenu. The distance for offset is 0.25 units from Line A towards the bottom of the screen. Repeat the offset for Line B but the side for offset is towards the top of the screen. Notice that the two offset lines are not joined. To join these lines, select either the CHAMFER or the FILLET command: Radius = 0 option. Select Lines A and B. The Offset lines are now joined. Draw an offset to the arc through point 9,4. Repeat the command but use 7,4 as the point. Figure 14-6 shows the solution to this example.

Example 14-3(b): Let's continue Example 14-3(a) by drawing an offset to a trace. Clear the screen. Draw a trace (0.1 unit wide) from 1,5 to 5,4 to 3,3. Offset the trace with a distance of 0.5. Nothing will happen because the OFFSET command cannot

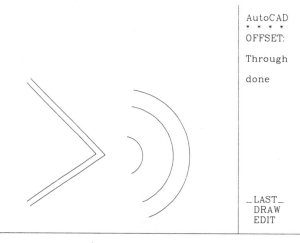

Figure 14–6   Solution to Example 14–3(a)

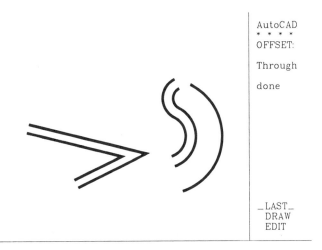

Figure 14–7 Solution to Example 14–3(b)

be used with a TRACE command. Erase the trace. Draw a PLINE, Start and Ending width = .1; same points as the trace. Use the through point of 4,4.625. Note that there is an offset on both lines and they are joined. Continue on with the PLINE command but in the Arc option: Initial point = 7.25,7.25; Start and Ending width = 0.1; arc; 7.25,5.625; 7.125,4. Draw an offset Through the point 8,5.5. Repeat the OFFSET command, using the first offset line and a Through point of 9,6. Notice that the arc at the bottom of the Pline offset does not curl in the opposite direction. The solution to Example 14-3b is shown in Figure 14-7.

Example 14-4: Clear the screen. Draw a six-sided polygon with the edge 2 units long, Starting at 3,3. Pick the OFFSET command, distance option of .5 units. Offset towards the outside of the polygon. Note that all sides were offset automatically. This is because the polygon is considered a block. To prove this theory, use the EX-PLODE command (listed under the EDIT Submenu) on the original polygon. Repeat the OFFSET command but offset towards the Center of the polygon. Select the bottom edge. Note that only the base or bottom edge of the polygon was offset. The solution to this example is shown in Figure 14-8.

14.3 ROTATE Command

The ROTATE command is also located on the flip side of the EDIT Submenu and is shown in Figure 14-9.

The Command Sequence for the ROTATE command is listed in Figure 14-10.

The ROTATE command enables the operator to rotate an entity about a stated Basepoint. The Basepoint will be the Center of rotation. A positive angular displacement of 35° will rotate the entity or object 35° in the CCW direction. An angular displacement of -35° will rotate the object 35° in the CW direction. The ROTATE command is operational for all entities (line, arc, circle, trace, polyline). The Rotation point must be selected with care.

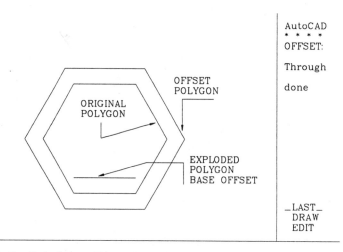

Figure 14–8 Solution to Example 14–4

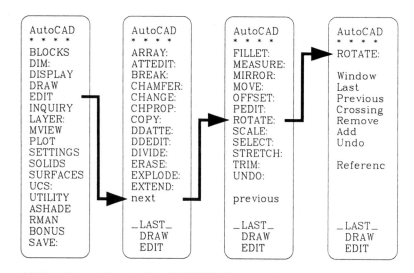

Figure 14–9 Menu Map for the ROTATE Command

```
Command: ROTATE
Select objects: 1 selected, 1 found
Select objects: (R)
Base point:

    PROMPTS FOR NUMERIC VALUE:
    <Rotation angle>/Reference: 35

    PROMPTS FOR REFERENCE OPTION
    <Rotation angle>/Reference: R
    Reference angle <0>: 0
    New angle: 45
```

Figure 14–10 Command Sequence for the ROTATE Command

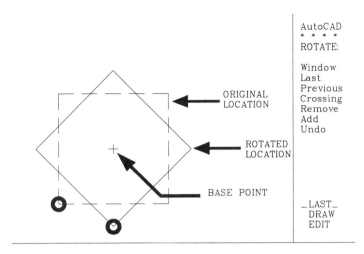

Figure 14–11 Solution to Example 14–6

Example 14-5: Bring up a new drawing called ROTATE. Draw a four-sided polygon, using the Edge method, located at 2,2; each edge is 3 units long. Select the RO-TATE command from the EDIT Submenu. Pick and confirm the selection (square) and establish the Basepoint at 2,2. Input an angular displacement of 45°. The box is now rotated CCW, 45° about the 2,2 point. Repeat the example but use -75 as the angular displacement. The box is rotated 75° in the CW direction. As indicated in the Command Sequence (Figure 14-10), the operator may use the Reference method. Repeat the example but this time input R; the reference angle is -30 and the new angle is 0. The box should appear as it was originally drawn at the start of this example.

Example 14-6: Add a donut (ID =0.25; OD =0.5) to the existing drawing; Center at 2,2. Select both the box and donut and confirm the selection. Use the Center of the box as the Basepoint. Input 45° as the angular displacement. The box and donut will be rotated 45° in the CCW direction. The solution is shown in Figure 14-11.

14.4 Transparent Commands

A new set of command options was developed and released in AutoCAD version 2.5 and updated in all subsequent releases. These commands are called Transparent commands and are identified by using the " ' " in front of the following commands:

'REDRAW	'HELP	'ZOOM	'PAN
'VIEW	'SETVAR	'GRAPHSCR	'TEXTSCR

These commands may be used anytime during any active command, without any disturbance to the active command. AutoCAD will stop the active command and perform the Transparent command and automatically return to the active command. There are several restrictions:

1. 'ZOOM, 'PAN, and 'VIEW cannot be performed while the VPOINT (a 3D command), ZOOM, PAN, or VIEW command is in progress.
2. The fast ZOOM mode must be ON for these commands to work as Transparent commands.
3. Any command that required regeneration (ie., ZOOM All; ZOOM Extents) cannot be used transparently.
4. 'REDRAW may be used only at a nontext prompt.
5. The Transparent commands cannot be used with either the PRPLOT, PLOT, SAVE, or END command.

14.5   Pull Down Menu for Chapter 14

Figure 14–12 represents the Pull Down Menu for Chapter 14.

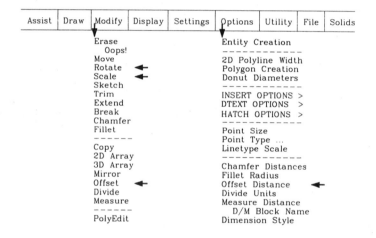

Figure 14–12   Pull Down Menu for Chapter 14

14.6   Template Reference—Chapter 14

Figure 14-13, on page 191, shows the location of the SCALE, OFFSET, and ROTATE commands. The Invisible or Transparent commands: ZOOM, PAN, and REDRAW are also indicated.

COMMAND SUMMARY

OFFSET   ROTATE
SCALE   TRANSPARENT

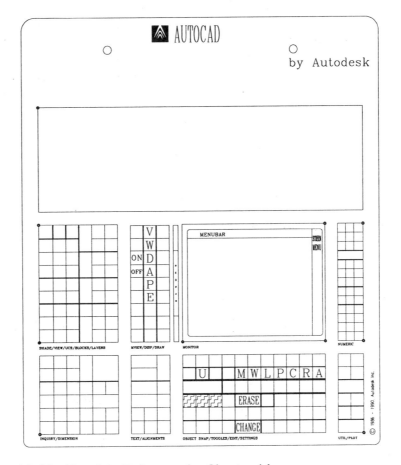

Figure 14–13 Template Reference for Chapter 14

GLOSSARY

Transparent commands: Commands that interrupt an existing command. There are eight such commands: HELP, REDRAW, VIEW, SETVAR, ZOOM, GRAPHSCR, PAN, and Text Screen.

OFFSET: The command that produces a line, arc, circle, or Pline a given distance from the reference entity or through a given point.

PROBLEMS

1. The OFFSET command can be found in which submenu?
2. True or False: The SCALE command is similar to using a ruler.
3. Name six of the eight Transparent commands.

15 Layers

Instructional Objectives

1. To understand the concept of overlay or layering a drawing
2. To be able to use the LAYER subcommands effectively
3. To understand that if a portion of the drawing appears on the screen, it can be modified
4. To understand the difference between the LAYER option OFF and LAYER option FREEZE
5. To be able to THAW a layer
6. To be able to establish a designated linetype (LTYPE) for a specified layer
7. To be able to use the LTSCALE command effectively
8. To be able to remove unwanted layers, blocks, or linetypes by using the PURGE command
9. To be able to change layer, linetype, and color by using either the CHANGE command or CHPROP command
10. To be able to change or RENAME a block, layer, ltype, style, or view

15.1 LAYER Command

15.1.1 Introduction

The purpose of the LAYER command is to provide one or more transparent overlays for a given drawing. These overlays or layers, are aligned so that the location of coordinating points on Layer 1 retains its location on the 1000th layer. The number of layers for a given drawing is unlimited. In addition to the alignment of the layers, it is possible to designate different colors and linetypes for each layer. The number of colors that are available depends upon the graphics card and Monitor found in each particular workstation. AutoCAD, with the proper graphics card and Monitor, can support 9 basic colors and 256 color shades. Currently, AutoCAD has 9 different linetypes (LTYPES) [8 basic linetypes with 3 options per linetype plus continuous (continuous represents an unbroken line)] stored in a library file named ACAD.LIN. Additional linetypes can be developed; the procedure is detailed in Appendix B of the AutoCAD Reference Manual. Typical applications of the layered drawing are: multilayered printed circuit board; as well as drawings used by an architect to designate different floor sections such as electrical requirements, plumbing, foundation.

15.1.2 Initial Settings of the LAYER Command

The LAYER command is listed on the Main Screen Menu as an active command. Figure 15-1 is the Menu Map for this command. Figure 15-2 lists the Command Sequence for the LAYER command.

15.1.3 LAYER Command Options

The LAYER command is listed on the Main Screen Menu. Upon selection of the LAYER command, the Screen Menu provides 10 modes or options. Each option (?/Make/Set/New/ON/OFF/Color/Ltype/Freeze/Thaw) is listed and defined below for ease of selection.

15.1.3.1 Definitions of the LAYER Command Option

The "?" stands for a listing or directory of current LAYER names, colors, linetypes, and layer status.

The New option is used to name the layers that will be used. The layer Name may contain up to 31 characters. (Only the first eight characters will be displayed on the left side of the Status line.) The operator selects the LAYER command and picks New from the Screen Menu or inputs N or NEW from the keyboard. The prompt will ask for the layer Names. All the layer Names can be typed at one time as long as the names are separated by a comma (,). A comma is not required after the last name. If by accident a layer Name has been omitted, it is possible to select the New option again to add the missing name(s). In some cases, the Make option is used to add one name.

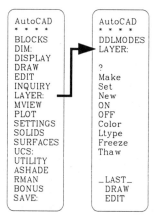

Figure 15–1 Menu Map for the LAYER Command

```
Command:  LAYER:  (R)
Command:  LAYER  ?/Make/Set/New/ON/OFF/Color/Ltype/Freeze/Thaw:
```

Figure 15–2 Command Sequence for the LAYER Command.

The Set option assigns a specific layer to be the current drawing layer. However, it is possible to modify a drawing as long as the drawing appears on the screen regardless of the Set layer.

The ON option permits the operator to make visible any or all layers either as a reference or for use in the drawing effort.

REMEMBER: If the drawing layer is visible, the drawing can be modified.

The OFF option turns the applicable drawing layer off and therefore the layer(s) is *no longer visible*. These layers (OFF) are still part of the drawing but do not appear on the screen. The drawing information contained on the OFF layer(s) cannot be modified, unless the layer is turned ON.

The Make option is a special option that permits the operator to Name and Set a new layer.

The Freeze mode removes the assigned layer(s) from the current work effort and is not affected when the drawing is regenerated. The Freeze mode is used to reduce the regeneration time. Those layers that are Frozen must be "THAWED" before any work on these layers is attempted.

The Thaw option is used to bring the FROZEN layer(s) back into the drawing. When the drawing is THAWED, the layer is automatically placed in the ON condition.

The Color option gives the operator the capability of assigning different colors to layers in addition to layer Names. All layers may have the same color or each layer may have a different color (depending on the graphics card and Monitor used). It is possible to have more than one color per layer. This is accomplished through the use of the CHANGE command discussed in paragraph 15.5 of this chapter.

The Ltype (Linetype) option is similar to the Color option in that the operator may assign one of the standard linetypes to any layer. As in the Color option, more than one Ltype is available per layer. These Ltypes are shown in Figure 15–3.

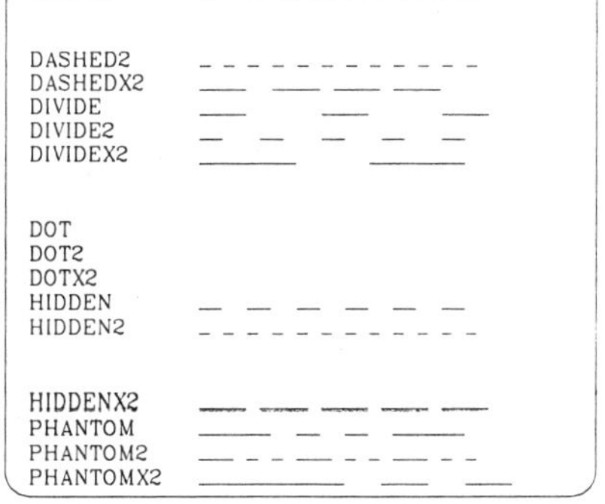

Figure 15–3 AutoCAD Library of Linetypes.

CAUTION: Tracking of color and Ltypes becomes difficult when more than one color or Ltype is used for a given layer.

The LTSCALE mode (Scale Factor for the length of the dash used in the linetypes, see paragraph 15.3) provides the ability to change the length of the dash. The default value is 1. A numeric value of less than 1 will make the dash smaller, and a value greater than 1 will make the dash longer.

Example 15–1: For illustrative purposes, start a new drawing called LAYER. This assignment requires four layers with layer Names, Colors and Ltypes specifications as listed below:

Layer Name	Layer Color	Layer Ltype
0	Red	Continuous
First-Floor	Blue	Dashed
Second-Floor	Green	Hidden
Roof	White	Border

NOTE: AutoCAD automatically establishes Layer 0 whose color is white, Ltype is continuous and current (Set). The layer Name "0" cannot be changed but the Color and Ltype can be changed. The layer Name may not have any empty spaces; therefore a dash or hyphen is used to separate the words. The AutoCAD program provides a dialogue box for the establishment of the layer (as shown in Figure 15–4) that may be used to define the layer Name, Color, and Ltype. The Dialogue Box for this example is shown in Figure 15–5.

The column VP (View Port) will not be used at this time.

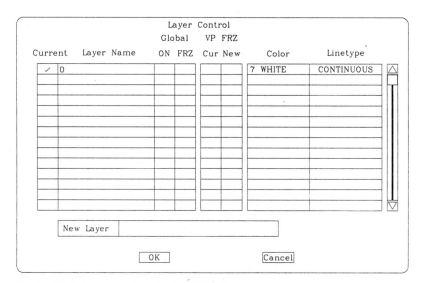

Figure 15–4 Dialogue Box for the LAYER Command

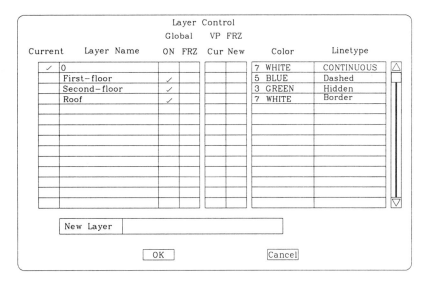

Figure 15–5   Completed Dialogue Box for Example 15–1

```
Command: LAYER:
Command: LAYER ?/Make/Set/New/On/Off/Color/Ltype/Freeze/Thaw : New
New layer name(s): First-Floor,Second-Floor,Roof
Command: LAYER ?/Make/Set/New/On/Off/Color/Ltype/Freeze/Thaw: (R)
```

Figure 15–6   Command Sequence for the LAYER Command—Layer Name

Figure 15–6 lists the prompts and correct replies to the prompts to specify the layer Names. The sequence used to input the layer Names does not affect the layers.

The operator must first establish the layer Name(s). However, the selection of Color, then Ltypes or Ltypes then Color makes no difference. Figure 15–7 is the Command Sequence used to select the layer Colors in accordance with the drawing requirements.

The Color selection for the layer may be any Color that the AutoCAD program and the equipment can support. The color selection is either assigned by Color name or number. Figure 15–8 lists seven basic Colors and their assigned numbers.

```
Command: LAYER:
Command: LAYER ?/Make/Set/New/ON/OFF/Color/Ltype/Freeze/Thaw: Color
Color: Red
Layer name(s) for color 1 (red) <0>: 0
Command: LAYER ?/Make/Set/New/ON/OFF/Color/Ltype/Freeze/Thaw: C
Color: Blue
Layer name(s) for color 5 (blue) <0>: First-Floor
Command: LAYER ?/Make/Set/New/ON/OFF/Color/Ltype/Freeze/Thaw: C
Color: Green
Layer name(s) for color 3 (green) <0>: Second-Floor
Command: LAYER ?/Make/Set/New/ON/OFF/Color/Ltype/Freeze/Thaw: C
Color: White
Layer name(s) for color 7 (white) <0>: Roof
Command: LAYER ?/Make/Set/New/ON/OFF/Color/Ltype/Freeze?Thaw: (R)
```

Figure 15–7   Command Sequence for the LAYER Command—Color Option

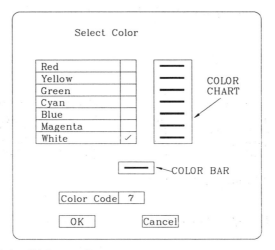

```
COLOR ASSIGNMENT
COLOR     NUMBER
RED          1
YELLOW       2
GREEN        3
CYAN         4
BLUE         5
MAGENTA      6
WHITE        7
```

Figure 15–8   Color Name and Number Assignment

Select Color

```
Red
Yellow
Green
Cyan
Blue
Magenta
White        ✓
```

COLOR CHART

Color Code   7

OK   Cancel

Figure 15–9   Color Dialogue Box

```
Command: LAYER ?/Make/Set/New/ON/OFF/Color/Ltype/Freeze?Thaw:  Ltype
Linetype (or?)<Continuous>: DASHED
Layer name(s) for linetype Dashed <0>:  First-Floor
Command: LAYER ?/Make/Set/New/ON/OFF/Color/Ltype/Freeze/Thaw:  Ltype
Linetype (or?)<Dashed>:  HIDDEN
Layer name(s) for linetype Hidden<0>:  Second-Floor
Command: LAYER ?/Make/Set/New/ON/OFF/?Color/Ltype/Freeze/Thaw/:  Ltype
Linetype (or?)<Hidden>:  BORDER
Layer name(s) for linetype Border<0>:  Roof
Command: LAYER ?/Make/Set/New/ON/OFF/Color/Ltype/Freeze/Thaw:  (R)
```

Figure 15–10   Command Sequence for the LAYER Command—Ltype Option

An extension of the layer Dialogue Box is the Color Dialogue Box shown in Figure 15–9.

The Ltype selection follows the pattern established for the Color assignment. Figure 15–10 lists the Command Sequence for the LAYER command, Ltype option. The AutoCAD program furnishes standard Ltypes. (See Figure 15–3.) The operator usually assumes that the selected linetypes have been loaded into the program. If the assumption is not true, then follow the procedure listed in paragraph 15.2.

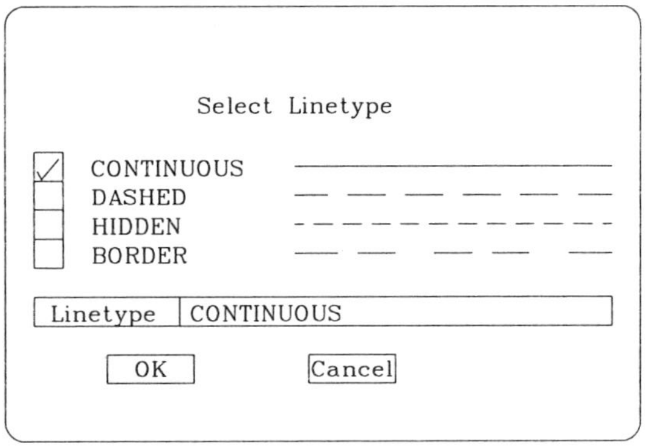

```
              Select  Linetype

  [✓]  CONTINUOUS    ────────────────
  [ ]  DASHED        ─  ─   ─   ─   ─   ─
  [ ]  HIDDEN        ‑ ‑ ‑ ‑ ‑ ‑ ‑ ‑ ‑ ‑
  [ ]  BORDER        ─  ─   ─  ─   ─

  Linetype │ CONTINUOUS

        [ OK ]          [Cancel]
```

Figure 15–11   Dialogue Box for LAYER Command—Linetype Option

```
  Layer name      State      Color        Linetype

  0               On         1(red)       CONTINUOUS
  First-Floor     On         5(blue)      DASHED
  Second-Floor    On         3(green)     HIDDEN
  Roof            On         7(white)     BORDER

  Current  layer:  0
```

Figure 15–12   Layer Directory

Figure 15–11 is the third Dialogue Box for the LAYER command designated as Linetype option. The Dialogue Box will display those linetypes that have been loaded into the drawing.

In addition to the Dialogue Boxes, a directory listing the layer Names, Color, Ltype, and Status is available by selecting the LAYER command. Pick the ? and depress the ENTER key twice. Figure 15–12 displays the Layer Directory. In addition to the Names, Colors and Ltypes, the directory shows which layer is ON, OFF, FROZEN, or CURRENT.

15.1.4 Application of the LAYER Command

Now that the layers have been established, Set Layer 0 using the procedure shown in Figure 15–13.

```
Command:  LAYER ?/Make/Set/New/ON/OFF/Color/Ltype/Freeze/Thaw:  Set
New  current  layer<0>:  0
```

Figure 15–13   Command Sequence for the LAYER Command—Set Option

NOTE: If the operator wants to use the Dialogue Boxes to setup the layer specifications, then the DDLMODES listing (on the Screen Menu) should be selected.

Example 15–2: Draw a circle with the Center located at 4,5 and a Radius of 2. If your workstation has a color Monitor, the circle should be in red with a CONTINUOUS LTYP. Using the same procedure as listed in Figure 15–9, assign Layer First-Floor as the current layer.

REMEMBER: The current layer Name (the first eight letters) is usually displayed at the left end of the status line prefixed by L or Layer.

Draw an inscribed polygon of six sides, with the Center located at 4,5, and a Radius of 2 units. The polygon should be blue and the Ltype is *dashed*.

Set the Second-Floor as the current layer. Draw a four-sided polygon whose edges are 4 units long, Starting at 2,3. The resulting drawing should be in green and the Ltype is *hidden*. The three drawings are displayed on the screen.

Set the Roof layer as the current layer. Draw a triangle, starting from 2,3 to 6,3 to 4,7, and close. The triangle should be in white and use a *border* Ltype. Figure 15–14 shows the drawings of the four layers. (Although the display is black and white, the Ltype defines the layers for each drawing.)

Example 15–3: This example demonstrates the use of the ON, OFF, Freeze, and Thaw modes. Explode the square and hexagon. Remember, if you can see the drawing, it is possible to modify a drawing located on another Layer that is ON. Erase the base of the hexagon. The Coordinates of the hexagon base are 3,3.2679 to 5,3.2679. Use the U command to replace the hexagon base. Now, using the Layer OFF option, change Layer First-Floor to OFF. The Command Sequence is shown in Figure 15–15.

Freeze Layer 0 and First-Floor. (Use the sequence shown in Figure 15–15, except replace OFF with Freeze.) When the prompt asks for the layer(s) Name, type 0, First-Floor, and (R). The circle and hexagon are no longer visible. They are still part of the drawing but will not be regenerated when the drawing or command calls for the

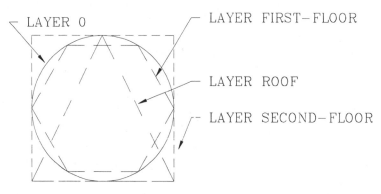

Figure 15–14 Solution to Example 15–1

```
Command: LAYER ?/Make/Set/New/ON/OFF/Color/Ltype/Freeze?Thaw:  OFF
Layer name(s) to turn off:  First-Floor
```

Figure 15–15 Command Sequence for the LAYER Command—OFF Option

automatic regeneration. Usually, those layers that contain text, hatch, or dimensions will slow down the regeneration time. Therefore, if the layer(s) is frozen, the program bypasses these layers and the Regen time is much faster. Now check the Layer Directory by using the LAYER command and ? plus two (R)s. The directory should read that Layers 0 and First-Floor are Frozen, Layer Second-Floor is ON, and Layer Roof is the current layer.

The hexagon has disappeared. Although the hexagon is not visible, we have the Coordinates of the base. Pick the ERASE command and input the Coordinates (3,3.2679 and 5,3.2679). Upon completion of the ERASE command, place Layer First-Floor ON (same sequence as the OFF option shown in Figure 15–15 but replace OFF with ON). The baseline is still there. The ERASE command has no effect on the hexagon baseline.

Freeze Layer First-Floor. The hexagon should not be visible. The Layer Directory should read that Layers 0 and First-Floor are Frozen, Layer Second-Floor is ON, and Layer Roof is the current layer. The Freeze option removes the layer from an active role in the drawing. In actual practice, the TEXT, HATCH, and DIMENSIONS commands would be located on their own layers and would be the last items to be completed. To bring the Frozen layers back, use the Command Sequence shown in Figure 15–15 but replace OFF with Thaw. Automatically, the FROZEN layers will return to the screen as an ON layer. The Layer Directory should show that Layers 0, First-Floor, and Second-Floor are ON and that Layer Roof is the current layer. Save this drawing because it will be used for further applications.

15.2 LINETYPE Command

The LINETYPE command is used to store the linetype patterns (library) and load the linetypes into any specified drawing, as well as assist the operator in creating new linetypes. We will restrict our work to the loading procedures from the library to the drawing. The LINETYPE command is listed in the Settings Submenu and is shown in Figure 15–16. The LINETYPE command may be used on a line, arc, circle, and polyline. All other entities are restricted to the CONTINUOUS line.

The Command Sequence is listed in Figure 15–17.

A directory or listing of the available linetypes may be obtained by the use of the ? symbol. Figure 15–3 shows the available linetype patterns and names for each pattern. The Linetype option Set allows the operator to bring up the requested linetype for all new entities. AutoCAD will search its files for the requested linetype. If the linetype has not been loaded into the drawing, the prompt will show "Linetype (name) not found". Use the Load option to load it. To load any of the standard linetypes, select Load from the Screen Menu or input from the keyboard. The prompt

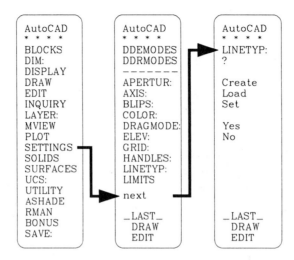

Figure 15-16 Menu Map for the LINETYPE Command.

```
Command: LINETYPE
?/Create/Load/Set: Load
Linetype(s) to load: Hidden
File to search <ACAD>: (R)
Linetype Hidden Loaded.
```

Figure 15-17 Command Sequence for the LINETYPE Command

will ask you from which file. Use the default file <ACAD>. The loading of the specific linetype will require one of three specific replies (BYLAYER, BYBLOCK, or ?). The BYLAYER reply will change the linetype selected for the specific layer being used. The BYBLOCK reply automatically makes the linetype CONTINUOUS until the block is completed. When a block is inserted into a specific layer, the block will then assume the linetype of that layer.

15.3 LTSCALE Command

The LTSCALE command (Scale Factor for linetypes) controls the length of the dash used in the LINETYPE command. This command will set the Scale Factor for all linetypes used in a given drawing. The LTSCALE command is located in the Settings Submenu as shown in Figure 15-18. The Command Sequence is listed in Figure 15-19.

Example 15-4: Start a new drawing called LTSCALE. Assign the color yellow and linetype Hidden to Layer 0. Draw a line from 3,5 to 8,5. Count the number of dashes in the line (14). Pick the LTSCALE command from the Settings Submenu. Use 2 as the Scale Factor. Again, count the number of dashes (7). Change the Scale Factor to 0.5 and count the dashes (28). Quit the drawing.

Example 15-5: Bring up the existing drawing called LAYER. Make Layer First-

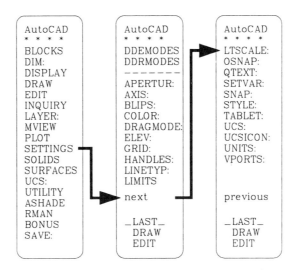

Figure 15–18 Menu Map for the LTSCALE Command

Command: LTSCALE New scale factor <1.0000>: 0.5

Figure 15–19 Command Sequence for the LTSCALE Command

Floor the current layer (Set option) and turn off all other layers. Change the Scale Factor for the linetypes to 2. The dashes used in the polygon are twice as long as before. Turn all layers ON. Notice that all linetypes using a dash have been changed to double size.

Another application of the LTSCALE command deals with the size of the dashes when the upper limit of the drawing is changed. The default or present LTSCALE value is 1. This setting assumes that the drawing limits will be 0",0" for the lower limit and 12", 9" for the upper limit. If the upper limits were changed to 12' (144"), 9' (108"), the linetype dashes would not be recognizable (because of the change in limits). The LTSCALE value must be changed to compensate for the change of limits. The new LTSCALE value will be the value of the ratio of the X value of the new limit divided by the X value of the prior limit. For example: A drawing calls for upper limits of 12',9'. The ratio would be 144"/12" or 12. Pick the LTSCALE command from the Settings Submenu and change the value from 1 to 12. Now when an entity is drawn (using dashes), the resulting Ltype will have the proper appearance. If the limits are reduced, then the LTSCALE must also be reduced in like manner.

REMEMBER: The LTSCALE command effects all the linetypes used in the drawing.

15.4 PURGE Command

Blocks, Linetypes, Layers, Shapes, and Styles that are specified for a drawing but are not needed will add to the drawing memory. In order to conserve disk space (either hard or floppy disk) AutoCAD has provided the PURGE command. To be effective, the PURGE command must be the *first* command used on a drawing. The PURGE command is found in the UTILITY Submenu and is shown in Figure 15–20. The Command Sequence is listed in Figure 15–21.

The keyword in this command is "unused". If a Layer, Block, Linetype, Shape, or Style has been specified for a given drawing, but does not contain any entities, the Layer, Block, Linetype, Shape, or Style is considered "unused". This is demonstrated in the following example.

Example 15–6: Start a new drawing called PURGE. Establish five layers (0, 1, 2, 3, 4) and select whatever colors you wish for each layer. Set Layer 2 and draw a line from 2,2 to 7,7. Check the Layer Directory for the established layers. End the drawing. Bring the drawing back using Menu option 2 (Edit an EXISTING drawing). Select PURGE from the Settings Submenu and input ALL. (All Layers, Blocks, Linetypes, Shapes, and Styles will be reviewed by AutoCAD to be purged.) AutoCAD will list all the unused layers one at a time: "Purge layer 1? (N):". Reply with Y for YES. Notice that Layer 2 is not listed. (There is an entity on that Layer.) The final prompt will read "No unreferenced Blocks, Linetypes, Shapes, and Styles found". Bring up the Layer Directory to see what Layers are available. The directory should list Layer 0 and Layer 2. Layer 0 cannot be Purged.

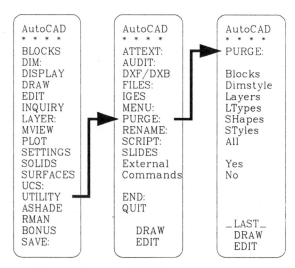

Figure 15–20 Menu Map for the PURGE Command

```
Command: PURGE
Purge unused Blocks/LAyers/LTypes/SHapes/Styles/All:  All
```

Figure 15–21 Command Sequence for the PURGE Command

15.4.1 Purge of Blocks

A Reference Block may be purged if it is no longer required for the drawing. The procedure to be used is: (1) Erase the block; (2) End the drawing (ending the drawing makes the Reference block an UNREFERENCE block); (3) Bring back the drawing and pick the PURGE command as the first command of the drawing; (4) Type or select ALL from the Screen Menu in response to the PURGE command prompt; and (5) When the Block name appears, answer with Y or YES to purge the block.

15.5 CHANGE B Command

Paragraph 11.1 of this text details the CHANGE command as related to the Change Point (CHANGE A) option. The second CHANGE command (CHANGE B) provides for changes to entity properties such as Color, Layer, Linetypes, Elevation, and Thickness. The CHANGE commands for Elevation and Thickness are associated with the 3D commands and are not discussed in this text. The operator may choose between two commands that will change the entity property: CHANGE or CHPROP (CHange PROPerties). The CHANGE command provides either the option to Change Point (CHANGE A or B) or Change Properties, while the CHPROP command (CHANGE B) is restricted to Change Properties. The CHANGE command is described in Chapter 11. The CHPROP is described below. The CHPROP command is found in the EDIT Submenu and is shown in Figure 15–22.

The Command Sequences for the CHPROP in Color, Layer, or Ltype commands are discussed in detail in paragraphs 15.5.1, 15.5.2, and 15.5.3. The initial sequence is the same for the three modes of operation and is listed in Figure 15–23.

Figure 15–23 lists the standard object selection procedure used for most of the commands listed in the EDIT Submenu. Select the object(s) and then confirm the selection.

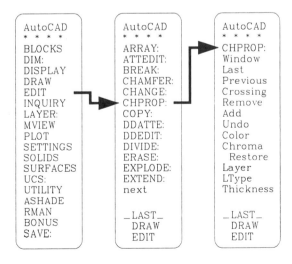

Figure 15–22   Menu Map for the CHPROP Command

```
Command: CHPROP:
Select objects:    Select objects: 1 selected, 1 found.
Change what properties (Color/Layer/LType/Thickness)?:  C
New color <BYLAYER>:  RED
Change what properties (Color/LAyer/LType/thickness)?:  (R)
```

Figure 15–23 Command Sequence for the CHPROP Command—Color Change

15.5.1 CHPROP Command—Color

The CHPROP command, Color may be used in one of three options:

1. Change the entity color.
2. Change the entity color for a specified layer color (BYLAYER).
3. Change the block color to the layer color (BYBLOCK).

15.5.1.1 CHPROP in Entity Color

After the object(s) has been selected and confirmed, select COLOR from the Screen Menu. This will automatically bring up the COLOR Command Menu that is located in the Settings Submenu. Select the required color from the menu (Figure 15–24) and the entity color will change.

If the keyboard is used, the Command Sequence is shown in Figure 15–25. After the selection and confirmation process has been completed, key in P (for Properties, then C for Color). The prompt "New color <BYLAYER>:" must be answered with the new color and *not* a layer Name.

Bring back the drawing called LAYER. Set Layer 0 as the current layer (red circle). Using the CHPROP command, Color, change the circle color to yellow. Pick the CHPROP command from the EDIT Submenu, select and confirm the circle as the

Figure 15–24 COLOR Menu Map for the CHPROP Command—Entity Color

```
Command : COLOR
New entity color <BYLAYER>: RED
```

Figure 15–25 Command Sequence for CHPROP Color—Keyboard Input

object to be changed. Pick COLOR from the Screen Menu, and select yellow from the Color Menu. The circle is now yellow. Follow the same procedure but use the keyboard input to change the color to blue.

15.5.1.2 *CHPROP Entity Color to Layer Color*

The procedure to CHPROP the Entity color to Layer color is similar to the method used in 15.5.1.1 with the exception of substituting BYLAYER and the layer Name for the color. The drawing called LAYER is still on the screen. Change the blue circle to red by using the BYLAYER method. Select and confirm that the circle is the object to be changed. Select BYLAYER from the Color Menu and depress the ENTER key twice. The entity will take on the color of the Layer that is Set. The circle is now red.

15.5.1.3 *CHPROP Entity Color to Block Color*

Follow the procedure as outlined in paragraph 15.5.1.2 with the exception of replacing BYLAYER with BYBLOCK.

15.5.2 CHPROP in Entity Linetype

The change in entity Linetype follows the same procedure as the CHPROP in Entity color. Select the object(s) and confirm the selection. Using the Screen Menu, pick LTYPE and the Screen Menu will change to the LTYPE menu (located in the Settings Submenu) which is shown in Figure 15–26. Figure 15–3 lists the standard LTYPE

```
AutoCAD
* * * *
LTYPE

bylayer
byblock

contin.
dashed
hidden
center
phantom
dot
dashdot
border
divide

_LAST_
DRAW
EDIT
```

Figure 15–26 Menu Map for the LINETYPE Command

```
Command: CHPROP
Select objects: 1 selected, 1 found
Select objects: R
Change what property (Color/Layer/LType/Thickness) ?:  LT
New linetype <bylayer>: Hidden
Change what property (Color/Layer/LType/Thickness) ?:  (R)
```

Figure 15–27   Command Sequence—Keyboard Input

options that are part of the AutoCAD program. The drawing will take on the new linetype upon completion of the command. If the keyboard is used, refer to the procedure detailed in paragraph 15.5.1.1 but replace Color by Linetype.

The drawing called LAYER is on the screen. Set Layer 0 as the current layer. Turn all other layers to OFF. Using the Screen Menu, select and confirm the circle as the object to be changed. Pick LTYPE from the Screen Menu. Note the new Linetype Menu (Figure 15–26).

Pick Dashed from the Screen Menu. The circle has the Dashed linetype. If the keyboard is used, select and confirm the circle as the object to change. Then key in P for Properties and then Ltype. Type in the Ltype name and (R). Figure 15–27 lists the Command Sequence for the keyboard input.

The CHPROP BYLAYER and CHPROP BYBLOCK will follow the same type of sequence as used in the Color Change.

15.5.3   CHPROP in LAYER Command

After the initial selection and confirmation of the object(s) have been completed, pick Layer from the Screen Menu. The prompt will ask "New layer <0>:". The name shown in <> is the layer that is current or Set. Input the new Layer name and (R). The drawing will disappear from the screen momentarily and return. When the drawing returns, its appearance will have the layer's color and linetype. For keyboard input, after the selection process has been completed, input P for Properties and then Layer. Reply with the new layer Name and (R). The drawing will disappear and reappear with the new layer's color and linetype. On your screen is the circle in red with a Continuous Linetype. Select and confirm the circle selection. Pick Layer; reply to the prompt with First-Floor and (R). The circle will disappear. (Layer First-Floor is OFF.) Using the LAYER command, turn Layer First-Floor ON. The circle should appear in blue with a Dashed linetype.

15.4   RENAME Command

The RENAME command permits the operator to rename the following items: Block, LAyer, LType, Style, or View. This command is listed in the Utilities Submenu and is shown in Figure 15–28.

The Command Sequence is shown in Figure 15–29.

The initial response to the RENAME command must be a choice of one of the following: Block, LAyer, LType, Style, or View. You may use either the complete word or capital letters (shown above). After you have selected what you want to change,

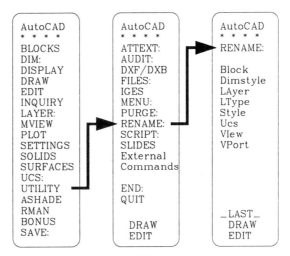

Figure 15–28 Menu Map for the RENAME Command

```
Command:  RENAME  Block/LAyer/LType/Style/View:  B
Old  block  name:  notebk1
New  block  name:  notebk2
```

Figure 15–29 Command Sequence for the RENAME Command

input the current name and (R), then the new name and (R). Certain names cannot be changed. For example: Layer 0 will always remain Layer 0; the Continuous Ltype will always carry the same name.

15.5 Pull Down Menu for Chapter 15

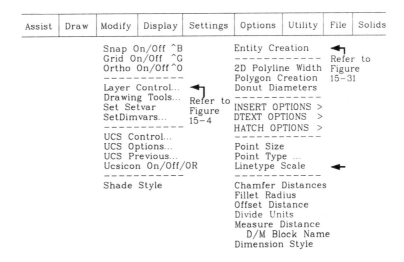

Figure 15–30 Pull Down Menu for Chapter 15

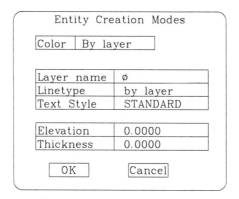

Figure 15–31   Dialogue Box for Entity Creation Menu

15.6 Template Reference—Chapter 15

Figure 15–32 highlights those Template areas for the commands described in this chapter. Note that PURGE is not displayed on the Template.

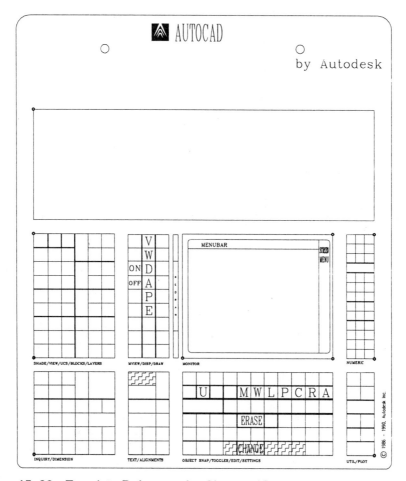

Figure 15–32   Template Reference for Chapter 15

COMMAND SUMMARY

LAYER	CHPROP IN COLOR
PURGE	CHPROP IN LTYPE
RENAME	CHPROP IN LAYER
LTYPE	LTSCALE

GLOSSARY

Set: To establish which layer will be current.

Freeze: An option that does not allow information contained in a particular layer to be updated. This permits the regeneration of the drawing to occur at a faster rate.

Thaw: A command that removes the layer from the frozen state to the ON state.

Ltype: A shorthand label for the LINETYPE command.

Color: Assigned to a layer for ease of identifying the drawing on that layer.

Properties: Used in the CHPROP command which designates that the change will deal with color, Ltype, or layer.

PROBLEMS

1. Is it possible to change the linetype of Layer 0?
2. The name of a layer (ASSY2) is incorrect. The correct name should be INSERT 3. List the steps required to make the change.
3. What is the correct procedure to purge a layer?
4. Explain the procedure required to make a change on that layer that has been Frozen. Assume Layer 4 has been Frozen.

16 Standard Dimensioning Commands and Options

Instructional Objectives

1. To be able to define the special terms used in the Dimensioning command
2. To be able to set the Dimension variables for any given drawing assignment
3. To be able to change any of the Dimensioning Default values
4. To understand the difference between DIM: and DIM1: commands
5. To be able to use the five major Dimensioning commands
6. To be able to apply the Dimension Utility commands
7. To be able to use the AutoCAD DIMENSIONING "semi-automatic" and the "automatic" options for LINEAR Dimensioning
8. To be able to apply either the Baseline or Continue Dimensioning modes

16.1 Definitions of the Dimensioning Terms and Variables

Before proceeding with the details of the Dimensioning commands, AutoCAD makes use of a number of special terms in the command prompts and Screen Menus. These terms are defined and listed below.

Dimension Line A line with arrows (or tick marks) at either end, drawn at the angle at which the dimensioning has been measured. See Figure 16–1.

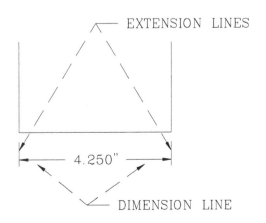

Figure 16–1 Dimension Lines used in Linear Measurements

213

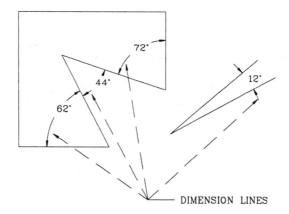

Figure 16–2 Dimension Lines used in Angular Measurements

The Dimension Lines for Angular Measurement are shown in Figure 16–2. When the text cannot be placed between theAarrowheads or Tick Marks, the text is placed on the side of the last object picked.

Depending upon the drawing requirements, the measurement value may either be located at the Center of the Dimension Lines or at the top of the Dimension Lines.

Arrowheads or Tick Marks The selection of Arrowheads or Tick Marks depends upon the industry's drafting standards. In general, individuals in the engineering profession use the Arrowheads while architects usually use Tick Marks. Arrowheads are shown in Figures 16–1 and 16–2, and Tick Marks in Figure 16–3. The Arrowhead size is governed by the Dimension Variable (Dim Var) called DIMASZ, whereas the size of the Tick Mark is governed by the value of DIMTSZ.

Extension Lines Lines drawn to show the two endpoints of the entity to be measured.

Dimension Text The textstring that contains the distance or angular value or other related data. AutoCAD calculates the distance which is shown in the prompt as

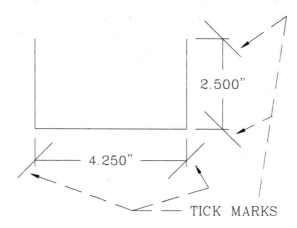

Figure 16–3 Examples of Tick Marks

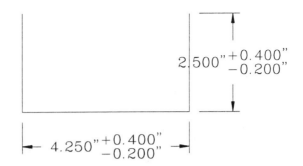

Figure 16–4 Examples of Dimensioning Tolerance.

"<value>:". The operator may either accept the value by (R) or input another value. The STYLE of the text is the current STYLE of the drawing. The height of the text is governed by the Dim Var called DIMTXT (if the height value in the STYLE option = 0).

Tolerance Defines the limits of a given entity. The limits may be specified as a numerical value (+.01"–.005") or the actual limits of the line. Figure 16–4 illustrates these alternatives. The Dim Vars for the Tolerance are DIMTP, DIMTM, and DIMTOL. (See paragraph 16.10.2 for definitions.) The Dim Var for limits is DIMLIM.

Alternate Units Inch and/or Metric units may be used by inputting the proper value for Dim Vars: DIMALT, DIMALTF, and DIMALTD. The Alternative unit may either be inches or metric and the value will appear in [] of the Dimensioned Text. Those illustrations with Dimensioned lines, radii, or diameter of arcs or circles will either be in units (if the inch mark is not used) or in inches. Generally, inch or feet/inch marks are used in Dimensioned drawings.

Leaders are lines that point to a selected item. The Leader may be used for notes or labels that appear on the drawing. When Dimensioned Text cannot fit inside the Dimensioned Line for Diameter, Radius, or Angular Measurement, the prompt will ask for the location of the text through the use of a Leader.

Center Mark or Center Lines Cross hairs [or a Plus (+) sign] are used to locate and mark the Center of a circle or arc. The Center Lines are extensions of the Center Mark. Figure 16–5(a) illustrates the Center Mark and Figure 16–5(b), the Center Lines. The Dim Var for these functions is DIMCEN. If a negative value of DIMCEN is used, Center Lines appear. When the positive value of DIMCEN is used, only the Center Mark appears.

NOTE:
1. Dimension lines, text, extension lines, arrowheads, tick marks, leader lines, and text are considered separate entities.
2. The dimensioned data take on the color and linetype of the Set or current layer.
3. Except for minor dimensioning tasks, a separate layer is used for all dimensioning efforts. This enables the operator to Freeze the Layer after the dimensioning effort has been completed.

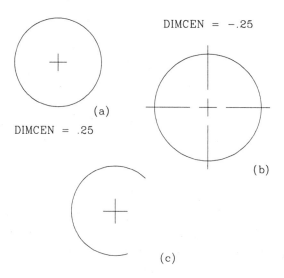

Figure 16–5 Examples of Center Marks and Center Lines.

16.2 Dimensioning Program

The Dimensioning command (DIM) is listed on the Main Screen Menu. The initial submenu provides six additional menus as shown in Figure 16–6.

16.2.1 Dimension Command Organization

AutoCAD treats dimensioning as an independent program. The DIM1: command allows the operator to make a single DIMENSIONING command before the system returns the standard AutoCAD program. The DIM: Command is used for two or more DIMENSIONING commands. To exit the DIM command, the operator may use the following commands: EXIT, DRAW, EDIT, or ^C.

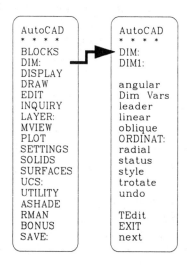

Figure 16–6 Menu Map for the DIMENSIONING Command

16.3 Dimension Commands

The Dimension commands are divided into four options:

Linear Dimension options
Angular Dimension option
Radial Dimensioning option
Utility option

16.3.1 Linear Dimensioning Option

The Linear Dimensioning option provides for four modes of measurements:

Horizontal Measurements mode
Vertical Measurements mode
Aligned Measurements mode
Rotated Measurements mode

These modes may either be selected from the Screen Menu as shown in Figure 16–6 or keyed in from the keyboard. If the keyboard is used, then the first three letters of each option is sufficient to invoke the mode (HOR, VER, ALI, or ROT).

> **CAUTION:** Although the operator can see the points to be measured, the actual coordinate values are resident within the drawing memory. OSNAP commands (* * * *) should be used to insure accurate dimensioning.

Example 16–1(a): Start a new drawing called DIMS. Set the units for engineering and 3 decimal places, Angular to decimal and zero decimal place. Draw a six-sided polygon, using the Edge method, Starting at 3",3" with an Edge length of 3". Establish a second Layer called TEXT. Label the corners (inside the polygon) of the polygon as follows: Pt A near 3",3"; Pt B near 6",3". Label the remaining corners in a CCW direction. Place the labels on Layer Text. The polygon and the lettering are shown in Figure 16–7. This drawing will be used to illustrate the Linear Dimensioning modes.

16.3.1.1 Horizontal (HOR) Dimensioning Option

This command is located by selecting Linear from the DIM: Submenu. Then pick horiz (HOR) as shown in Figure 16–8.
The Command Sequence is listed in Figure 16–9.

Example 16–1(b): We want to measure the horizontal distance between Pt A and Pt B located in Figure 16–7 [initial drawing for Example 16–1(a)]. Set Layer 0. Pick DIM: from the Main Screen Menu; then Linear; then horiz. Using OSNAP (INT), pick Pt A and then Pt B. The Dimension Line location is at 4.5,2. The Dimension text will show a numerical value of 3.000". Press ENTER and the value, dimension lines and arrowheads will appear on the drawing at a selected location. Now dimension Pts

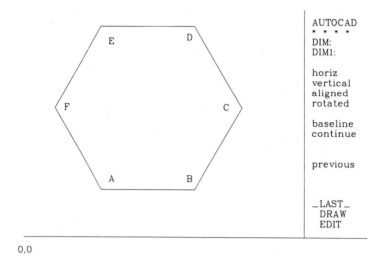

Figure 16-7   Initial Drawing for Example 16-1(a)

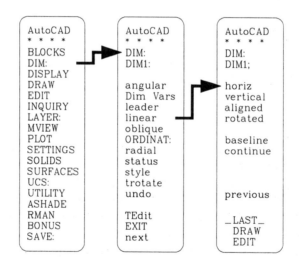

Figure 16-8   Menu Map for the HORIZONTAL Dimensioning Command

```
Command: DIM
DIM: horiz
First extension line origin or RETURN to select:
Second extension line origin:
Dimension line location
Dimension text <1.234>:
```

Figure 16-9   Command Sequence for the HORIZONTAL Dimensioning Option

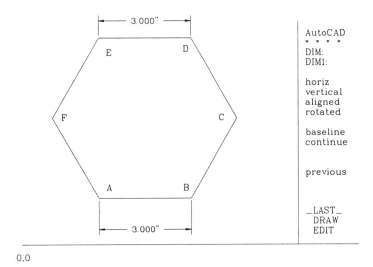

Figure 16-10 Solution to Example 16-1(b)

D and E (use OSNAP and pick a suitable location for the Dimension Line). The solution is shown in Figure 16-10.

16.3.1.2 Vertical (VER) Dimensioning Option

The Vertical option sequence is similar to the Horizontal sequence except for the name.

Example 16-1(c): Using the drawing DIMS (Figure 16-7), select the Vertical option (VER) and measure the vertical distance between Pt B and Pt C. Pick a suitable location for the Dimension Line. Repeat the sequence for Pts A and F. The solution is shown in Figure 16-11.

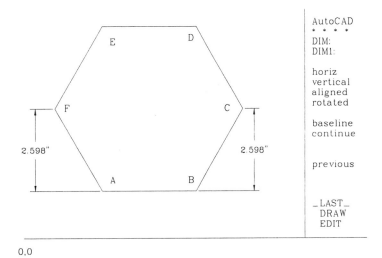

Figure 16-11 Solution to Example 16-1(c)

16.3.1.3 Align Dimensioning (ALI) Option

The Align option measures the distance between two points that are drawn on an angle as compared to the HOR option which measures the horizontal distance between two points or the VER option which measures distance in the vertical plane. The option Command Sequence is similar to the HOR or VER commands.

Example 16–1(d): Substitute ALI for either HOR or VER to develop the distance value. The drawing DIMS is on the screen. Using the ALI Command, measure the distances between Pts D and C as well as the distances between Pts A and F. Figure 16–12 reflects the solution to Example 16–1(d) (ALI Dimensioning problem).

16.3.1.4 Rotated Dimension (ROT) Option

The Rotated option is the least used dimensioning option. It provides the measurement of the Linear distance, where the measurement points are at a specified angular displacement. The Command Sequence is similar to the other Linear options with the exception of the first prompt which asks for a Rotated Dimension Angle. The Command Sequence is listed in Figure 16–13.

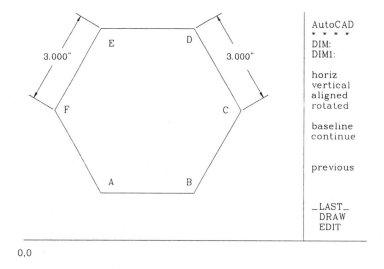

Figure 16–12 Solution to Example 16–1(d)

```
Command:  DIM
Dim:  rotated dimension line angle <0>:  (R)
First extension line origin or RETURN to select:  line AB
Second extension line origin:
Dimension line location:
Dimension text <value>:
```

Figure 16–13 Command Sequence for the Rotated Dimension Option

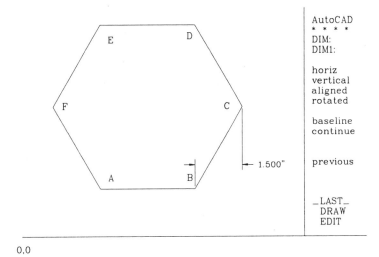

Figure 16–14 Solution to Example 16–1(e)

Example 16–1(e): The data shown in Figure 16–13 refer to the drawing DIMS and the polygon. The solution to this Example is shown in Figure 16–14.

16.3.1.5 Baseline (BASE) Mode

The examples developed in prior dimensioning problems are considered the measurement of a single entity. The dimensioning of a drawing using a single reference point or datum line is called the "Baseline" mode. This mode is selected after the first measurement has been completed. The location of the Baseline (BASE) subcommand is shown in Figure 16–15. The Command Sequence for the example is listed in Figure 16–16. Select the datum or reference point for the drawing and the endpoint of a specific line. Follow the command prompt questions. After the dimen-

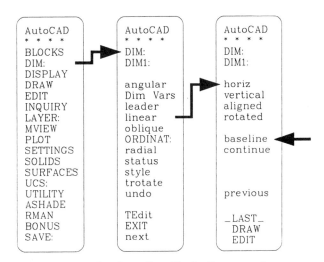

Figure 16–15 Menu Map for the Baseline Mode Command

```
Command: DIM
Dim: horiz
First extension line origin or RETURN to select: Pt A
Second extension line origin: Pt B
Dimension line location: 4",4.5"
Dimension text<1.625">: (R)
Dim: BASELINE
Second extension line origin: Pt C
Dimension text<3.250">: (R)
Dim: BASELINE
Second extension line origin: Pt D
Dimension text<5.000">: (R)
```

Figure 16–16   Command Sequence for the Baseline Example

sions appear on the drawing, select baseline. Pick the endpoint of the second line. The computer will complete the command and place the dimension above the first dimension. Select the next endpoint or intersection and continue until the dimensioning (either HOR or VER) task has been completed.

Example 16–2(a): End the previous drawing and start a new drawing called DIMOPTS. This drawing will require three layers (layer Names: 0, Baseline, Continue). Layer Baseline will be red. Layer Continue will be green. Linetypes (Ltypes) will be Continuous for all three layers. Draw the following figure on Layer 0: Draw a continuous line from 3,2; 8,2; 8,2.625; 6.25,2.625; 6.25,3.5; 4.625,3.5; 4.625,4; 3,4 and close. Label 3,4 as Pt A; 4.625,3.5 as Pt B; 6.25,3.5 as Pt C; and 8,2.625 as Pt D. Place labels (Simplex font, 0.2 height below each line). Change the current layer to Baseline using the Set command. Follow the Command Sequence listed in Figure 16–16.

The solution to Example 16–2(a) is shown in Figure 16–17. Note that the reference or datum point is located at Pt A.

16.3.1.6   Continue (CONT) Mode

The alternative for the Baseline option is the Continue (CONT) mode, where the dimensions are given for each dimensioned entity. The Menu Map for the Continue

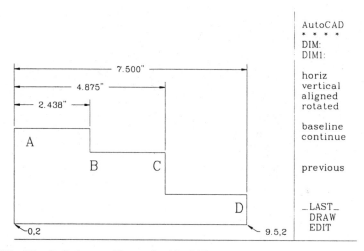

Figure 16–17   Solution to Example 16–2(a)

```
Command:  DIM:
Dim:  horiz
First  extension  line  origin  or  RETURN  to  select:  Pt  A
Second  extension  line  origin:  Pt  B
Dimension  line  location:  4",4.5"
Dimension  text  <1.625">:  (R)
Dim:  CONTINUE
Second  extension  line  origin:  Pt  C
Dimension  text  <1.625">:  (R)
Dim:  CONTINUE
Second  extension  line  origin:  Pt  D
Dimension  text  <1.750">:  (R)
```

Figure 16–18 Command Sequence for the Continue Mode

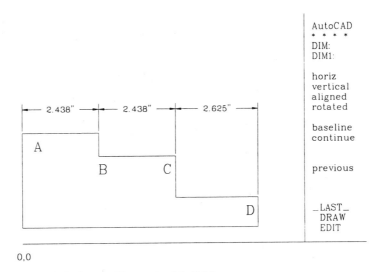

Figure 16–19 Solution to Example 16–2(b)

mode is the same as that shown for the Baseline mode (Figure 16–15) with the exception of using Continue instead of Baseline.

Example 16–2(b): The Command Sequence for the Continue mode example is listed in Figure 16–18. The drawing is shown in Figure 16–19.

NOTE: The Baseline and Continue modes are *only* used with the Horizontal and Vertical Dimensioning modes.

16.4 Dimensioning Shortcut

AutoCAD remembers every command and the location of every point used in a drawing. Note that the first line of the Command Sequence for the HOR, VER, or ALI options will call out as a part the prompt "First extension line origin or RETURN to select". We have used the first part of the prompt in prior exercises. If (R) is used,

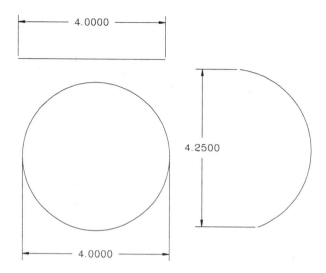

Figure 16-20 Solution to Example 16-3

we have another prompt: "Select line, arc, or circle." The operator's task has been simplified in that the entity, not the two endpoints (to be measured), is selected. After the entity has been selected, the prompt will ask for the location of the Dimensioned Text. Although this method is a short cut, it can only be used effectively with single entity measurements and not the Baseline or Continue modes.

Example 16-3: End the current drawing and bring up a new drawing called SHORT-CUT. Draw a line from 3,625 to 7,625; a circle whose Center is 5.125,3.625 and whose Radius is 2; 3P arc: 9,6; 10.5,5.125; and 9.5,1.75. Select the DIM: command; Linear and HOR option. Use the "RETURN and select line, arc or circle" and pick the line. Place the Dimension Text at 5,7.25. Repeat the sequence for the VER measurement of the arc with the text at 8,4. Complete the example with the HOR measurement of the circle and locate the text at 5,1. The solution to the example is shown in Figure 16-20.

16.5 Angular (ANG) Dimensioning Option

The Angular Dimensioning option is located on the DIM: Submenu as shown in Figure 16-21 and the Command Sequence is listed in Figure 16-22.

The purpose of this command is to measure the angular displacement between two nonparallel lines.

Example 16-4: End the existing drawing. Start a new drawing called ANGULAR. Draw two lines: 3,2; 6,2; 5,7. Measure the included angle. Refer to the Command Sequence (Figure 16-22): Select DIM: Angular and pick the line 3,2; 6,2; now pick the other line. Enter the location of the Angular Measurement text at 4.5,3.5; use the same location for the Dimensioned Text (79°). Now repeat the exercise but choose line 6,2; 5,7 first. Use 7.5,3.5 as the dimension and arrow location. The angular displacement is 101°. Figure 16-23 is the solution to this example.

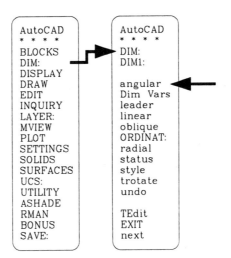

Figure 16–21 Menu Map for the Angular Measurement Option

```
Command: DIM
Dim: angular
Select arc, circle, line, or RETURN:
Enter dimension line arc location:
Dimension text <270>:
Enter text location:
```

Figure 16–22 Command Sequence for the Angular Dimension Option

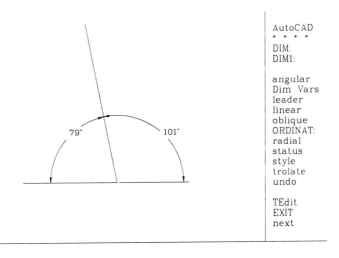

Figure 16–23 Solution to Example 16–4

16.6 Radial Measurements

The Dimension commands Diameter and Radius are located in the Radial Submenu as shown in Figure 16–24.

16.6.1 Diameter (DIAM) Dimension Option

AutoCAD has a semi-automatic Diameter Dimensioning Option mode that permits the operator to pick any part of a circle or arc circumference and AutoCAD will compute the numerical value. The location of this command is shown in Figure 16–24, and the Command Sequence is shown in Figure 16–25.

After the DIM:, diameter, and the arc or circle have been selected, AutoCAD will calculate the diameter and show the value as a default number. The operator may either select the default value by (R) or input any other text. The symbol φ replaces the word diameter on the drawing.

Example 16–5: End the drawing on the screen and bring back drawing SHORTCUT. Erase all Dimensioned Lines and data. Determine the Diameter of the circle and the arc. The solution is shown in Figure 16–26. Note the automatic extension of the arc for the Diameter placement.

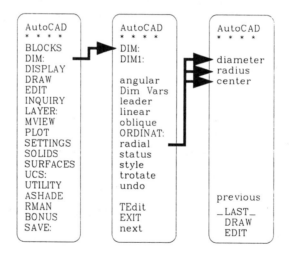

Figure 16–24 Menu Map for the Radial Subcommands

```
Command: DIM
Dim: diameter Select arc or circle
Dimension text <1.2345>:
Enter leader length for text:
```

Figure 16–25 Command Sequence for the Diameter Dimensioning Option

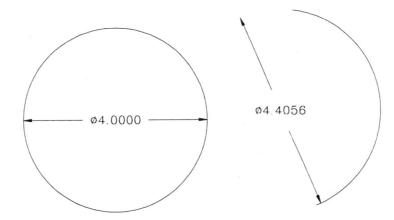

Figure 16–26 Solution to Example 16–5

16.6.2 Radius (RAD) Dimension Option

The Radius Dimension option is located in the DIM: Submenus and is shown in Figure 16–24. The Command Sequence for this command is listed in Figure 16–27.

Example 16–6: Use the same drawing (SHORTCUT). Erase all Dimension Lines, straight lines, and textstrings. Select: DIM:; Radius; and pick the circle. The default value of the Radius is 2.000. Repeat the Command Sequence, but this time pick the arc. The default value of the Radius is 2.2028. The capital R represents the Radius in the same fashion as the ϕ represents the Diameter. The solution is shown in Figure 16–28.

16.6.3 Placement of Diameter/Radius Information

The placement of the Diameter or Radius measurement data depends upon the settings of the following Dim Vars: DIMCEN, DIMTIX, and DIMTOFL. Figure 16–29 defines the status of the particular Dim Var and the placement of the Diameter/Radius information.

```
Command: DIM
Dim: radius Select arc or circle:
Dimension text <1.2345>:
Enter leader length for text:
```

Figure 16–27 Command Sequence for the Radius Dimension Command

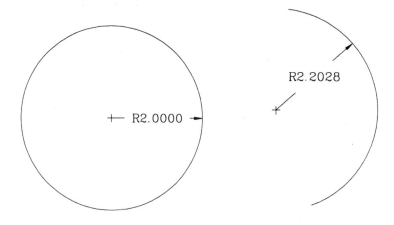

Figure 16–28 Solution to Example 16–6

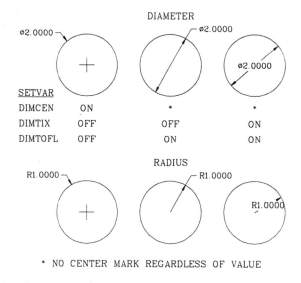

Figure 16–29 Placement of Diameter/Radius Information

16.7 Dimension Utilities Option and Command

The operator has seven Dimension Utilities options and commands that may be used separately (in nondimension tasks) or as part of the dimensioned drawing:

CENTER	LEADER	STATUS	UNDO
EXIT	REDRAW	style	

REDRAW, UNDO, and STYLE commands perform the same functions as in the non-

DIM: commands. These commands (except for the CENTER command) are listed in Figure 16–6. The Center command is shown in Figure 16–24.

16.7.1 Center Option

The Center option will draw the Center Mark (+) or Center Lines of either a circle or an arc. The command is found in the DIM: Submenu. (See Figure 16–24.) The Command Sequence is shown in Figure 16–30.

The selection of Center mark or Center Lines and the size of the lines are controlled by another command called DIMCEN. DIMCEN may take one of three values:

If DIMCEN = 0; No Center Marks or Lines
If DIMCEN = + value; Center Marks whose length are equal
        to the numerical value
If DIMCEN = –value; Center Lines whose length are equal to
        the numerical value

NOTE: The Dim Vars variables, DIMTIX and DIMTOFL control the appearance of the Center Mark and Lines. If either variable is on, the Center Mark will not appear.

Example 16–7: End the existing drawing. To demonstrate the CENTER command, start a new drawing called CENTER. Draw two circles: Circle 1: Center at 2.625,6.25; Radius = 1.25; Circle 2: Center at 7,6.25; Radius = 2.125. Draw an SCA arc: Start point = 3,4.5; Center point = 3,3.125; Angle = 285°. Select DIM:, Dim Vars (shown in Figure 16–31), and DIMCEN. Set DIMCEN to 0.25.

Select Center and pick Circle 1. The Cross Marks (0.25 units in both directions) will appear at the Center of the circle. Repeat the variable command setting procedure for DIMCEN but set the value to 0. Return to the CENTER command and pick the arc. Since DIMCEN = 0, there will be no Cross Marks. Repeat the Dim Vars setting procedure for DIMCEN. Set the value = -0.25 units. Pick Circle 2. Cross Lines will appear. These Center Marks and Center Lines are shown in Figure 16–32.

16.7.2 EXIT Command

The EXIT command is listed in the same DIM: Submenu as shown in Figure 16–6. This command is one of four commands that permit the operator to leave the DIM: program. ^C, DRAW, and EDIT are the other three commands. To leave the DIM: program, pick EXIT. AutoCAD automatically returns to the Main Screen Menu.

```
Command: DIM
Dim: center Select arc or circle
```

Figure 16–30 Command Sequence for the Center Option

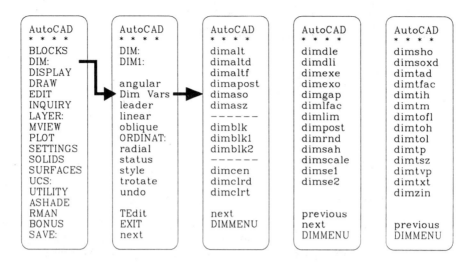

Figure 16–31 Menu Map for Dimension Variables (Dim Vars)

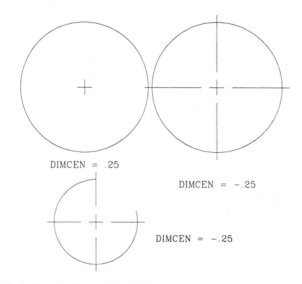

Figure 16–32 Solution to Example 16–7

16.7.3 LEADER Command

The LEADER command provides the operator with the following capabilities: (1) an arrow pointing to a specified point; (2) a line (whose length and direction are variable); and (3) the capability to place a textstring at the end of the line. When the leader line has been completed, the default value (showing the distance) is displayed. If the operator wishes to use this value, a (R) is required. If the operator wants to replace the default value with a different textstring, the default value is set aside and the new textstring is input. The LEADER command is located in the DIM: Submenu as shown in Figure 16–6. The Command Sequence is shown in Figure 16–33.

```
Command: DIM
DIM: leader Leader start:
To point:
To point:
To point: (R)
Dimension text <>:
```

Figure 16–33 Command Sequence for the LEADER Command

Example 16–8: Using the existing drawing called CENTER, erase all dimensional data. Select the LEADER command and use location 6.5,4.625 (as the Start point); 7.125,3.25; 8.375,3.25; (R). The prompt will read "Dimension text <1.3750>:". Input the following message "AutoCAD reduces the work effort"; and (R). If no text is required, use ^C to end the command.

16.7.4 STATUS Option

The STATUS option will list the 42 dimensioning variables (Dim Vars), their current values, and a brief description of the variable. These variables are defined in paragraphs 16.8.1 and 16.8.2. Figure 16–31 lists all the Dim Vars.

16.8 Dimensioning Variables (Dim Vars)

The Dimensioning Variables are divided into three categories:

- Variables used in the dimensioning process
- Variables controlling the size and distance data
- Variables controlling the text and text placement

The Dim Vars Menu is located in the DIM: Submenu as shown in Figure 16–31.

16.8.1 Dim Vars Used in Dimensioning Process

There are 24 Dim Vars in this category. Each variable may act as a toggle switch and/or specify a default value. The listing calls out what the variable controls, its default value, and any toggle switch action.

DIMALT (Alternate Unit display): A toggle switch. If DIMALT is ON the metric value will be added to the dimension inside a [] next to the feet/inch text. Default value = OFF.

DIMALTD (Alternate Unit decimal): Sets the decimal places to be used in the alternate dimensions. Default value = 2.

DIMALTF (Scale Factor for Alternate Units): Sets the conversion factor to convert the inch to millimeters. Default value = 25.4 units.

NOTE: The current AutoCAD release (11) provides an additional dimensional feature called Associative Dimensioning. The Associative Dimensioning program automatically checks the dimensions of a drawing when the STRETCH command is used. The dimension variables DIMASO and DIMSHO control this feature.

DIMASO (Associative Dimensioning): A dimension variable that, together with DIMSHO, controls the Associative Dimensioning program. When DIMASO is ON, the entities used for dimensioning (line, arc, arrowhead, and text) are treated as a block and will be changed to reflect the true dimensions of the drawing. If DIMSHO is OFF, these entities revert to individual items and the dimensions will not be changed.

DIMCEN (Size of the Center Mark): Controls the size of the Center Mark. Default value = 0.09 units.

DIMDLE (Dimension Line extension): A toggle switch. If DIMTSZ (tick control) is ON and DIMDLE is greater than zero, the Dimension Line will extend past both Extension Lines for proper tick mark placement. Default value = 0.

DIMDLI (Dimesion Line increment): Determines the increment used in either Baseline or Continue modes of dimensioning. Default value = .38 units.

DIMEXE (Extension above Dimension Line): Determines the distance the Extension Line is drawn past the Dimension Line. (Refer to Figure 16–34.) Default value = 0.18 units.

DIMEXO (Extension Line offset): Offsets distance between the line being measured and the start of the Extension Line. Default value = 0.0625 units. (Refer to Figure 16–35.)

DIMGAP: Gap from dimension line to text. Default value = 0.0900.

DIMLFAL: Linear unit Scale Factor. Default value = 1.0000.

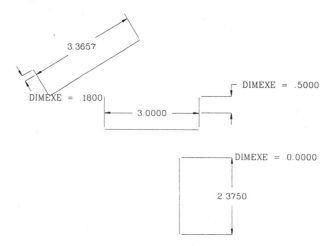

Figure 16–34 Example of the DIMEXE Command

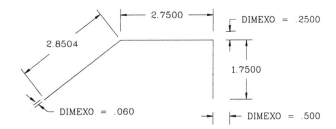

Figure 16–35 Example of DIMEXO Command

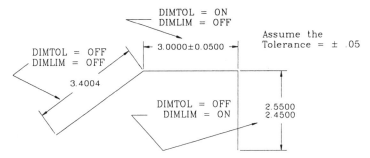

Figure 16–36 Example of the DIMLIM Command

DIMLIM (Dimensional Limits): A toggle switch. If DIMLIM = ON, the limits are placed on the drawing. Default value = OFF. (Refer to Figure 16–36 for an example.)

> **NOTE:** DIMTOL and DIMLIM may be OFF at the same time. To activate either DIMTOL or DIMLIM, only one variable may be ON at any one time.

DIMRND (Rounding off value): Defines the rounding off factor. If DIMRND = 1, all numerical values will be rounded off to an integer. If DIMRND = .5, all numerical values will be rounded off to .5 increments. DIMRND does not apply to angular measurements. Default value = 0.0000.

DIMSCALE (Scale Factor): The overall Scale Factor to be used with the Dimension command. Its primary application is to change the size of the arrowheads and textstring when the limits of the drawing have been changed. The initial value of DIMSCALE is 1 when the limits are 12,9. If the limits are increased, the size of the arrowheads and textstring will remain as if the limits were not changed. This makes the arrowheads and text data very small. To compensate for the change in limits, the DIMSCALE value is determined by dividing the new limits (X value only) with the old limits (X value only). Assume that the new limits are 120,90; old limits were 12,9. The DIMSCALE value is 120/12 or 10. Pick Dim Vars from the Screen Menu, and then DIMSCALE. Input 10 for the new value. Pick UPDATE command from the DIM: Submenu. Window the dimension data to be changed and (R). A secondary application is to change the size of the text when the text data exceed the space inside the Extension Lines. It is *not* applied to tolerances or measured lengths and angles. Default value = 1.0000 units. (Refer to Figure 16–37.)

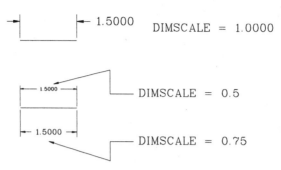

Figure 16–37 Example of DIMSCALE Command

DIMSE1 (Suppress Extension Line 1): A toggle switch. Default value is OFF. When the default value lists ON, the first extension line will be suppressed.

DIMSE2 (Suppress Extension Line 2): A toggle switch. Default value is OFF. When the default value lists ON, the second extension line will be suppressed.

DIMSHO: This Dim Var, with the DIMASO variable, controls the Associative Dimensioning program. DIMSHO controls the change in dimensioning during the "drag" period. If DIMSHO is ON, the Dimensioned Lines that are changed will be changed, on the screen, during the "drag" period. If DIMSHO is OFF, then the change in dimensioning will occur after the change in the drawing has been completed. Table 16-1 shows the four conditions.

DIMSOXD: Surpress outside extension dimension. Default value is OFF.

DIMSTYLE: Current dimension style (read only).

DIMTM (Minus Tolerance): Same as DIMPT but is used to place the negative Tolerance of the dimension. Default value = 0. (Refer to Figure 16–38.)

DIMTP (Plus Tolerance): Defines the value of the Tolerance in the plus (+) side to be placed on the drawing. Default value = 0. (Refer to Figure 16–38.)

DIMTOFL: Forces line inside extension line. Default value is OFF.

DIMTOL (Tolerance): A toggle switch. If DIMTOL is ON, Tolerance of the dimension is added to the textstring. Default value = OFF (Tolerance not shown). (Refer to Figure 16–39 for an example.)

DIMZIN (Zero editing): A toggle switch. When DIMZIN is ON, if feet or inches = 0, the dimensioned text will not display the 0 unit. For example: given the dimension 3'0", if DIMZIN is OFF, the text will read 3". Default value = OFF.

Table 16-1

Condition	DIMASO	DIMSHO	Effect
1	OFF	OFF	Associative dimensioning OFF
2	OFF	ON	Same as Condition 1
3	ON	OFF	Dimension changed after command has been finished
4	ON	ON	Dimensional changes during "drag" period

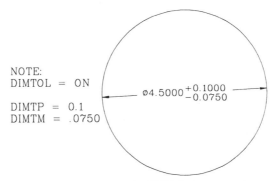

Figure 16–38 Example of DIMTP and DIMTM Commands

16.8.2 Text Variables

DIMAPOST: Suffix for Alternate Unit.

DIMPOST: Default suffix (inches/feet) for dimension text.

DIMTAD (Text above Dimension Line): A toggle switch. Text appears above the Dimension Line if DIMTAD = ON. Default value = OFF. Text appears between the arrows. (Refer to Figure 16–40 for an example.)

DIMTFAC: Tolerance text height Scaling Factor. Default value = 1.0000.

DIMTIH (Text inside horizontal): A toggle switch. The textstring fits between Extension Lines. If DIMTIH = ON, the textstring is horizontal; if DIMTIH = OFF, the

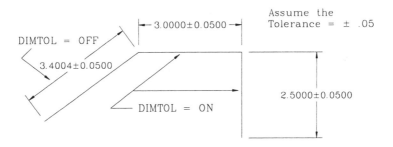

Figure 16–39 Example of the DIMTOL Command

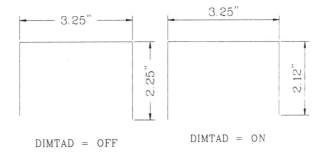

Figure 16–40 Example of DIMTAD Command

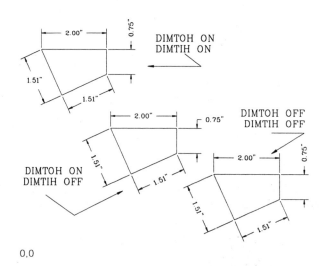

Figure 16–41 Examples of Dim Vars: DIMTIH and DIMTOH

textstring will assume the angle of the Dimensioned Line. Default value = ON. (Refer to Figure 16–41 for examples.)

DIMTOH (Text outside Horizontal): A toggle switch. Same as DIMTIH except that the textstring is drawn outside the Extension Line. If DIMTOH = ON, text is horizontal. If DIMTOH = OFF, text assumes the angle of the dimension line. The default value = ON. (Refer to Figure 16–41.)

DIMTIX: Place text inside Extension Lines. Default value is OFF.

DIMTVP: Text vertical position. Default value = 0.0000.

DIMTXT (Text height): Establishes the text height. Default value = 0.18 units. The text STYLE will be the current STYLE used in the drawing, but STYLE height = 0.

16.8.3 Dimension Variables (Size and Distance) Command

The remaining Dim Vars commands deal with either the size or distance (not the actual drawing that is being dimensioned) of lines.

DIMASZ (Arrowhead size): Controls the size of the arrowheads. Default value = 0.18 units.

DIMBLK: Arrowhead block name.

DIMBLK1: First arrowhead name.

DIMBLK2: Second arrowhead name.

DIMCLRD: Dimension line color. Default value = BYBlock.

DIMCLRE: Color of extension line including leader. Default value = BYBlock.

DIMCLRT: Color of text. Default value = BYBlock.

DIMSAH: Separate arrow blocks. Default value is OFF.

DIMTSZ: (Tick size): A toggle switch. If DIMTSZ is ON, a tick mark will be made in lieu of arrowheads. Default value = 0.

16.9 Pull Down Menu for Chapter 16

Figure 16–42 (Pull Down Menu for Chapter 16) is an excellent example of adopting the Dialogue Box and associated Icons to minimize the number of keystrokes needed to activate a command. When the operator selects "Set Dim Vars" from Figure 16–42, a number of Dialogue Boxes are available to set the various dimension variables for a given dimension assignment. There are seven (Figure 16–43 to Figure 16–49) Dialogue Boxes displaying Icons or visual images of the dimension variables. Figure 16–47 (Set Display of Leading and Trailing Zeroes) shows numbers in the lower right corner of the Icons. The numbers 0, 1, 2, and 3 effect the display (Dim Var = DIMZEN) of only feet and inches. The +4 is used to supress the leading zeroes. The +8 is used to suppress the trailing zeroes. The +12 is a combination of +4 and +8 in order to suppress both the leading and trailing zeroes.

Figure 16–42 Pull Down Menu for Chapter 16

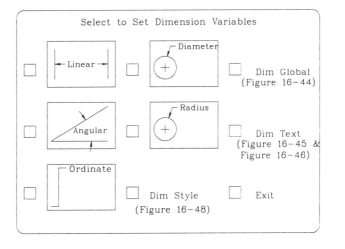

Figure 16–43 Select to Set Dim Vars

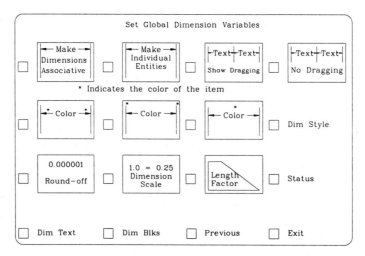

Figure 16–44   Global Dimension Variables

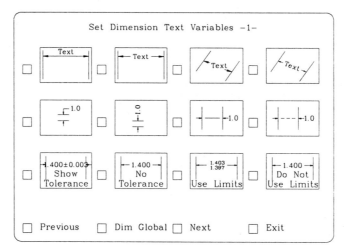

Figure 16–45   Dimension Text Variables -1-

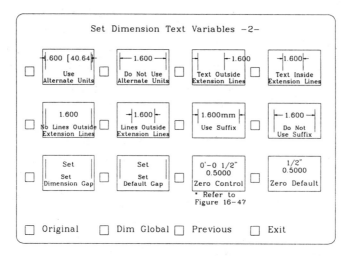

Figure 16–46   Dimension Text Variables -2-

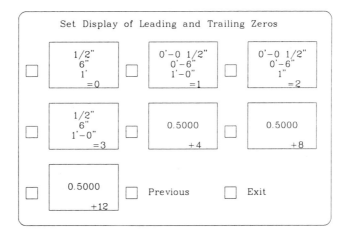

Figure 16–47 Set Display of Leading and Trailing Zeroes

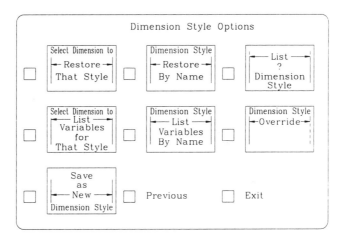

Figure 16–48 Dimension Style Options

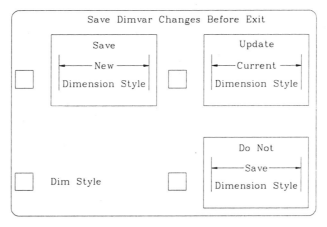

Figure 16–49 Save Dim Var Changes Before Exit?

16.10 Template Reference—Chapter 16

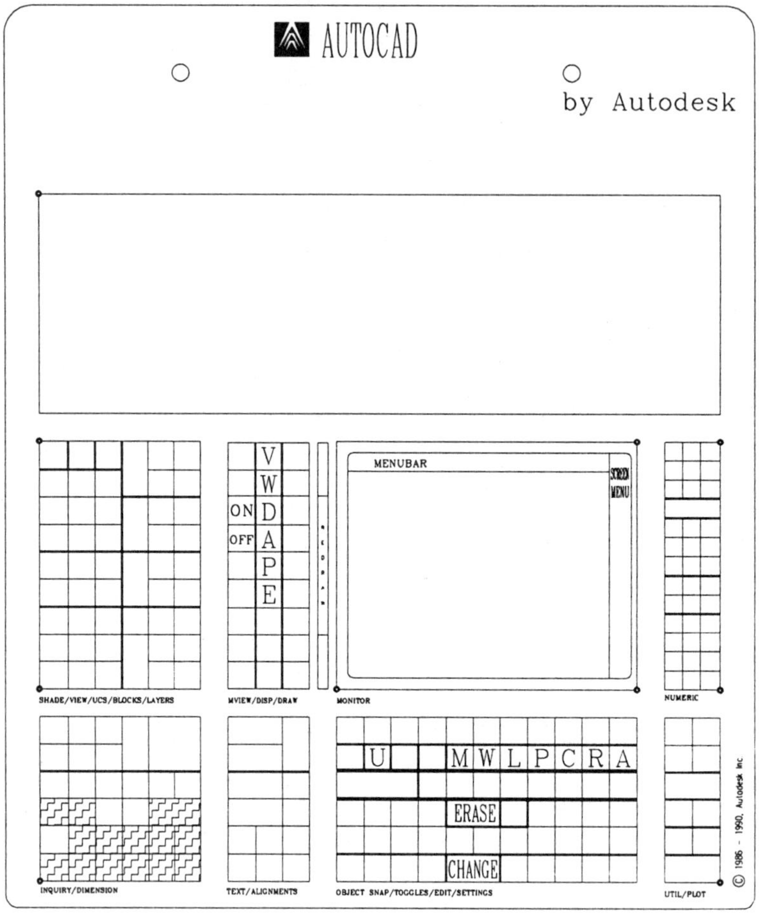

Figure 16–50 Template Reference for Chapter 16

COMMAND SUMMARY

All of the Standard Dimension commands and variables have been discussed.

GLOSSARY

Dim Vars: Variable terms (size of text, size of arrowhead, etc.) used in the Dimensioning command.

DIM1: DIM1 is the same command as DIM with the exception that DIM is a repetitive command while DIM1 is a single command.

PROBLEMS

1. Draw a five-sided polygon using the Edge method: Starting point = 2,3; each edge = 3 units. Prior to measuring the horizontal edge, set the Dim Vars so that there is a .25 unit spacing between the measurement point and the Extension Line. Call this drawing 16A. Do a PRPLOT, half scale. End the drawing.

2. Bring up drawing 16A. Make a copy of this drawing and call it 16B. Quit drawing 16A. Bring back 16B. Add the following Tolerances to the horizontal dimensions: +.05 and -.01. Erase the existing Dimension Line. Dimension the horizontal base of the polygon and add the Tolerances to the dimensions. Do a PRPLOT, half scale. End drawing.

3. Bring up drawing 16A and make another copy of the drawing but call the drawing 16C. Quit and bring up 16C. Change the Tolerance configuration so that the limits of the measurement are called out. Do a PRPLOT, half scale. End the drawing.

17 Advanced Dimensioning Commands and Options

Instructional Objectives

1. To activate the ASSOCIATIVE DIMENSIONING command and options
2. To save the Dimensioning Style (group of dimensioning variables) for recall in the future
3. To be able to determine the differences between Dimension Styles
4. To activate the OBLIQUE command to rotate the dimension lines
5. To understand the TROTATE and TEDIT commands as they apply to the dimension text location and orientation
6. To be able to apply the ORDINATE command
7. To understand and apply the three UPDATE commands: HOMETEXT, UPDATE, and NEWTEXT

17.1 ADVANCED DIMENSIONING Options

This chapter reviews the advanced or Associative Dimensioning options of the Dimensioning commands. These options provide the ease of operation necessary for the required accuracy for dimensioning in general. Before proceeding with the implementation of the Associative commands or options, it should be noted that the Dim Vars DIMASO and DIMSHO must be ON. The Pull Down Menus developed for Chapter 16 (Figure 16–42 to Figure 16–49) are applicable for the ADVANCED DIMENSIONING options.

17.2 ASSOCIATIVE DIMENSIONING Commands

Associative Dimensioning permits the operator to change a dimensioned point by moving it to another location. When the new location is identified, the dimensioned value is automatically changed to the new value. If the Dim Var DIMSHO is ON, then the change in dimensioned value will dynamically appear (on the screen) as the point is moved to the new location. Any one of three Edit commands may be used to change the dimension of an item: STRETCH, EXTEND, or TRIM. These commands are listed in the EDIT Submenu as described in Chapter 13.

17.2.1 ASSOCIATIVE DIMENSIONING—STRETCH Option

The STRETCH command (refer to Chapter 13) may be used to change the location of a dimensioned point. It is important to remember that the Crossing Window mode

243

is used to define the selected objects. Go to the EDIT Submenu, select the STRETCH command, and Cross Window the required objects. The basepoint is usually one of the endpoints of the dimensioned line. Pick the basepoint to be moved and the new point location. The dimensioned text will be changed to its new value. If DIMSHO is ON, the operator will see the dimensioned text change as the point is moved to its new location.

Example 17–1: Start a new drawing called ASSOC. Draw an eight-sided polygon with the Edge method, First point = 2,3; Second point = 4,3. Label the upper right line as Line A; the right vertical line as Line B; and the lower right line as Line C. Dimension each line. Use the Align Dimensioning mode for Lines A and C. Use the Vertical Dimensioning mode for Line B. Place the text approximately 0.5 units to the right of each line. Make sure that variables DIMASO and DIMSHO are ON. Select the STRETCH command from the Edit Submenu. The Crossing Box should cut Lines A and C (near the midpoints of the lines). Use the coordinates 4.75,8.375 for the First point of the Crossing Window and 9.0000,3.3750 as the Second point of the Crossing Window. Now move the midpoint of Line B to 9.0000,5.4142. Before inputting the new point, move the cursor and note that the dimensions for Lines A and C change with a change in cursor position. The solution is shown in Figure 17–1.

17.2.2   ASSOCIATIVE DIMENSIONING—EXTEND Command

The operator may use the EXTEND command in a similar way to the STRETCH option. The Command Sequence of the EXTEND command is given in Chapter 13. Dimension the drawing and then determine which end of the drawing will be extended and its new location. The EXTEND command will only work if the lines to be extended will cross the Extend Boundary Line.

Example 17–2: Erase the current drawing and redraw the polygon used in Example 17–1. Explode the polygon. Dimension Lines A, B, and C. Draw the Extend Boundary

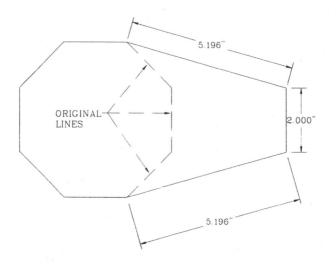

Figure 17–1   Solution to Example 17–1

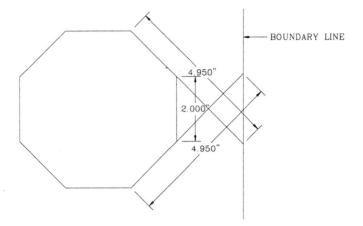

Figure 17-2 Solution to Example 17-2

Line from 7.5000,8.5000 to 7.5000,2.000. Pick the EXTEND command from the EDIT Submenu. Pick the Boundary line. Pick: Line A; include the dimension line and text to be extended. Repeat the command for Lines B and C. Note that the dimensions of Lines A and C will change but the dimensions of Line B will remain the same. The solution to this example is shown in Figure 17-2.

17.2.3 ASSOCIATIVE DIMENSIONING—TRIM Command

The TRIM command will also change the dimensions of a drawing. The Command Sequence is similar to that of the EXTEND option. The TRIM command is listed in the EDIT Submenu and is described in Chapter 13.

Example 17-3: Clear the screen and replace the polygon as in Figure 17-1. Dimension the right three faces as in the prior examples. The drawing is to be modified by trimming the right faces of the polygon to a vertical line that goes through the midpoints of Lines A and C. Draw this line. Select the TRIM command from the EDIT Submenu. Pick this vertical line as the cutting line. Trim Lines A and C, and the dimension data. The solution to this example is illustrated in Figure 17-3.

17.3 OBLIQUE Command

The OBLIQUE command is used to set the extension lines, dimension lines, and text data at a selected oblique angle. It is usually used when one set of dimension lines (such as horizontal dimension lines and data) makes another set of dimension lines hard to read or interpret. The OBLIQUE command is listed in the main DIM: Menu Map as shown in Figure 17-4. The Command Sequence is shown in Figure 17-5.

Example 17-4: Start a new drawing called OBLIQUE. Draw a 3P Arc with the following coordinates: pt 1 = 1.288,4.820; pt 2 = 3.715,4.092 and pt 3 = 5.228,2.060. Draw

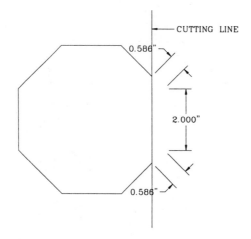

Figure 17–3 Solution to Example 17–3

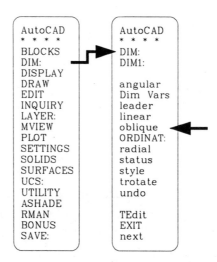

Figure 17–4 Menu Map for the OBLIQUE Command

```
Command:  DIM:
Dim:  oblique
Select objects: 1 selected, 1 found
Select objects: (R)
Enter obliquing angle (Return for none): 60
```

Figure 17–5 Command Sequence for the OBLIQUE Command

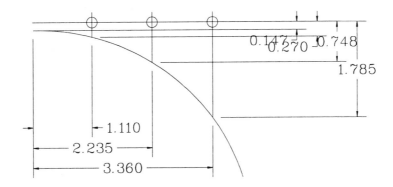

Figure 17–6 Initial Setting for Example 17–4

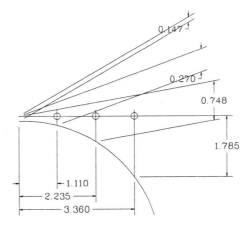

Figure 17–7 Solution to Example 17–4

a line from 1.273,4.967 to 5.773,4.967. Divide this line into four equal parts. Use PD mode (Point Symbol) = 34 and a PD size (Point Symbol size) = 0.20. Draw a vertical line from each DIVIDER NODE or SYMBOL to the edge of the arc. Dimension the horizontal values between each of the intersections (where the vertical line meets the edge of the arc) using the Baseline option. The datum point is the left endpoint of the arc. Dimension the vertical distance, bringing the data to the right side of the arc. This is shown in Figure 17–6.

It is difficult to read the vertically dimensioned data. Select the OBLIQUE command from the DIM: Menu. Set the angle for 30° and select the 0.147 dimension line and data. Set the angle to 20° and pick the 0.270 dimensioned line and data. Set the next angle to 10° and select the 0.8527 dimension line and data. The new drawing should look like Figure 17–7.

17.4 Changing Dimension Text

New to Release 11, AutoCAD introduces two commands: TROTATE and TEDIT. Both commands deal with the placement and orientation of the dimensioned text data.

17.4.1   TROTATE Command

The TROTATE command is listed in the DIM: Menu and is shown in Figure 17–8. The Command Sequence is listed in Figure 17–9.

This command permits the operator to rotate the text data using the Insertion point as the basepoint. One or more dimension texts may be selected to be rotated at a specific angle.

Example 17–5:   Recall the drawing in Figure 16–17. Select TROTATE from the DIM: Submenu and an Angle of 45°. Pick the three Horizontal Baseline text data. Upon completion of the Selection process, all the texts will be rotated 45° as shown in Figure 17–10.

17.4.2   TEDIT Command

The TEDIT command is also listed in the DIM: Submenu as shown in Figure 17–11. This command permits the operator to change the location and/or rotation of the dimension text data. The operator may specify that the text data be moved to the Left Justified position, or Right Justified position on the dimension line as well as an angular rotation of the text. The main difference between the rotation capabilities of

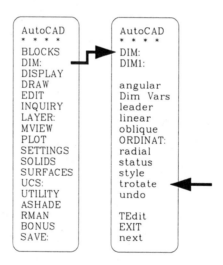

Figure 17–9   Command Sequence for the TROTATE Command

```
Command: DIM
Dim: trotate
Enter new text angle: 45
Select objects: 1 selected, 1 found
Select objects: (R)
```

Figure 17–8   Menu Map for the TROTATE Command

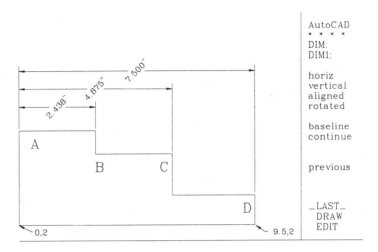

Figure 17-10   Solution to Example 17-5

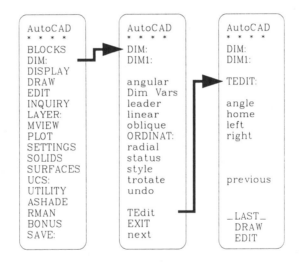

Figure 17-11   Menu Map for the TROTATE Command

the TROTATE command and the TEDIT command is that with the TROTATE command one or more dimension text data may be rotated at the same time. The TEDIT command works on *one* dimension line at a time. The Command Sequence is shown in Figure 17-12.

Example 17-6: The drawing on the screen represents Figure 16-17 with the text data rotated at a 45° angle. There are three lines of dimension text. Assign number 1 to the 2.438″ text data; number 2 to the 4.875″ data and number 3 to the 7.500″ data. Select the TEDIT command and line 1. Place the text so that it is left justified. Repeat the command but select line 2 to be right justified. Select line 3 and rotate the text by 75°. The solution is shown in Figure 17-13. Quit the drawing.

```
Command:  DIM
Dim:  TEDIT
Select  dimension:
Enter  text  location  (Left/Right/Home/Angle):  left
```

Figure 17–12   Command Sequence for the TEDIT Command

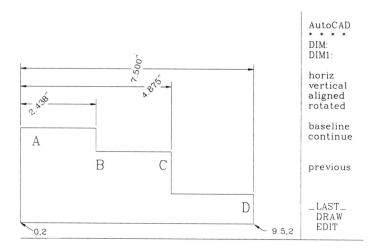

Figure 17–13   Solution to Example 17–6

17.5   Additional Dimension Text Options

There are three additional commands/options that may be used to modify the dimension text data. They are the HOMETEXT, NEWTEXT, and UPDATE options.

17.5.1   HOMETEXT Option

The operator, during the dimensioning portion of any drawing, may have to move the dimensioned text data from its original position (due to the use of either the TEDIT or STRETCH commands). The operator can return the dimensioned text data to its original or home position by using the HOMETEXT option. The HOMETEXT option is located in a submenu of the DIM: Submenu and its location is shown in Figure 17–14. The Command Sequence for this option is listed in Figure 17–15.

Example 17–7:   Return Figure 16–17 to the screen. Modify the dimensioned data by using the TEDIT command as follows: Move the top and bottom dimension text data to the Right Justified position. Repeat the operation for the Center dimensioned text data to the Left Justified position. The drawing should look like Figure 17–16. Select the DIM: Submenu, then next, then HOMETEXT, and select each dimensioned text data. Confirm the selection and the dimensioned text data will automatically return to its "home" location. The solution to this example is shown in Figure 17–17.

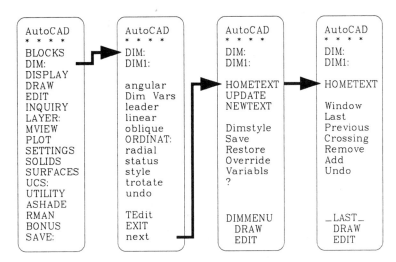

Figure 17–14 Menu Map for the HOMETEXT Option

```
Command: DIM:
Dim: HOMETEXT
Select objects: 1 selected, 1 found
Select objects: (R)
```

Figure 17–15 Command Sequence for the HOMETEXT Option

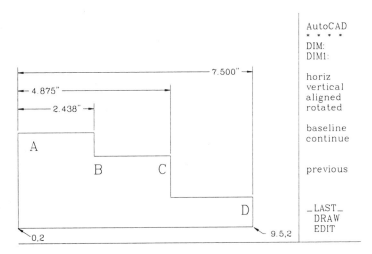

Figure 17–16 Initial Setting for Example 17–7

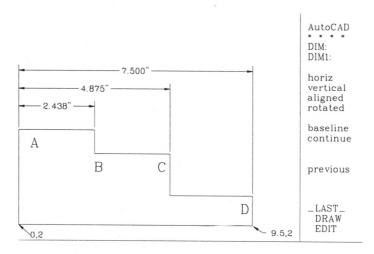

Figure 17–17 Solution to Example 17–7

17.5.2 UPDATE Option

This option is used to update a selected dimensioned text data to the current set of dimension variables, text style, or UNIT setting. The location of this option is shown in Figure 17–18. The Command Sequence is shown in Figure 17–19.

Example 17–8: Figure 17–17 is on the screen. Change two Dim Vars: DIMASZ and DIMTXT. Set DIMASZ (arrowhead size) to 0.25 and DIMTXT (text size) to 0.50. One way to change the arrowhead and text size is to erase the current dimensions and redimension. However, the UPDATE option makes this chore easier. Select UPDATE from the DIM: Submenu and either select each dimension or window all three dimensioned lines. The end result should look like Figure 17–20.

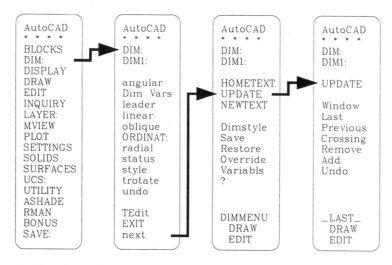

Figure 17–18 Menu Map for the UPDATE Option

```
Command: DIM:
Dim: UPDATE
Select objects: 1 selected, 1 found
Select objects: (R)
```

Figure 17–19 Command Sequence for the UPDATE Option

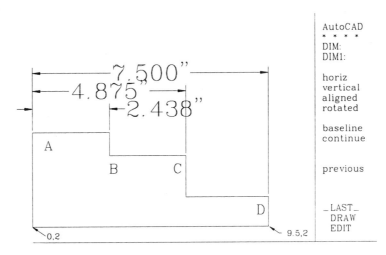

Figure 17–20 Solution to Example 17–8

17.5.3 NEWTEXT Option

The Menu Map for this option is illustrated in Figure 17–21. Figure 17–22 is the suggested Command Sequence to be used. The purpose of this command/option is to change the text of (similar to the CHANGE command) one or more dimensioned text data lines.

Example 17–9: Figure 17–20 is on the screen. Return the DIMASZ and DIMTXT

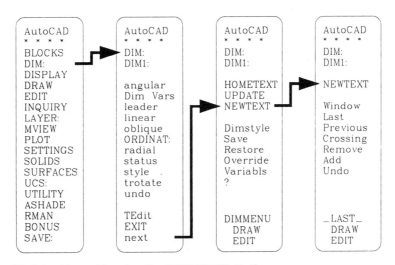

Figure 17–21 Menu Map for the NEWTEXT Option

```
Command: DIM:
Dim: NEWTEXT
Enter new dimension text: TBD
Select objects: 1 selected, 1 found
Select objects: (R)
```

Figure 17–22   Command Sequence for the NEWTEXT Option

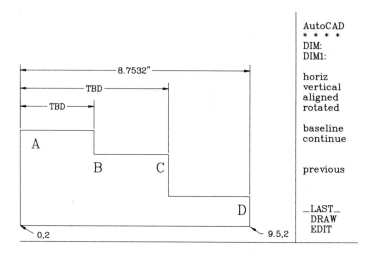

Figure 17–23   Solution to Example 17–9

variables to their default values (DIMASZ = 0.1800; DIMTXT = 0.1800). Use the UPDATE option to update all dimensioned text data in the drawing. The operator wants to change the dimension text for the top line to 8.7532″ and the two other lines to TBD (To Be Determined). These changes will be accomplished in two steps. The first step is to change the top line. Select NEWTEXT. Type in the new value (8.7532). Select the top dimension line and (R). The top line should read 8.7532″. Repeat the NEWTEXT selection. Type in TBD for the second change. Pick the Center and bottom dimensioned lines and (R). The solution to this example is shown in Figure 17–23.

17.6   Ordinate Dimensioning

Ordinate Dimensioning is not restricted to the Associative Dimensioning option. It may also be used in the Standard Dimensioning option. (See Chapter 16.) The Ordinate Dimensioning command provides either the X or Y values from a given origin. The World Coordinating System (WCS) has its origin at 0,0,0. This origin may be moved to another location by using the User Coordinating System (UCS). The new origin point is given a name for file purposes. The UCS command is listed on the flip side of the SETTINGS command.

The ORDINATE command is listed in the DIM: Submenu (refer to Figure 17–24) and the Command Sequence is shown in Figure 17–25.

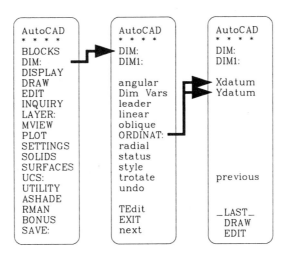

Figure 17-24 Menu Map for the ORDINATE Command

```
Command: DIM:
Dim: ordinate
Select Feature: Center of circle
Leader endpoint: ( Xdatum/Ydatum): Xdatum
Leader endpoint: 4,3
Dimension text <4.2314>: (R)
```

Figure 17-25 Command Sequence for the ORDINATE Command

When the command prompt requests "Select Feature:," The program is requesting the point of measurement. For example: The Select Feature for a circle is the Center of the circle. The Second prompt question Xdatum/Ydatum calls for either the X or Y dimension data. If a number of X values are to be measured, the answer to the third question is a (R). The leader endpoint location is the point where the leader ends and the data begins.

Example 17-10: Clear the screen. Set the UNITS to 3. Draw a line from 2,3 to 5,3 to 5,5.5 to @ -2.5,0 to @0,-0.5 to @ -0.5,0 and close. Fillet all outside corners with a Radius of 0.25. Place the first circle at 3,4 with a Radius of 0.5. Draw the second circle at 4,5 with a Radius of 0.375. Set DIMCEN = 0.09, DIMASZ = 0.1, and DIMTXT = 0.2. It will help if the GRID and SNAP are used and set to 0.25. Dimension the drawing using the ORDINATE command. Include the overall X and Y dimension, and Centers of all circles and arcs. The solution is displayed in Figure 17-26.

NOTE: Change the origin of the drawing (via UCS) to the upper left corner of the drawing.

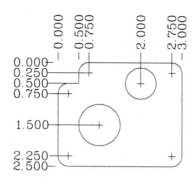

Figure 17–26 Solution to Example 17–10

17.7 Dimension Style

Figure 17–27 (Menu Map for the DIMENSION STYLE and options) shows the location of Dimension Style and the options listed below. This command is different from the STYLE command used with the TEXT command. DIMENSION STYLE command is a grouping of Dim Vars that is in current use for a dimensioning task. When a DIMENSION STYLE is saved, a name must be assigned for the purpose of recall. The DIMENSION STYLE command has four options: SAVE, RESTORE, OVERRIDE, and VARIABLES.

17.7.1 SAVE Option

The Command Sequence is listed in Figure 17–28.

NOTE: This option does *not* save the drawing.

The default DIMENSION STYLE name (default settings of Dim Vars) is *UN-

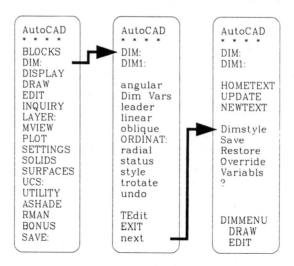

Figure 17–27 Menu Map for the DIMENSION STYLE and Options

```
Command: DIM:
Dim: Save
?/Name for new dimension style: dims1
```

Figure 17–28 Command Sequence for the DIMENSION STYLE—SAVE Option

NAMED. The operator may use up to 31 characters for the DIMENSION STYLE name. There are three modes to this option: 1) a listing of all the DIMENSION STYLE names (use the ? and *); 2) to name the current DIMENSION STYLE; and 3) the listing of the Dim Vars difference between the current DIMENSION STYLE name and any other DIMENSION STYLE name. The last mode is accomplished by placing a tilde (~) before the DIMENSION STYLE name. The screen will flip to the Text Screen and display the difference on a Dim Var level. When a name is SAVED, that name is assigned to the current DIMENSION STYLE.

Example 17–11: Call the current DIMENSION STYLE DIMS1. Change the following Dim Vars: DIMASZ = 0.25 and DIMTXT = 0.50. Save the current DIMENSION STYLE as DIMS2. Place the DIM: Submenu on the screen, select next, SAVE, and input ~Cad1. The Text Screen will show the difference between Cad1 and Cad2 in the DIMASZ and DIMTXT values. End the drawing.

17.7.2 RESTORE Option

Figure 17–29 is the Command Sequence for the RESTORE option. This option permits the operator to change the DIMENSION STYLE as required. It will also list the differences between DIMENSION STYLES using the tilde (~).

17.7.3 OVERRIDE Option

The operator may Override any one variable during a dimensioning task. Figure 17–30 is the Command Sequence for this option. The command prompt will ask for the variable and the new state/value. In addition, a second prompt will ask if this new value should be included in the current DIMENSION STYLE.

17.7.4 VARIABLES Option

The Command Sequence for this option is shown in Figure 17–31. This command provides a listing of all Dim Vars for a named DIMENSION STYLE.

```
Command: DIM:
Dim: Restore
Current dimension style: DIMS1
?/Enter dimension style or Return to select dimension: (R)
Select dimension:
```

Figure 17–29 Command Sequence for the RESTORE Option

```
Command: DIM:
Dim: Override
Dimension variable to override: DIMASZ
Current value <0.1000> New value: 0.500
Select object: 1 selected, 1 found
Select object: (R)
Modify dimension style "DIMS1"? <N> (R)
```

Figure 17–30 Command Sequence for the OVERRIDE Option

```
Command: DIM:
Dim: VARIABLES
Current dimension style: dims1
?/Enter dimension style name or RETURN to select dimension: dims1
 --LISTING OF ALL Dim Vars --
```

Figure 17–31 Command Sequence for the DIMENSION STYLE—VARIABLES Option

17.8 Pull Down Menu for Chapter 17

The Pull Down menu for Chapter 17 is shown in Figure 17–32.

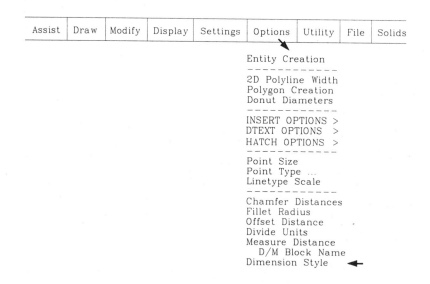

Figure 17–32 Pull Down Menu for Chapter 17

17.9 Template Reference—Chapter 17

See Figure 17–33 on page 259.

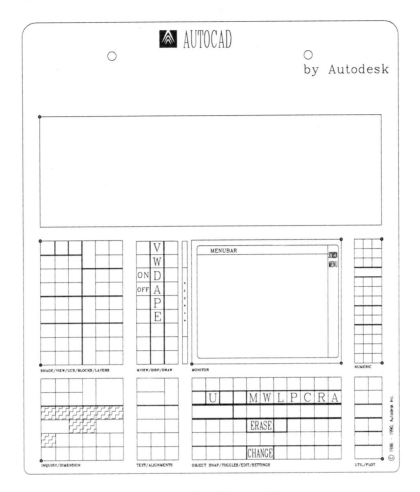

Figure 17–33 Template Reference for Chapter 17

COMMAND SUMMARY

ASSOCIATIVE DIMENSIONING	RESTORE
DIMENSION STYLE	SAVE
HOMETEXT	TEDIT
NEWTEXT	TROTATE
OBLIQUE	UPDATE
ORDINATE	VARIABLE
OVERRIDE	

PROBLEMS

1. Draw a five-sided polygon whose Center is located at 5,5, Radius = 2, using the Inscribed mode. Dimension the upper and lower right faces. Set DIMASO and DIMSHO to ON. Use the engineering units and two decimal places. The sides are 2.35" long. Using the STRETCH command, move the intersection of the two

right faces for a distance @2<45. The new dimensions are: upper right face = 3.32"; lower right face = 4.23". Reposition the Dimension Text data to its original "HOME" position by using the HOMETEXT command. Make a PRPLOT, Display mode and half scale.

2. What is the difference between the TEDIT and TROTATE commands?
3. What happens when the tilde (~) is used before the DIMENSION STYLE name?
4. When and why is the HOMETEXT command used?
5. Does the UPDATE command change the dimensioned value?

18 Hatch Command

Instructional Objectives

1. To be able to understand the requirement for complete boundaries when hatching a specific area
2. To be able to use the three styles of hatching effectively
3. To be able to use the HATCHING command successfully
4. To be able to select any one of 41 established HATCHING patterns
5. To be able to change the scale and rotational angle of any pattern
6. To be able to design a hatching pattern during the Command Sequence

18.1 HATCH Command

The purpose of the HATCH command is to highlight or fill a given drawing area with a selected Hatch pattern. Release 11 provides for fifty-three specific patterns. A number of these patterns are in accordance with the American National Standards Institute (ANSI). The PULL DOWN Menus, under the OPTION heading, enable the operator to select any one of the fifty-three patterns. These patterns are illustrated in Figures 18–18 to 18–21. The HATCH command is found in the DRAW Submenu and is shown in Figure 18–1.

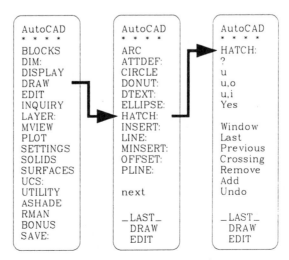

Figure 18–1 Menu Map for the HATCH Command

```
Command: HATCH
Pattern (? or name/u, style): ANSI31
Scale for pattern <1.0000>:(R)
Angle for pattern <0>: (R)
Select object(s):
```

Figure 18–2 Command Sequence for the HATCH Command

Figure 18–2 lists the Command Sequence for this command.

The Hatch pattern is a specific series of lines (consisting of dots and/or dashes) at a specified rotational alignment and spacing. Fifty-three hatching patterns are part of the AutoCAD program, and the pattern structure is located in the ACAD.PAT file. Each pattern can be modified by changing the Scale Factor (default value = 1) or the Rotational Angle (default value = 0). The name appearing beneath each box is the name of that pattern.

CAUTION: When inputting the pattern name, care must be used to select the letter I and the number 1 or letter O and the number 0. If the wrong character is used (letter or number), AutoCAD will not accept the improper item and will return to the command prompt.

The Scale Factor for each pattern has a default value of 1. A positive numerical value (greater than zero) is used to change the size of the pattern. A Scale Factor of .5 makes the pattern 50% smaller. Figure 18–3 illustrates the effect of Scale Factor from 0.5 to 4.

Figure 18–4 shows the difference between the Rotational Angles of 0°, 30°, 60°, and 90°. Any angle whose value is less than 360° is acceptable.

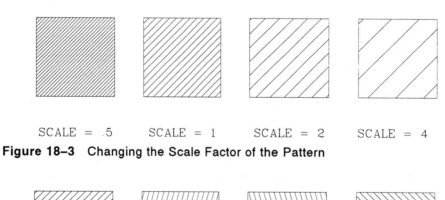

SCALE = .5   SCALE = 1   SCALE = 2   SCALE = 4

Figure 18–3 Changing the Scale Factor of the Pattern

ANGLE = 0   ANGLE = 30   ANGLE = 60   ANGLE = 90

Figure 18–4 Effects of Rotational Angle on the Hatch Pattern

NOTE: The 0° position of the pattern may not be the same as the 0° position for circle or arc.

18.2 Applying the HATCH Command

The operator must be able to specify the *closed* boundaries of the hatching area (using either lines, arcs, circles, or polylines) to obtain an acceptable hatch. If the boundary lines are not contiguous or touching, the resulting hatching pattern will either spill over to the next set of lines or be incomplete. In either case the resulting drawing is not acceptable. Consider the drawing in Figure 18–5.

Example 18–1: Start a new drawing called HATCH and draw the figure shown in Figure 18–5. Use the LINE command: draw a line from 3,2; 8,2; 8,6; 3,6; and close. Draw the two diagonals. Label (on the outside of the box) point 3,6 as Pt A; 8,6 as Pt B; point 8,2 as Pt C; and 3,2 as Pt D. Do *not* label point E. The Hatch Pattern ANSI31 will be used in this exercise. The HATCH Command Sequence is listed in Figure 18–2. Select the triangle AEB. The resulting hatched drawing (shown in Figure 18–6) is unsatisfactory. Note the hatching pattern in AED and BEC area.

Remove the hatching pattern by using either the ERASE or U command. Break line ED (remove .5 units starting at point E towards Pt D. Repeat the procedure for

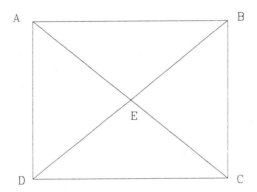

Figure 18–5 Example of Boundary Selection

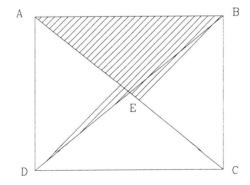

Figure 18–6 Improper Solution to Example 18–1

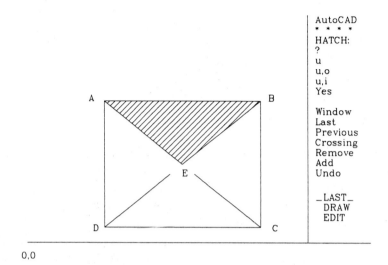

Figure 18–7   Proper Solution to Example 18–1

line EC. The remaining lines AEB will present a closed boundary to the HATCH command. Repeat the Hatching Sequence and again select points AEB. The resulting acceptable hatch pattern is shown in Figure 18–7.

Example 18–2: Remove the hatch pattern. Repeat the sequence used in Example 18–1 but select points AED. Notice the space where the boundary line breaks. (See Figure 18–8.)

Remove the hatch pattern and try points DEC. A similar pattern will be drawn on the screen. Another way to break the line is to use the @ for the second point in the BREAK command. This method breaks the line using minimal spacing. The line appears not to be broken.

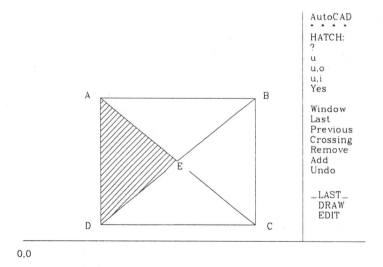

Figure 18–8   Solution to Example 18–2

18.3   Hatching Styles

Three Hatching Styles (refer to Figure 18–22) are used in the HATCH command. They are as follows:

Normal (letter N): the program will hatch every other boundary.

Outermost (letter O): will hatch the outside boundary.

Ignore (letter I): will hatch the complete drawing.

These Styles are best illustrated by using an example.

Example 18–3:   Start a new drawing called STYLES. There will be five layers: 0, Normal, Outermost, Ignore, and Text. The colors for these layers are: red for Layer Normal; green for Layer Outermost; blue for Layer Ignore; and white for Layers Text and 0. Draw the following on Layer 0: six-sided polygon, Edge option, 3.5,3; each edge 3 units long; a circle whose Center is the Center of the polygon with a Radius of 2.3; a square (four-sided polygon) whose edge is located at 3.5,4.25, with edge length 3 units; a triangle whose points are 3.75,4.5; 6.25,4.5; 5,6.6651 and close; text: using Complex font, Middle option at 5,5 and height of .5. Input the word "CAD." The drawing should look like Figure 18–9.

Example 18–3a: Set Layer Normal; use the Pattern ANSI31,N (for Normal Style); Scale Factor 1 and rotational angle 0°. Window the drawing or select each object including the word CAD. The resulting hatch will be similar to that shown in Figure 18–10. The Hatch area will appear in red.

NOTE: The text area has not been hatched. AutoCAD places an invisible fence around the textstring to prevent hatching. (Refer to Figure 18–10.) If the text area must be hatched, then use the Ignore Style. (Refer to Figures 18–12 and 18–13.)

Example 18–3b: Set Layer Outermost as the current layer and turn OFF Layer Normal. Repeat the above procedure, with the exception of the pattern input: Use

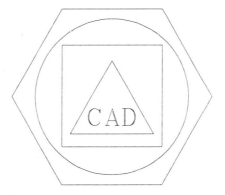

Figure 18–9   Solution to Example 18–3

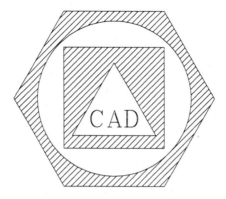

Figure 18–10 Solution to Example 18–3a

ANSI31,O. (Window the drawing or select each boundary.) The resulting drawing is shown in Figure 18–11. The hatched pattern will be green in color.

Example 18–3c: Repeat the above procedure but set Layer Ignore, turn Layer Outermost OFF, and use ANSI31,I. The resulting HATCH pattern should appear in blue, and the complete drawing, including text, will be hatched. The solution to this example is shown in Figure 18–12.

Example 18–3d: Set the Layer Text and turn OFF Layer Ignore. The text is treated in the same fashion as lines, arcs, and circles. Use ANSI31,I and select the text to be hatched. The text will be hatched as shown in Figure 18–13.

18.4 General Comments

The Hatching pattern is considered a block and should be treated as such. If the Hatch pattern is to be erased, then use either last, Window, or pick the Hatch pattern. If the operator wants to use the Hatch pattern in the Nonblock mode, prefix the pattern with an "*".

Figure 18–11 Solution to Example 18–3b

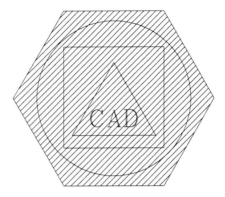

Figure 18–12 Solution to Example 18–3c

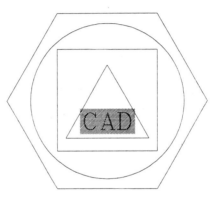

Figure 18–13 Solution to Example 18–3d

You may design your own hatch pattern as you are using the AutoCAD program. This is accomplished by using the letter U in lieu of the pattern name. The Command Sequence is shown in Figure 18–14.

Example 18–3e: Set Layer 0 and turn OFF all other layers. Follow the sequence shown in Figure 18–14. Use the new pattern to Hatch the complete drawing. (Use the Window option to select the objects.) Figure 18–15 is the new Hatch pattern.

```
Command: HATCH
Pattern (? or name/U,style)<ANSI31>: u
Angle for crosshatching lines <0>: (R)
Spacing between lines <1.0000>: 0.5
Double hatch area? <N>: Y
Select objects: 1 selected, 1 found
Select objects: (R)
```

Figure 18–14 Command Sequence for the Design of a Hatch Pattern

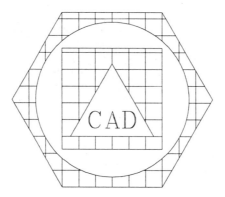

Figure 18–15 Solution to Example 18–3e

NOTE: The Hatch program assumes the Normal Style whether or not N is used.

To obtain a listing of the current patterns, reply to the pattern prompt with a "?". When you end the current drawing, note the number of bytes used in the development of the drawing. The hatch program ranks either first or second in the amount of memory required to produce a small drawing. Therefore, to save time (in the Regeneration mode), try to do all hatching at the end of the drawing.

18.5 Pull Down Menus for Chapter 18

Figures 18–16 through 18–21 illustrate the Hatch patterns.

NOTE: To activate a specific hatch pattern from the dialogue box, pick the box to the left of the icon.

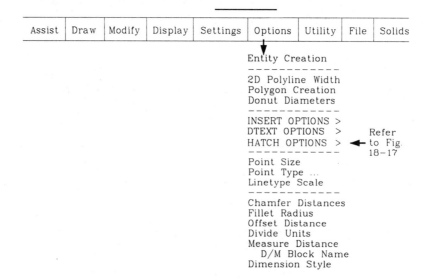

Figure 18–16 Initial Pull Down Menu for Chapter 18

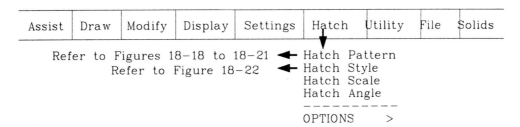

Assist	Draw	Modify	Display	Settings	Hatch	Utility	File	Solids

Refer to Figures 18-18 to 18-21 ← Hatch Pattern
Refer to Figure 18-22 ← Hatch Style
                                 Hatch Scale
                                 Hatch Angle
                                 - - - - - - - - -
                                 OPTIONS   >

Figure 18–17   Secondary Pull Down Menu for Chapter 18

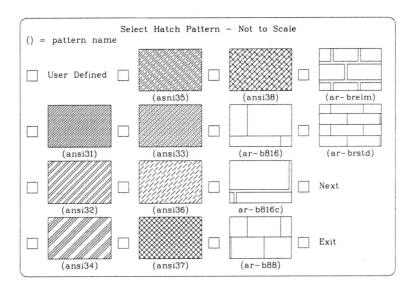

Figure 18–18   Select Hatch Pattern (Page 1 of 4)

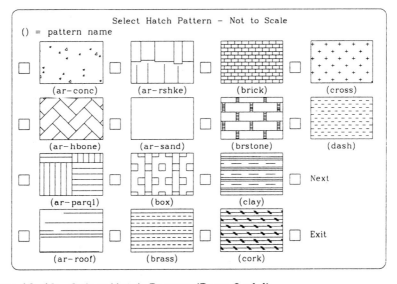

Figure 18–19   Select Hatch Pattern (Page 2 of 4)

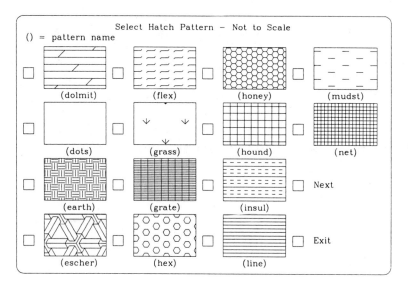

Figure 18–20 Select Hatch Pattern (Page 3 of 4)

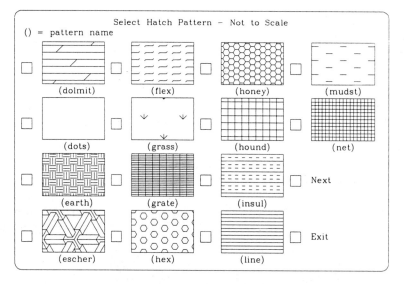

Figure 18–21 Select Hatch Pattern (Page 4 of 4)

18.6 Template Reference—Chapter 18

The Template does not support the Hatching Program.

COMMAND SUMMARY

All styles and options listed for the HATCH command were discussed in this Chapter.

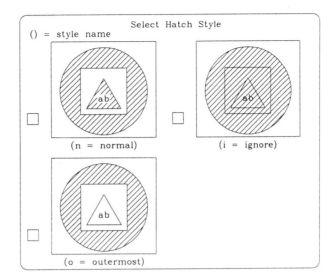

Figure 18–22 Select Hatching Style

GLOSSARY

ANSI: American National Standards Institute.

Contiguous: A word meaning that the lines are physically connected.

PROBLEMS

1. Draw an eight-sided polygon using the Edge method. The Starting point is 2,2; and the edges are 2 units long. Place a circle whose diameter is 4 units at the Center of the polygon. Draw an equilateral triangle whose sides are 2 units long. Place the Center of the triangle at the Center of the circle. Hatch the triangle using the ZIGZAG pattern, hatch the circle using the ANSI31 pattern, and for the polygon, use the HEX pattern. Use the default values.

2. Define the three styles:

   N

   O

   I

3. True or false: The Hatch pattern may be scaled in both scale and angle prior to hatching a particular drawing.

19 Attribute Commands

Instructional Objectives

1. To be able to define what is meant by an *attribute*
2. To be able to define the Attribute TAG for computer usage
3. To understand why the Attribute prompt is necessary for the operator
4. To understand the differences between the four ATTRIBUTE commands
5. To be able to apply the three operational modes correctly
6. To be able to display the Attributes regardless of the invisibility criterion
7. To be able to obtain a report, through the computer, by means of the ATTEXT.BAS program

19.1 Definition of an Attribute

The word attribute may be defined as a characteristic of a person or product. For example: A person may have brown hair, blue eyes, and a dimpled chin. The underlined words are the characteristics or attributes of the individual. A screw will have the following attributes: oval head, 6–32 thread, and 2 in. length. When a floor plan is required, the attributes may be the individual's name seated at the desk, the telephone extension number, and the individual's badge number.

19.2 ATTRIBUTE Commands and Modes

The ATTRIBUTE commands are divided into four applications: Attribute Definition (ATTDEF), Attribute Edit (ATTEDIT), Attribute Display (ATTDISP), and Attribute Extraction (ATTEXT).

19.2.1 Attribute Definition (ATTDEF) Command

The ATTDEF command is used to define specific attributes of a given drawing. The end result of this command is a special block that contains a drawing and/or text material (which defines the Attribute). The BLOCKS and DRAW Screen Submenus contain the ATTDEF command. The Menu Map is shown in Figure 19-1.

273

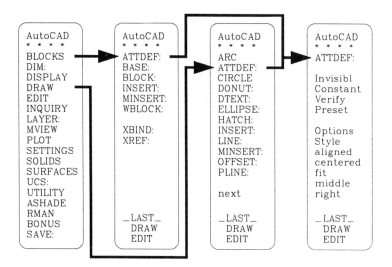

Figure 19–1 Menu Map for the ATTDEF Command

19.2.1.1 ATTDEF Modes

There are four modes that must be established before utilizing the ATTDEF command. These modes are: INVISIBLE, CONSTANT, VERIFY, and PRESET. The Invisible mode makes the Attribute data visible or invisible on the Monitor. The Constant mode provides for either a Variable Attribute value or a Constant Attribute value. The Verify mode permits the operator to verify the Attribute value or accept the value as input. The Preset mode enables the operator to preset certain values before entering the ATTRIBUTE command.

19.2.2 Command Sequence for the ATTDEF Command

The initial Command Sequence requires answers to the four modes. After the mode specifications have been established, then the Attribute Tag, Attribute Prompt, Attribute Default, and Text data (text style, location, height, and rotation) will be requested. This procedure is repeated for each Attribute that is used.

The Attribute Tag is the name (a maximum of 31 characters with no spaces) of the Attribute (brown hair, length of screw, badge number, etc.) that will be used by the program as a filename. The Attribute Prompt is similar to that of the Attribute Tag but is used by the operator (a maximum of 31 characters with spaces). The Attribute Default is used if the Attribute value has a common term for all Attributes. One application of the Attribute is a floor plan. A typical floor plan will require three Attribute values: (1) Name of the employee; (2) Telephone extension number; and (3) The employee's badge number. The Command Sequence listed in Figure 19–2 calls out the sequence used for Example 19–1 and the Attribute names and values are listed in Table 19–1.

Example 19–1: Start a new drawing called ATT. Set the Limits to 0",0" for the origin and 18',13'6" for the upper limits. ZOOM All. You have been given the task to de-

```
Command: ATTDEF
Attribute mode  -Invisible: N Constant: C Verify: V Preset: P
Enter (ICVP) to change, Return when done:  (R)
Attribute tag:  Employee's-Name
Attribute prompt:  Employee's Name
Default Attribute value:  Not available
Justify/Style/<Start point>:  X1,Y1
Height <0.2000>:  (R)
Rotation <0>:  (R)
Attribute mode  -Invisible: N Constant: C Verify: V Preset: P
Enter (ICVP) to change, Return when done:  (R)
Attribute tag:  Telephone-Extension-Number
Attribute prompt:  Telephone Extension Number
Default Attribute value:  Not available
Justify/Style/<Start point> :  (R)
Attribute mode  -Invisible: N Constant: C Verify: V Preset: P
Enter (ICVP) to change, return when done:  I
Attribute mode  -Invisible: Y Constant: C Verify: V Preset: P
Enter (ICVP) to change, Return when done:  (R)
Attribute tag:  Badge-Number
Attribute prompt:  Badge Number
Default Attribute value:  Not available
JustifyStyle/<Start point>:  (R)
```

Figure 19–2 Command Sequence for Example 19–1

velop a floor plan for the typing pool. This room has space for four people but only three individuals have been hired. The Attribute names and values are shown in Table 19–1. Three Attributes will be used. The first two Attributes (employee's Name and telephone extension numbers) will be visible but the third Attribute (Badge Number) will be invisible. The values will be variable, there is no need to verify the values, and no value will be preset. The complete Command Sequence is described in Figure 19–2.

Draw the top of the desk (4' wide and 2'6" deep). Use the GRID/SNAP setting of 3 in. The text data is as follows: height = 2", and font = Simplex. The Start point of the text is to be 6" from the top of the desk and 6" from the left side of the desk. Select ATTDEF from either the BLOCKS or DRAW Submenus. Input the values of the four modes as shown in Figure 19–2. Continue with the Attribute Tag, Attribute Prompt, and Attribute Default names. The command prompt will call for the location of the text data (6" from the desk top and 6" from the left side of the desk). Set Text height to 2" and rotation to 0. Upon completion of the text data, the first Attribute Tag (Employee's Name) will appear in the upper left corner of the desk. Continue with the second Attribute by pressing (R). The ATTDEF command is an automatic repeat command. The command prompt should ask for the inputs to the

Table 19-1

Tag Names:	Employee's Name	Telephone Ext. No.	Badge No.
	Rosie Candle	1392	1011212
	April Moon	4739	4798526
	Lilly White	5683	n/a

four modes; then the Attribute Tag and Names. The command prompt will ask for the text data. Press the ENTER key for an automatic listing of the second Attribute Tag. Again press the ENTER key to repeat the sequence for the third Attribute value. This time the Badge Number is to be invisible. Using the letter I, turn the Invisible (N) to Invisible (Y) and return. Complete the sequence with the third Attribute Tag and Name. Figure 19-3 shows the three Attribute Names in the upper left corner of the desk.

The initial Attribute definition has been completed. Using the BLOCK command, block the desk and the Attribute values. Call the block PLAN. The Insertion point is the lower left corner of the desk. If the Block is successful, the screen will be empty.

Draw a room using PLINE. (Set Width to 0.50".) The room is 16' wide by 12' deep. The Start point is 1',1'. Place a 3" door in the middle of the lower wall. Insert Desk 1 (Block name PLAN) 2' from the left wall and 2' from the bottom wall. The Block PLAN is a special block as it contains the Attribute names. When the block is in place, the command prompt will ask for the Employee's Name, then Telephone Extension Number, and Badge Number. The Attribute values will then be placed on the screen. Insert Desk 2, 2' from the right wall and 2' from the bottom wall. Answer the command prompt questions. Repeat the sequence for Desk 3. Place Desk 3, 2' from the top wall and 2' from the left wall. Place Desk 4, 2' from the top and 2' from the right wall. For the Attribute values of Desk 4, input N/A since the desk is Not Assigned. The room layout is shown in Figure 19-4.

19.2.3 Attribute Edit (ATTEDIT) Command

There are three methods to update existing Attribute values:

1. Use the DDATTE listed in the EDIT Submenu.
2. Use the ATTEDIT command, also listed in the EDIT Submenu.
3. Erase the data and insert the block PLAN with revised information.

The easiest method is DDATTE. The Dialogue Box is shown in Figure 19-5. Using the DDATTE method, change the values of Desk 3 to: Employee's Name: Fran

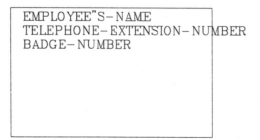

Figure 19-3 Attribute Listings for Example 19-1

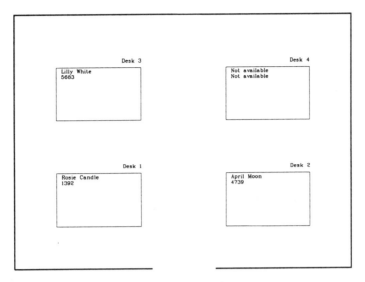

Figure 19–4 Room Layout for Example 19–1

```
                    Edit  Attributes

Badge  Number................10115
Telephone  Extension  Num 4367
Employee's  Name............Fran  Bonnie
```

Figure 19–5 DDATTE Dialogue Box for ATTRIBUTE Editing

Bonnie, Telephone Extension Number 4367, and Badge Number 10115. The revised floor plan is shown in Figure 19–6.

Another application would be a bill of material, where the Attribute Tags could call for model number, part number, manufacturer's name, and cost for each component.

19.2.4 ATTDISP (ATTribute DISplay) Command

The Attribute Display command is listed in the DISPLAY Submenu as shown in Figure 19–7. This command controls the Screen Display of the Attributes. There are three modes: Normal, ON, or OFF. The Normal display represents the initial mode of invisibility assigned to each Tag. Display ON turns all Tags ON. Display OFF turns all Tags OFF. Try this command on the drawing shown in Figure 19–4. Select ATTDISP, then ON. The three Tags should appear with the Identification Numbers visible. Now pick ATTDISP and OFF. All Tags will disappear. Select ATTDISP and NORMAL; this will return the Attributes to their configured display.

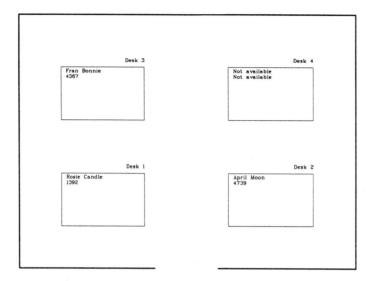

Figure 19–6   Revised Floor Plan

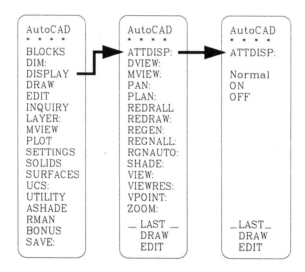

Figure 19–7   Menu Map for the ATTDISP Command

19.3   ATTEDIT (Attribute EDIT) Command Manual

This command as well as the DDATTE command is listed in the EDIT Submenu as shown in Figure 19–8.

If the ATTEDIT command is used, a number of restrictions are placed on the editing of the Attributes. These restrictions deal with what can or cannot be changed. The ATTEDIT command should be used by the more experienced operator. At this time, if any changes are required, the use of the DDATTE command should be used.

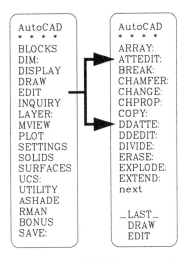

Figure 19-8 Menu Map for the ATTEDIT Command

19.4 ATTEXT (ATTribute EXTraction) Command

A printout of the floor plan may be obtained by taking the existing drawing information [either by means of Comma Delimiting Format (CDF) or Semicolon Delimiting Format (SDF)] and converting the data for use in a spreadsheet program. For those work areas where the spreadsheet programs are not available, a parts printout may be obtained by using the Drawing Interchange Format (DXX) with the ATTEXT.BAS file.

NOTE: The DXF format will produce the DXX file.

The ATTEXT command is located in the UTILITY Submenu and is shown in Figure 19-9.

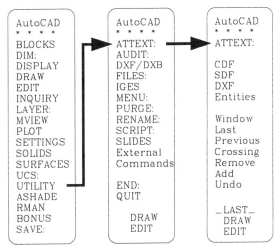

Figure 19-9 Menu Map for the ATTEXT Command

Example 19–1a: Pick ATTEXT from the Screen Menu, then select DXF. When DXF is selected, AutoCAD formats the drawing information into a .DXF file type. The next prompt will read "DXF Extract filename < >:." Reply with (R) or select another filename. The final prompt will read "XXX entities in Extract file." This procedure will produce a .DXX file for the drawing. End the drawing. If ATTEXT.BAS is not available, skip the next paragraph.

> **NOTE:** It is prudent to check the ACAD Directory for the ATTEXT.BAS file before proceeding to obtain a hard copy. If ATTEXT.BAS is not available, skip the next paragraph.

Leave the ACAD program and change to the DOS directory and bring up the BASIC program. Load the file ATTEXT (do not use the extension) by pressing the F3 (Load) function key and input: C:\ACAD\ATTEXT (R). When the screen shows "ok", press the F2 (Run) function key and input the drawing name: C:\ACAD\FILENAME (no extension). Press (R) and relax. The Monitor screen produces a listing of the floor plan using the Tag names as the heading. Press the Print Screen button on the keyboard. This will provide a hard copy readout of the floor plan.

19.5   Pull Down Menus for Chapter 19

There are no Pull Down Menus for Chapter 19.

19.6   Template Reference—Chapter 19

The Template has two of the ATTRIBUTE commands (ATTDEF and ATTEDIT). The Template reference is shown in Figure 19–10 on page 281.

COMMAND SUMMARY

Except for the ATTEDIT command, all phases of the Attributes have been discussed.

ATTDEF   ATTDISP   ATTEXT

GLOSSARY

CDX: Comma delimiting format for Attributes.

SDF: Semicolon delimiting format for Attributes.

DXF: A binary form used for Attributes.

Tag: Attribute name for program identification.

Prompt: Attribute name for operator input.

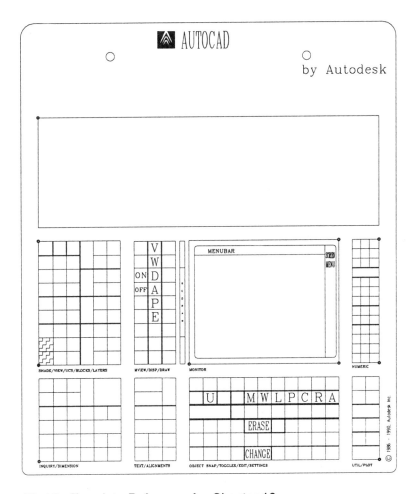

Figure 19–10 Template Reference for Chapter 19

PROBLEMS

1. What is meant by the Attribute Tag?
2. What is meant by the Attribute Prompt?
3. The command prompt shows that the Attribute will be invisible but the operator wants that Attribute visible. What are the procedures to change the Invisible to Visible Attributes?

20 Inquiry Commands

Instructional Objectives

1. To understand that the commands listed in this chapter deal with the *status* of the drawing entities and/or layers
2. To be able to determine the AREA of a closed entity
3. To be able to obtain the DISTANCE between two points
4. To be able to define the location of any point (ID) within the limits of the drawing
5. To be able to obtain a description of all entities on a given drawing
6. To be able to understand the Status information for each layer and linetype
7. To be able to effectively keep track of the time that is used for each drawing

20.1 AREA Command

The AREA command provides the operator with dual capabilities: (1) to determine the area and the perimeter of either a portion or the completed drawing; and (2) to determine the net area, taking into account those areas (e.g. holes) that must be subtracted. The AREA command is listed in Figure 20-1.

The Command Sequence used for determining a single AREA is listed in Figure 20-2. Figure 20-3 lists the Command Sequence used to determine the net area of a drawing.

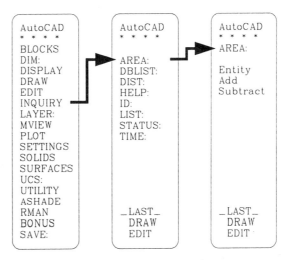

Figure 20-1   Menu Map for the AREA Command

```
Command:  AREA
<First point>/Entity/Add/Subtract:  2,3
Next point:  6,3
Next point :  6,7
Next point:  2,7
Area  =  16 Perimeter  =  16
```

Figure 20–2 Command Sequence for the Determination of an AREA

```
Command:  AREA
<fIRST POINT>/Entity/Add/Subtract:  Add
<First point>/Entity/Subtract:  Point  A
(Add mode) Next point:  Point  B
(Add mode) Next point:  Point  C
(Add mode) Next point:  Point  D
(Add mode) Next point:  (R)
Area  =  16.0000,  Perimeter  =  16.0000
Total area  =  16.0000
<First point>/Entity/Subtract:  Subtract
<First point>/Entity/Add:  Entity
(Subtract mode) Select circle or  polyline:  Circle
Area  =  3.1416,  Circumferance  =  6.2832
Total area  =  12.8584
(Subtract mode) Select circle or  polyline:  Polyline
Area  =  0.4330,  Perimeter  =  3.0000
Total area  =  12.4254
(Subtract mode) Select circle or  polyline:  (R)
```

Figure 20–3 Command Sequence Used to Obtain the Net Area of a Drawing

20.1.1 Area of an Entity

AutoCAD uses two methods to determine the area of an entity. The first method is to outline the drawing using the location of specific points, and the second is to select an entity.

Example 20–1: Bring up a new drawing called AREA: Draw the following entity: A rectangle with lower left corner located at 2,3; upper right corner located at 6,7. Label the lower left corner as Pt A, the lower right corner as Pt B, the upper right corner as Pt C, and the upper left corner as Pt D. Place the labels outside the rectangle.

Pick the INQUIRY Submenu and select the AREA command. Refer to Figure 20–2 for the Command Sequence. Use the Pointer (set ONSAP to INT) to pick the labeled points in sequence (A, B, C, D, and back to A). Remember that the computer knows exactly where those points are. It is recommended that the OSNAP commands be used to pick the five points. After the fourth point is picked, depress the ENTER button. The prompt should read Area = 16 Perimeter = 16.

Draw a circle inside the rectangle whose Center is located at 4,5 and whose Radius is 1. Draw a three-sided polygon using the Edge method, with the first point located at 4.5,3.5 and an edge length of 1 unit. The area of the circle and the three-sided polygon (triangle) is determined by picking entity from the Screen Menu, then the circle and/or the triangle (polygon). Since the circle and triangle are closed entities, the operator need only identify the circle and triangle. The program knows the points of each entity, and so the area will be calculated automatically. The area of the circle = 3.1416 with a circumference of 6.2832. Select the triangle. The area = 0.4330 and the perimeter is 3.0000.

NOTE: The units of AREA will be square units, square inches, square feet, and so on. The prompt readout assumes that the operator knows which drawing units have been assigned to the drawing.

20.1.2 Net Area of a Drawing

Example 20–2: The net area of the rectangle will be the area of the rectangle less the areas of the circle and the triangle. Follow the Command Sequence listed in Figure 20–3. Pick the AREA command from the INQUIRY Submenu. Pick Add and use the OSNAP commands to pick the four points (A through D). The prompt should show area = 16. Pick Subtract from the Screen Menu or input S from the keyboard. Pick the entity (circle) whose area is being subtracted from the rectangle. Notice that the prompt shows Subtract mode. The prompt should read 12.8584. Now subtract the triangle. The net area is listed in the prompt as 12.4254. The drawing is shown in Figure 20–4.

20.2 DBLIST Command

The DBLIST commands list the detailed drawing data for every drawing entity. The DBLIST command is listed in the INQUIRY Submenu as shown in Figure 20–5.

There is no Command Sequence for the DBLIST command. The DBLIST command is picked from the Screen Menu and AutoCAD automatically displays the details of each entity on the Text Screen. The operator must be prepared for the information to scroll across the screen. To stop the scrolling, use either the keyboard PAUSE button or ^S. To restart the listing, use either the Space Bar or ENTER button.

Example 20–3: Clear the screen and bring up a new drawing called DBLIST. Draw a circle (Center at 3.75,6; Radius = 1); draw a line from 3.25,2.5 to 8.5,4.5. Using the TEXT command place the word DBLIST at 6.5,7; Complex font; letter height = .25; rotation angle = 30. (Refer to Figure 20–6.) Select the DBLIST command. The screen will automatically change to the Text Screen and list the data for the circle, line, and text. The data are shown in Figure 20–7.

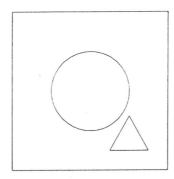

Figure 20–4 Solution to Example 20–2

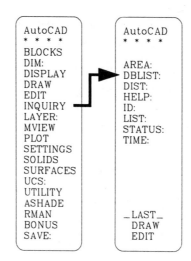

Figure 20–5 Menu Map for the DBLIST Command

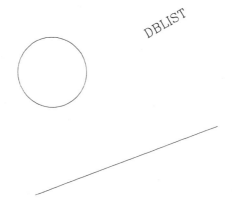

Figure 20–6 Drawing for Example 20–3

```
Command                         Circle Layer 0
DBLIST                              Space: Model space
         center point, X=       3.7500    Y=    6.0000   Z=  0.0000
            radius    1.0000
  circumference    6.2832
            area    3.1416

                      LINE         LAYER: 0
                                   Space: Model space
           from point, X=       3.2500    Y=    2.5000   Z=  0.0000
             to point, X=       8.5000    Y=    4.5000   Z=  0.0000
   Length =    5.6181,      Angle in X-Y Plane =       21
              Delta X=       5.2500,  Delta Y =   2.0000  Z =    0.0000

                      TEXT         LAYER: 0
                                   Space: Model space
       Style = STANDARD               Font file = complex
       start point, X=            6.5000    Y=   7.0000  Z=  0.0000
      height    0.2500
        text DBLIST
    rotation angle               30
     width scale factor             1.0000
  oblique angle         0
  generation normal
```

Figure 20–7 Solution for Example 20–3

20.3 DIST Command

The DIST (distance) command determines the distance and angle from one point to another. The command is listed in the INQUIRY Submenu as shown in Figure 20–8. The Command Sequence is listed in Figure 20-9.

The operator must identify the two points. (OSNAP is recommended.) When the Second point is identified, AutoCAD computes the distance (delta X and delta Y) and angle between the two points. The information will be listed in the prompt area.

Example 20–4: Start a new drawing called DIST. Draw a line from 2,2 to 6,8. Now select the INQUIRY Submenu and the DIST command. Select the first point then the second point. The distance between the two points is 7.2111, angle = 56; delta X = 4, delta Y = 6.

20.4 ID Command

The ID command, listed in the INQUIRY Submenu, is shown in Figure 20–10. The purpose of this command is to identify any point whether or not that point is within the limits of the drawing. It is recommended that the OSNAP commands be used in the accurate location of a given point.

The X, Y, and Z Coordinates for the specified point will be listed in the prompt area.

Example 20–5: Bring up a new drawing called ID. Draw a circle whose Center

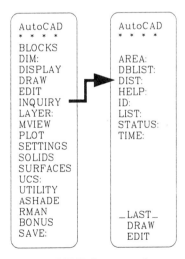

Figure 20–8 Menu Map for the DIST Command

```
Command: DIST First point:   Second point:
Distance = 7.2111, Angle in X-Y Plane = 56, Angle from X-Y Plane = 0
Delta X = 4.0000, Delta Y = 6.0000 Delta Z = 0.0000
```

Figure 20–9 Command Sequence for the DIST Command

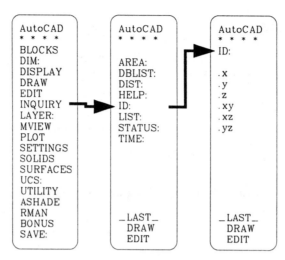

Figure 20–10   Menu Map for the ID Command

is 3,4 and whose Radius is 2. Although you have input the Coordinates of the circle Center, you want to verify the Center point. Pick INQUIRY, select ID, and using the OSNAP Center option, pick the circle. The prompt will list X = 3.0000 and Y = 4.000. The number of decimal places for this and any other command listed in the INQUIRY Submenu is determined when the units are specified at the start of a drawing.

20.5   LIST Command

The LIST command provides detailed information for a specific entity or group of entities. The Menu Map for this command is shown in Figure 20–11.

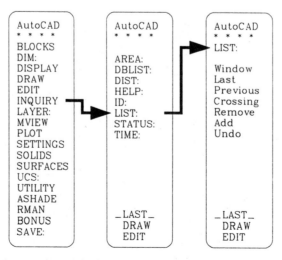

Figure 20–11   Menu Map for the LIST Command

The operator may select either a single entity or multiple entities, using the standard object selection procedures.

Example 20–6: Draw the following entities:

Circle: Center at 9.625,7.125; Radius = 0.8750

3P arc: Pt 1 = 6,8; Pt 2 = 5,7.125; Pt 3 = 5.5,6.5

Line: 1.375,6.875 to 3.5,4.375

Trace: width = .150 from 5,5 to 7,5

Pline: from 3,2.5 to 7,4.5; width 0.25 (Start and End)

Select any or all entities. The AutoCAD program will use the Text Screen and scroll the data. As in the DBLIST command, the scrolling might present a problem. To minimize scrolling, limit the identification of two entities at any one time.

20.6 STATUS Command

The STATUS command provides the general data concerning any drawing. The data will cover such items as: Limits, Units, Display limits, Insertion base, Snap resolution and Grid spacing. The second part of the STATUS command describes the Layer data: Current layer name, color, linetype, and elevation. In addition, the STATUS command will display the status (ON/OFF) of: AXIS, FILL, GRID, ORTHO, QTEXT, SNAP, and TABLET. The Menu Map for this command is listed in Figure 20–12.

The Command Sequence is minimal. Select the STATUS command from the screen or input STATUS from the keyboard. AutoCAD automatically flips to Text Screen and presents the information.

20.7 TIME Command

The TIME command, listed under the INQUIRY Submenu (refer to Figure 20–13 for

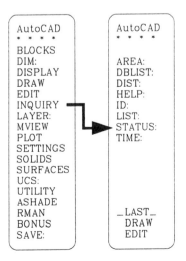

Figure 20–12 Menu Map for the STATUS Command

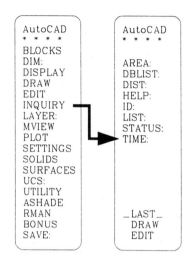

Figure 20–13 Menu Map for the TIME Command

```
Command: TIME
Current time:             15 Mar 1991 at 21:19:08.700
Drawing created:          15 Mar 1991 at 21:18:54.970
Drawing last updated:     15 Mar 1991 at 21:18:54.970
Time in drawing editor:   0 days 02:00:13.630
Elapsed timer:            0 days 00:00:13.630
Timer on.
Display/ON/OFF/Reset:     (R)
```

Figure 20–14 Time Record

the Menu Map), keeps a time record for each drawing. This record is shown in Figure 20–14.

The operator has no control over the time shown in Figure 20–14 with the exception of the elapsed time data. The elapsed time may be turned ON, OFF, or reset. It should be pointed out that the time listed does not include the time for printing or plotting a drawing.

20.8 Pull Down Menu for Chapter 20

Figure 20–15, on page 291, is the Pull Down menu for Chapter 20.

20.9 Template Reference—Chapter 20

Figure 20–16 highlights the Template area that contains the commands described in this chapter.

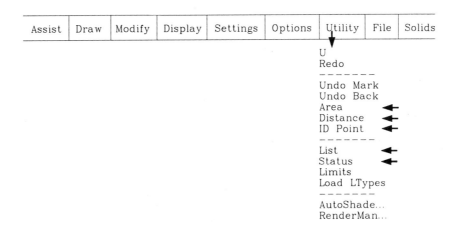

Figure 20–15 Pull Down Menu for Chapter 20

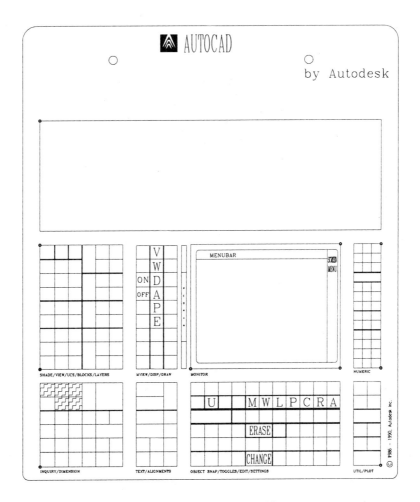

Figure 20–16 Template Reference for Chapter 20

COMMAND SUMMARY

This chapter describes those commands that are listed in the INQUIRY Submenu, as detailed below:

AREA	DBLIST	ID	DIST
LIST	STATUS	TIME	

PROBLEMS

1. Name the methods used to stop the scrolling of data.
2. True or False: The elapsed time indicator may be reset by the operator.
3. Draw a four-sided polygon whose sides are 4″ long. Describe the procedure to determine the area of the square.
4. Place a circle in the Center of the square (Problem 3) whose Radius is 1″. Determine the area of the circle and the net area remaining in the square.

21 Tablet Commands

Instructional Objective

1. To be able to configure the AutoCAD Template
2. To be able to use the AutoCAD Tablet Menus effectively

21.1 INTRODUCTION

The TABLET command is divided into four separate operating modes (ON/OFF/CAL/CFG). The first mode, Configure (CFG), utilizes a special overlay, or Template, designed by AutoDESK for the AutoCAD program. The second mode, Calibration (CAL), is used to transfer or digitize existing hard-copy drawings into the AutoCAD format. The CAL mode is considered an advanced topic and is not covered in this text.

The primary focus of this text is the selection of a specific command from either the Screen Menu or as input from the keyboard. As stated in Chapter 3, there is a third method of entering commands. This method will use the TABLET command with the Template in place. This Template was developed by AutoDESK (see Figure 21–1) and contains approximately 80% of the AutoCAD commands. In addition to the Template, a Digitizer (not Mouse) must be used.

NOTE: A number of Templates have been designed to work with the Tablet Command and the AutoCAD subprogram called "ACAD.MNU". The configuration procedures listed in this chapter are designed solely for the AutoCAD Template. The use of any other Templates may require changes in the ACAD.MNU and configuration process.

21.2 TABLET Command

As stated above, there are four options to the TABLET command:

1. Configure (CFG) option permits the operator to pick a command shown in the Template with the same result as picking the command from the Screen Menu or typing from the keyboard. The configuration procedure divides the Template into four specific Menu and Screen Presentation areas. Each menu area is again subdivided into rows and columns. The

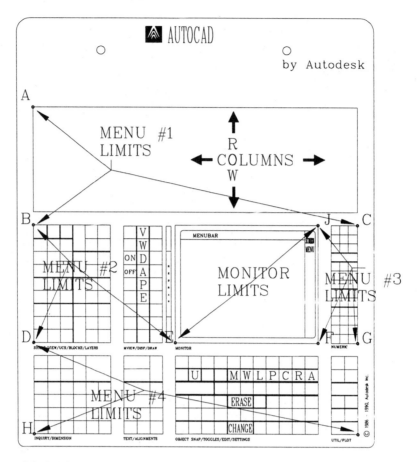

Figure 21–1 AutoCAD's Template

operator, by using the Digitizer Pointer, picks the command from the Template. The command location is converted (by the ACAD.MNU) to the actual command.

2. Calibration (CAL) option removes the configuration alignment and permits the operator to calibrate the Tablet and trace a drawing.
3. ON: Activates the TABLET command.
4. OFF: Deactivates the TABLET command.

The TABLET command is located on the flip side of the SETTINGS Submenu as shown in Figure 21–2.

21.3 AutoCAD's Template

The Template is divided into four menu areas and one screen presentation area. The Menu and Screen Presentation areas are highlighted in Figure 21–1 with the use of capital letters.

Menu 1: Defined by letters ABC

Menu 2: Defined by letters BDE

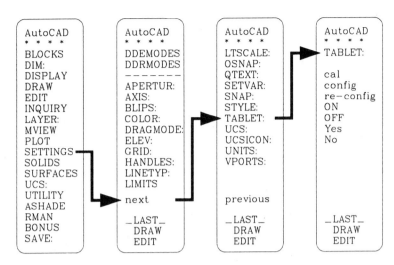

Figure 21-2 Menu Map for the TABLET Command

Menu 3: Defined by letters JFG

Menu 4: Defined by letters DHI

Screen Presentation Area: Defined by letters EJ

The actual Template does not have letters but rather black donuts to indicate the limits of each menu. The Template is used to reduce the necessary keystrokes per command (to reduce the time it takes to activate a command).

REMEMBER: The AutoCAD's Template does not contain all the commands but only those that are used most often. Each menu area must be specified as to location or be configured (CFG), and the Screen Pointing area must be established before the Template becomes functional. Figure 21-3 illustrates the Command Sequence necessary to CFG the Tablet.

NOTE: The Tablet is a peripheral device (sometimes called a digitizer). The Template (usually a plastic sheet) must be securely placed on top of the Tablet and is operational when the CFG procedure has been completed. The Tablet remains operational until the TABLET command is changed.

The TABLET command has four modes: ON/OFF/CAL/CFG. The ON and OFF options will toggle the TABLET command ON or OFF after the CFG procedures have been successfully completed. Place AutoCAD's Template on the Tablet. (Center the Template in the middle of the Tablet.) Make sure that the Template is secured to the Tablet and is within operating limits of the Tablet. The operating limits may be checked by moving the Digitizer Pointer from top to bottom of the Template as well as from side to side. In all areas, the cursor must be present on the Monitor screen.

```
Command: TABLET Option (ON/OFF/CAL/CFG): CFG Enter
            number of tablet areas desired (0 −4): 4
Digitize upper left corner of menu area 1: Point A
Digitize lower left corner of menu area 1: Point D
Digitize lower right corner of menu area 1: Point C
Enter the number of columns for menu area 1: 25
Enter the number of rows for menu area 1: 9
Digitize upper left corner of menu area 2: Point B
Digitize lower left corner of menu area 2: Point D
Digitize lower right corner of menu area 2: Point E
Enter the number of columns for menu area 2: 11
Enter the number of rows for menu area 2: 9
Digitize upper left corner of menu area 3: Point J
Digitize lower left corner for menu area 3: Point F
Digitize lower right corner for menu area 3: Point G
Enter the number of columns for menu area 3: 9
Enter the number of rows for menu area 3: 13
Digitize upper left corner for menu area 4: Point D
Digitize lower left corner for menu area 4: Point H
Digitize lower right corner for menu area 4: Point I
Enter the number of columns for menu area 4: 25
Enter the number of rows for menu area 4: 7
Do you want to respecify the screen pointing area: Y
Digitize lower left corner of screen pointing area: Point E
Digitize upper right corner of screen pointing area: Point J
```

Figure 21–3 Command Sequence for the Tablet Configuration

21.4 Configuration Procedure

AutoCAD's Template is divided into four specific regions or menus. These menus are shown in Figure 21–2 and are defined by black-filled donuts. The letters (A through J) were added by the author for ease of identification. Each Template Menu area lists a number of Screen Menu titles such as DRAW, EDIT, BLOCKS, etc. Beneath these titles are the commands that are the same as those listed in the Screen Menus. Each Menu area is subdivided into a specific number of rows and columns, so that the commands can be picked by use of a Digitizer Pointer. Table 21–1 lists the command Submenu Names.

Table 21-1

Menu Area Number	Submenu Titles
1	To be customized by the operator
2	3D/ASHAE, BLOCKS, LAYERS, TOGGLE, DISPLAY, DRAW, UCS, VIEW, MVIEWS
3	NUMERIC INPUT
4	INQUIRY, DIMENSION, TEXT, SETTINGS, OSNAP, EDIT, UTILITY PLOT

To start the Configuration process, select the TABLET command from the Screen Menu or input TABLET from the keyboard. Each Menu area has a different number of row and column values. Table 21–2 lists the Menu areas and their row and column values. Refer to Figure 21–3 for the answers to the command prompts.

It is suggested that the Screen Pointing area be respecified after the Menu areas have been configured. The Screen Pointing area is defined by points E and J. The

TABLE 21-2

Menu Area	Limits Points	No. of Columns	No. Rows
1	ABC	25	9
2	BDE	11	9
3	JFG	9	13
4	DHI	25	7

configuration of the Template is now complete. The CAL procedure is not part of this text.

NOTE: Let's review the AutoCAD's Template:
1. The Screen Pointing area is used to display the drawn entities and is viewed on the Video Monitor.
2. Where possible, pick the command from the Template. These commands will then be displayed in the command prompt area on the Monitor.

REMEMBER: The Screen Menu (on the Monitor) is also available for input information. All data and commands (not found on the Template) may be input from the keyboard or selected from the Screen Menu.

Once the Tablet has been configured, the configuration procedure will not be required again in the normal use of the system.

Example 21-1: Using the Template only for the command and numbers, draw a line from 2,2 to @3,3. Draw a circle; Center at 3,4; Radius 1. Draw a six-sided polygon using the Edge method; start at 6,3; edge length is 2 units. Figure 21-4 is the solution to this example.

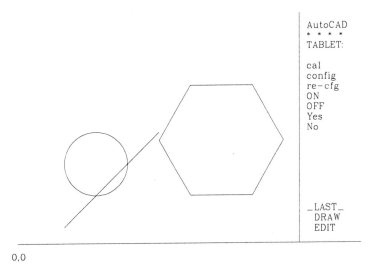

Figure 21-4 Solution to Example 21-1

21.5 RECONFIGURE Command

Figure 21–2 lists a RECONFIGURE command (as part of the Screen Menu). This command automatically assumes that the operator wants to use AutoCAD's Template. This command has been programmed to answer the rows and column questions for each Menu area.

21.6 Pull Down Menus for Chapter 21

The TABLET command is not listed in the Pull Down Menus.

COMMAND SUMMARY

The TABLET command will permit the operator to configure any Template that is designed using the same or similar techniques as called out for the AutoCAD's Template. Each Template can have a different configuration of points for the number of Menu areas, rows, and columns.

GLOSSARY

Configure: The process by which the grouping of the specified command shown in the Template is located under the AutoCad program.

Template: A grouping of commands under specified submenus that are linked to the ACAD.MNU.

A Keystroking with AutoCAD

A1.0 Introduction

The thought of sitting down in front of a computer and operating the system may cause considerable stress and strain on the first-time student or operator. The unknown is frightening. The purpose of this Appendix is to assure the student that the workstation is "user friendly" and is designed to take considerable abuse without breaking down. The introduction to the computer will follow the steps outlined below.

1. Turn the workstation ON.
2. Log ON to AutoCAD.
3. Start a new drawing.
4. Edit an existing drawing.
5. Draw a line, arc, or circle.
6. Exit from a drawing.

There is no doubt that mistakes will be made. The AutoCAD program is designed to inform the operator when a mistake is made and to try the command again. In the event that the computer "hangs up" (computer does not accept any additional commands) and the ^C Command does not help, depress the CTRL, ALT, and DEL keys at the same time. This will restart or "reboot" the computer to the opening C:\> prompt.

NOTE: If you are in the AutoCAD program, the combined use of the CTRL, ALT, and DEL keys will automatically destroy your *drawing. Be careful!*

A1.1 Power ON

Every component of the workstation (Computer, Monitor, Printer, etc.) has its own power switch. The accepted method of applying AC power to the system, is to plug all the components into a power strip equiped with a circuit breaker and spike eliminator. In this way, all the components of the workstation will be turned ON by pressing one button. In some installations, the individual items must be turned ON one at a time. Take a few minutes to find the power ON/OFF switch for each component and sketch the location for reference use.

A1.2 Log In Procedure

Turn the computer ON and the C:\> prompt appears at the upper left corner of the screen. Using the keyboard, type in CD ACAD and press the ENTER key.

NOTE: To complete any command, you must press the ENTER key which may be indicated as (R).

The next display on the screen will be C:\ACAD>. Type ACAD for the second time and (R). The Main Menu will appear as shown in Figure A-1.

CAUTION: In some installations, the drive letter (C:) or the initial input to the ACAD program (ACAD) may be different than listed.

If a new drawing is to be started, type 1 (R) for the Menu Selection. Type the filename of the drawing and (R). Do *not* add the extension .DWG to the filename. The AutoCAD program will do this automatically. The Video or Monitor screen is activated as shown in Figure A-2. A filename is limited to eight characters.

Example A1: The operator wants to start a new drawing called DAC.
Turn the equipment ON. Look for the C prompt (C:\) in upper left corner.

Type CD space ACAD (R). This will change the prompt C:\ to C:\ACAD>.

Type ACAD (R). This will bring up the Main Menu.

Type 1 for a NEW drawing. The computer will ask for the filename.

Type DAC (R). If there is a drawing called DAC in the file, the computer will inform the operator to either choose another name or select mode 2 (Edit an Existing Drawing) and use DAC as the filename.

A1.3 LINE Command

Example A2: Assume that the Root Screen Menu is on the screen. (Refer to Figure A-3.) Draw a line from a point located at 3,1 to a point located at 8,3.

```
Main Menu
    0   Exit AutoCAD
    1   Begin a NEW drawing
    2   Edit an EXISTING drawing
    3   Plot a drawing
    4   Printer Plot a drawing
    5   Configure AutoCAD
    6   File Utilities
    7   Compile shape/font description file
    8   Convert old drawing file
    9   Recover damaged drawing


    Enter selection:
```

Figure A-1 Main Menu

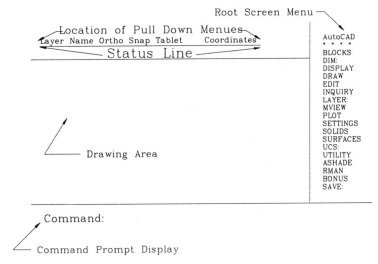

Figure A-2   Operational Video/Monitor Screen

Figure A-3   Root Screen Menu

Step 1: Use the Pointer to highlight and pick the DRAW Submenu.

Step 2: Refer to Figure A-4. The DRAW Screen Menu will appear. Highlight and pick "Line:."

Step 3: The right-hand Screen Menu (Figure A-4) will appear on the screen. Pick "line."

Step 4: Look at the command prompt area (bottom of the screen). The message to the operator asks for the point location of the From point. Use the keyboard and press 3, then comma (,) then 1, then (R). A bright spot should appear on the screen. (The bright spot is the location of the From point.) In addition to the point, there will be a line (sometimes called a rubber band or drag line) that is connected to the From point. The other end of the line is the Pointer or Cursor (cross hairs).

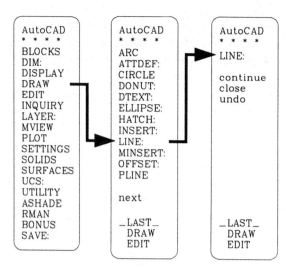

Figure A-4   Menu Map for the Line Command

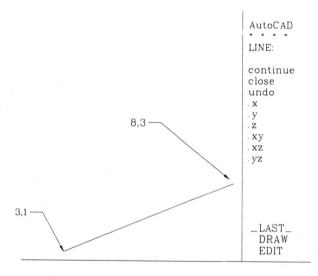

Figure A-5   Solution to Example A2

Step 5: The To point for this line is 8,3. Look at the command prompt. The message calls for the location of the TO point. From the keyboard, press the number 8, then comma, then 3, then press the ENTER button. The screen should show a line from 3,1 to 8,3 as illustrated in Figure A-5. The numbers shown in Figure A-5 are for reference only and will not appear on the screen. An additional return (R) will complete the Line command

A1.4   Return to Main Menu

There are two commands (QUIT and END) that will return the AutoCAD program to its Main Menu (Figure A-1).

The QUIT command is used when the operator has completed the drawing effort and finds that the drawing cannot be used. Type QUIT (R). The computer will ask "Are you sure (N):." If you are sure, type Y. If the you want another review of the drawing, type N.

The END command is used when the operator has completed the drawing and wants to keep the drawing for reference. Type END (R). The drawing will be placed on the hard disk.

There is a SAVE command. This command may be considered an interim END command. The difference between SAVE and END is that when the SAVE command is used, the current drawing data are committed to memory but the drawing remains on the screen. The SAVE command should be used on a periodic basis (every 15 minutes) to prevent the loss of the drawing information in the event of a power or equipment failure.

A1.5   The ARC

Refer to Figure A-6 for the listing of the ARC commands. The first three methods are broken down to the required keystrokes.

Example A3: Bring up a new drawing called ARCS. Draw a 3P arc where pt 1 = 3.75,6.75; pt 2 = 2,7.7, and pt 3 = 1.5,4.

Step 1: Bring up a new drawing called ARCS from the Main Menu. (Review the procedure to bring up or log in to AutoCAD.) This will be a new drawing, select the first option (Start a NEW drawing) and name the drawing ARCS.

Step 2: Pick the DRAW Submenu. (The ARC commands are part of this submenu.) Then pick ARC: (for the ARC command).

Step 3: Pick the 3P arc and provide the data called for by the command line. In answer to the 3P arc, type 3.75,6.75 (R) as the Start point. The Second point is now

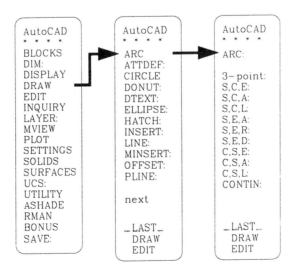

Figure A-6   Menu Map for the ARC Command

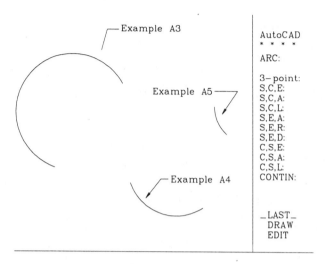

Figure A-7   Solutions to Example A3, A4, and A5

requested. Type 2,7.7 (R). The Third or End point is 1.5,4.0. Type this value and (R). The arc should look like the 3P arc in Figure A-7.

Example A4: Draw an arc with the following point locations. Given: Start point = 4,3.5; Center is located at 5.5,4; Included angle = 105.

Step 1: Assume that the drawing name has not changed and the ARC Submenu (right side of the Menu Map shown in Figure A-6) is on the screen.

Step 2: Using the Pointer, highlight and pick ARC then SCA (Start, Center, and Included angle).

Step 3: The command prompt (at the bottom of the screen) will ask for the Start point. Type 4,3.5 (R).

Step 4: The command prompt will ask for the Center location of the arc. Type 5.5,4 (R).

Step 5: The command prompt will ask for the Included angle. Type 105 (R).
The complete arc will look like that shown in Figure A-7 (SCA ARC).

Example A5: Draw an arc using SCL (Start, Center, Length of Arc) with the following data: (SCL) Start point = 6.75,6; Center location at 8,6 and Length of arc (L) = 1. Look at the data and determine which arc method will be used. Since we are given SCL, pick that method from the Screen Menu.

Step 1: The command prompt will ask for the Start point. Type 6.75,6 (R).

Step 2: The command prompt will now ask for the Center location. Type 8,6 (R).

Step 3: The command prompt will ask for the value of the length of the chord (distance from the Start of the arc to the End of the arc). Type 1 and (R). This arc will be the same as the SCL arc illustrated in Figure A-7.

A1.6   Circle

Refer to Chapter 4, paragraph 4.6.3 CIRCLE commands and the Menu Map for the CIRCLE commands in Figure A-8. The following two examples will provide the nec-

```
 AutoCAD        AutoCAD        AutoCAD
 * * * *        * * * *        * * * *
 BLOCKS         ARC            CIRCLE
 DIM:           ATTDEF:
 DISPLAY    ⌐⌐> CIRCLE     ⌐⌐> CEN,RAD:
 DRAW           DONUT:         CEN,DIA:
 EDIT           DTEXT:         2 POINT:
 INQUIRY        ELLIPSE:       3 POINT:
 LAYER:         HATCH:         TTR:
 MVIEW          INSERT:
 PLOT           LINE:
 SETTINGS       MINSERT:
 SOLIDS         OFFSET:
 SURFACES       PLINE:
 UCS:
 UTILITY        next
 ASHADE
 RMAN
 BONUS        _LAST_        _LAST_
 SAVE:        DRAW          DRAW
              EDIT          EDIT
```

Figure A-8   Menu Map for the Circle Commands

essary keystrokes to draw the circle. Remember that the diameter of any circle is twice the value of the Radius.

Example A6: Draw a circle whose Radius is 3 and whose Center is located at 5.5,5.5. Step 1: End the drawing on the Screen (ARCS). Bring up a new drawing called CIR-CLE. Highlight and pick the DRAW Submenu. Highlight and pick CIRCLE. Highlight and pick CEN,RAD: (method 1).

Step 2: Refer to the command prompt for the required data. AutoCAD calls for the value of the Center location (<Center Point>). Type 5.5,5.5 (R).

Step 3: Refer to the command prompt. AutoCAD calls for the value of the Radius (<Radius>). Type 3 (R).
The solution to this example is shown in Figure A-9.

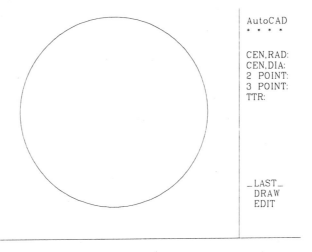

Figure A-9   Solution to Example A6 for the Circle Command

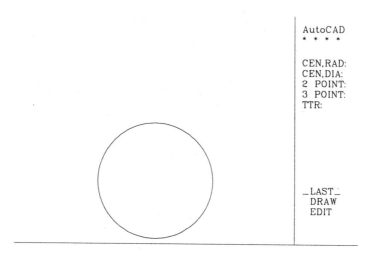

```
AutoCAD
*  *  *  *

CEN,RAD:
CEN,DIA:
2 POINT:
3 POINT:
TTR:




_LAST_
 DRAW
 EDIT
```

Figure A-10   Solution to Example A7

Example A7: Given three points (3P), draw the circle. Pt 1 = 4,2; pt 2 = @3<90; pt 3 = 7,3.5.

Step 1: Erase Example A6. Highlight and pick the EDIT Submenu. Highlight and pick ERASE. Move the cursor (using the Pointer) to the edge of the existing circle. Pick the circle. Notice the change in the outline of the circle. The command prompt will ask you to confirm the ERASE selection. If the selection is correct, then (R). If the selection is incorrect, then type ^(shift 6)C and start over.

Step 2: Return to the Draw Submenu, pick the CIRCLE Submenu, and select 3P option.

Step3: The command prompt will ask for the first point. Type 4,2 (R).

Step 4: The command prompt will ask for the Second point. Type @3<90. This command will tell AutoCAD that the location of TO point is relative (@) to the last point used. Type @ (shifted 2) 3 < (shifted comma) and 90 (for 90°).

Step 5: The command prompt will ask for the THIRD point. Type 7,3.1. This input will tell AutoCAD that the third point is located at 7,3.1 (Absolute Coordinates). The circle will be the same as shown in Figure A-10.

B Configure AutoCAD

B.1 Main Menu Options

As stated in Chapter 2, the individual who installed the workstation had a number of choices in the method that the computer was programmed to use to start or "boot-up." The end result is the presence of C:\> called the C prompt. From this point, any directory (within the C drive) may be selected. In our case, we want to activate the AutoCAD program (which has been loaded in the C drive) and display AutoCAD's Main Menu. Answer the C:\> with CD ACAD (R). The screen will answer with C:\ACAD>. Answer this prompt with ACAD (R).

The ACAD program will then process the input data (change in Directory to ACAD). The next screen display may be a message from Autodesk; answer the message with (R). This message may be deleted. The next Monitor display will be AutoCAD's Main Menu. (Refer to Figure B-1.)

B.2 Configure AutoCAD

Main Menu option 5 (Configure AutoCAD) enables the operator to program AutoCAD for specific peripheral devices that make up the workstation. There is a good possibility that the CAD operator will be asked to reconfigure AutoCAD if and when different input or output devices become part of the existing workstation.

```
Main Menu
    0   Exit AutoCAD
    1   Begin a NEW drawing
    2   Edit an EXISTING drawing
    3   Plot a drawing
    4   Printer Plot a drawing
    5   Configure AutoCAD
    6   File Utilities
    7   Compile shape/font description file
    8   Convert old drawing file
    9   Recover damaged drawing


    Enter selection:
```

Figure B-1 Main Menu

Although the AutoCAD software operates successfully with a large variety of external devices, the specific make and model number of the devices must be input into the Configuration program (Main Menu 5). The Video Monitor has to be configured first. Option 5 is selected, and the video Display will list the make and model number of the peripheral devices currently programmed into the software (refer to Figure B-2) for that workstation.

Press the ENTER key (R) and a second menu, similar to Figure B-3, will appear. This menu will enable the operator to select a specific device.

NOTE: Prior to the start of the configure or reconfigure effort, the operator should know the input/output devices by make and model number. This information is then programmed into the AutoCAD program as the actual device being used. The graphics Video Card is configured first (through the Video Display option). The technique used (the selection of the Make and Model number of the peripheral device) to configure the video card will be the same for the remaining devices.

Now that you are in the Configuration mode, select option 3, Configure Video Display. Select 3 (R). The next screen display will list those video graphics cards that will operate with the AutoCAD program. Select the proper Video Card by using its listing number. Then follow the messages or prompts on the screen. Initially, do not be concerned with the calibration of the screen. If the model and make of the video card is not listed, contact the video display card manufacturer and ask for the equivalent device that is listed in the AutoCAD program.

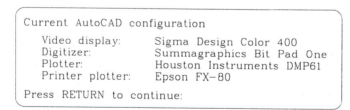

```
Current AutoCAD configuration

   Video display:      Sigma Design Color 400
   Digitizer:          Summagraphics Bit Pad One
   Plotter:            Houston Instruments DMP61
   Printer plotter:    Epson FX-80

Press RETURN to continue:
```

Figure B-2 Current Configuration Summary

```
Configuration menu

   0.     Exit to Main Menu
   1.     Show current configuration
   2.     Allow I/O port configuration

   3.     Configure video display
   4.     Configure digitizer
   5.     Configure plotter
   6.     Configure printer plotter
   7.     Configure system console
   8.     Configure operating parameters

Enter selection <0>:
```

Figure B-3 Configuration Menu

The Digitizer is usually configured next. In the event that neither the Digitizer, Plotter, and/or Printer are part of the workstation, select *none* from the list of devices and follow the screen display prompts.

NOTE: After the initial configuration has been completed, the selection of the COM ports (used for the Digitizer, Printer, and/or the Plotter) that connect the device to the correct input connector (called the I/O port) must be made. After this selection has been completed, and if the device cables are not disturbed, the operator will usually bypass the I/O port configuration.

Upon completion of the configuration effort, select Configuration Menu, option 0 (return to the Main Menu). Prior to the return to Main Menu, the program will place a message on the screen asking if the changes made during the Configure mode should be saved. The answer is Y for yes. When the Main Menu appears, the program has accepted the configure information and the AutoCAD program is ready for a work assignment. In some cases, it is prudent to recheck the configuration listing. Repeat the above sequence. Keep a written record of the peripheral devices (Make and Model number) and assigned COM locations as a reference.

Index